Software Reuse

Software Reuse

Domain Analysis and Design Processes

Jag Sodhi
Prince Sodhi

McGraw-Hill
New York San Francisco Washington, D.C. Auckland Bogotá
Caracas Lisbon London Madrid Mexico City Milan
Montreal New Delhi San Juan Singapore
Sydney Tokyo Toronto

Library of Congress Cataloging-in-Publication Data

Sodhi, Jag.
Software reuse : domain analysis and design processes / Jag Sodhi, Prince Sodhi.
p. cm.
Includes index.
ISBN 0-07-057923-7
1. Computer software—Reusability. I. Sodhi, Prince. II. Title.
QA76.76.R47S63 1998
005.1—dc21 98-38747
CIP

McGraw-Hill

A Division of The ***McGraw-Hill*** *Companies*

1 2 3 4 5 6 7 8 9 0 DOC/DOC 9 0 3 2 1 0 9 8

ISBN 0-07-057923-7

The sponsoring editor for this book was Simon Yates and the production supervisor was Tina Cameron. It was set in Century Schoolbook by North Market Street Graphics.

Printed and bound by R. R. Donnelley & Sons Company.

We dedicate this book to Lynda Sodhi and Kanwal Sodhi, who gave us the love and encouragement to complete this work.

Contents

Preface

Software reuse is a process of implementing or updating software systems using existing software assets. Assets can be defined as software components, objects, software requirement analysis and design models, domain architecture, database schema, code, documentation, manuals, standards, test scenarios, and plans. Software reuse may occur within a software system, across similar systems, or in widely different software systems. This process provides ways to reduce costs, shorten schedules, and produce quality products.

This book consists of six parts dealing with different aspects of the software reuse process. Part 1 introduces object-oriented software reuse strategies, the reuse paradigm, and reuse processes. Chapter 1 explains software reuse taxonomy, the importance of software reuse, reuse objectives, and software reuse evolution.

Chapter 2 deals with the software reuse paradigm. Software reuse is receiving much attention and recognition in the commercial industry as a computer software development component. This chapter introduces the analogy of software development as an iceberg and covers object-oriented software development characteristics and the importance of the software life cycle.

Chapter 3 presents object-oriented software reuse processes, advocating that an organization follow a disciplined software development approach that will provide a sound basis for establishing and measuring the effectiveness of integrating software reuse. This chapter includes definitions of domain, boundary, environment, and software reuse classifications.

Part 2 presents an object-oriented software reuse initiation plan. One size does not fit all when it comes to software reuse. Different types of domains may require different paradigms, processes, methods, and tools. The reusability process finds ways for existing software to be reused in new software development. The object-oriented approach provides convenient ways for pretested software to be reused. Software reusability results in closer alignment with object-oriented software engineering goals and principles and reduces the costs and schedule times associated with new software development, as well as during the postdeployment life cycle. This section covers activities involved in the software reusability process and domain analysis. The selection criteria for suitable reusable software and the establishment of a reusable library are also presented in these chapters. The primary objective of the portability strategy is the reduction of difficulty in identifying and changing parts of the software program that are necessary for acceptability on the target computer.

Chapter 4 discusses planning for software reuse, recommending that an organization establish a group to provide guidance in formalizing software reuse. One of the guidance criteria is to establish software reuse plans and standards at early stages. This chapter covers planning for software reuse, identifying the domain, establishing a software reuse dialogue among the practitioners, and educating them in software reuse to change the mind-set from that of "stovepipe" developments to domain development.

Chapter 5 covers object-oriented software reuse management. Management is an art for some professionals and a science for others. Techniques vary from person to person and are used to manage practitioners, systems, and projects. This chapter discusses some of the management techniques for software reuse projects.

Part 3 covers domain engineering. Object-oriented system software is usually the part of the domain that consists of other related systems software. Chapter 6 presents the basics of domain engineering, application engineering, and object-oriented software life-cycle models. This chapter also covers domain architecture for software reuse to be used in object-oriented software.

Chapter 7 examines the reusability process, which means finding ways that existing software can be reused in new software development. Software standards such as IEEE 1498 and International Standards clearly emphasize reusability. The object-oriented approach provides convenient ways in which pretested software can be reused. Software reusability results in a better chance of achieving object-oriented software engineering goals and closer adherence to its principles, as well as reducing the cost and schedule time required for new software development and during the maintenance life cycle. This chapter discusses software reusability, processes and activities, and repositories.

Chapter 8 deals with distributed object technology, which provides the mechanism for linking objects in a network. With distributed objects, users can better concentrate on what they need rather than on how to get it. This chapter covers distributed object technology, environments, and Common Object Request Broker Architecture (CORBA).

Chapter 9 discusses the CORBA framework and CORBA products available from various vendors, including Orbix, ObjectBroker, CORBAplus, and VisiBroker. Examples will also be presented.

Chapter 10 describes domain models, which represent graphical presentation for object-oriented software development. The reuse process necessitates that the customer's requirements first be understood and then graphically shown by logical models. The domain model determines objects and establishes the relationships among other objects within the domain infrastructure.

Part 4 examines the domain analysis process. Chapter 11 presents domain analysis methods. Domain analysis is a technique to systematically find commonality across related software systems to enable software reuse. This chapter covers the current methods for domain analysis: KAPTUR, DESIRE, Genesis, and IDEFo.

Chapter 12 presents the feature-oriented domain analysis (FODA) method, which focuses on the identification of prominent or distinctive features of software systems in a domain. These features are user-visible aspects or characteristics of the domain. They lead to the creation of a set of products that define the domain and also give the method its name.

Chapter 13 explains the joint object-oriented domain analysis (JODA) method. The Joint Integrated Avionics Working Group (JIAWG) Reuse Subcommittee has initiatives in several areas to demonstrate that reuse can effectively support the JIAWG programs and that the creation of reusable assets is an essential element of the reusability process. Domain analysis is the process that identifies what is reusable, how it can be structured, and how it can be used. Software objects are more understandable, more adaptable, and less likely to change than functions. This chapter covers some of the major characteristics of the JODA method.

Chapter 14 covers domain analysis and the design process method. The domain analysis and design process (DADP) method focuses on the software and systems reuse process. Software and systems reuse entails the application of a reusable asset to more than one application system. This chapter covers some of the major features of the DADP method.

Part 5 covers the domain design process. Chapter 15 presents domain design methods available in the industry that are object-oriented.

Chapter 16 deals with domain implementation, which implies the collection, classification, cataloging, browsing, and searching of assets. This chapter presents the domain implementation, repository mechanism, maintenance, certification, and validation processes.

Chapter 17 discusses application development with reuse. Application development with reuse software is a reality. The benefits of reusable software components are achieved if the reusable software is successfully used in another application development within the domain or in any other domain. This chapter covers the important issues involved in application development with reuse software, understanding the customer requirements, and future trends.

Part 6 presents samples for reuse. Chapter 18 provides a list of repositories and assets that are readily available and accessible on the Internet. Chapter 19 provides examples of various domain analysis and design processes. Chapter 20 presents a practical case study of the DCE/CORBA application.

Most acronyms used in this book are defined in Appendix A. A list of vendors, including contact information, is included in Appendix B. A list of reuse repositories appears in Appendix C. The name/date labels in square brackets [] throughout the book cite references that are listed in Appendix D. Appendix E consists of CORBA, DCE, and reuse success stories.

This book presents state-of-the-art material; it reflects what's currently happening in the object-oriented software reuse field. Use of the book's appendixes is encouraged. You can consult respective vendors for further information.

The information and data contained in this book has been compiled from various sources and is intended to be used for reference purposes. Neither the publisher nor the authors guarantee the accuracy of the information and data.

Acknowledgments

We thank the McGraw-Hill editors, staff, and friends who convinced us of the need for this book and supported us in its development. Their cooperation is appreciated and has contributed to the successful publication of this book.

We owe a great debt to our friends who have contributed to the development of this book: David Hart, KBSI, College Station, Texas; Heather Shaver, MESA Systems, Warwick, Rhode Island; Kathleen Gilroy, Software Compositions, Melbourne Beach, Florida; Charles Engle, Q-Labs, College Park, Maryland; Dr. Charles Lillie, SAIC, Morgantown, West Virginia; Donna Cornwell, MITRE, McLean, Virginia; Lorraine Cash, Raytheon, Sudbury, Massachusetts; Hugh Carroll, Expersoft, San Francisco, California; Paul Hickey, IONA Technology, Cambridge, Massachusetts; Todd Tornga, GCI, San Francisco, California; and Rachel Gauntlett, The Hoffman Agency for HP, Palo Alto, California.

We express our appreciation to those friends and relatives who contributed in other ways toward the completion of this book: G. Lynn and Shellie Orrell; Sonia and Sanjay, Keshav, Maulika Kohli; Anita Sodhi and Thomas Sodhi; Rani and Rajiv, Shaan, Alisha, Krisha Ranjan.

We thank wholeheartedly all our friends, students, and colleagues who contributed in different ways toward the completion of this book. It would be impossible to list them all. We thank all the people at McGraw-Hill who were involved in the editing and production of the text.

Finally, we commend members of our families, who diligently supported us so that this project could be finished successfully. Without their love and support, we would not have completed such a project.

Software Reuse

Part

1

Object-Oriented Software Reuse Strategies

Reuse provides ways to reduce cost, reduce schedule time, and produce quality products.

Chapter

1

Object-Oriented Software Reuse Taxonomy

Software reuse is a process of implementing or updating software systems using existing software assets. Assets can be defined as software components, objects, software requirement analysis/design models, domain architecture, database schema, code, documentation, manuals, standards, test scenarios, and plans. Software reuse may occur within a software system, across similar systems, or in widely different software systems.

There have been problems in the software development industry since its inception. The cost of software development is constantly increasing. Many projects are challenged but not completed. A challenged project is one that is completed with cost overruns and delays in schedule. The percentage of failure is greater than that of successfully completed projects (see Fig. 1.1).

Since the advent of computers, the industry has tried to reduce the costs and shorten the schedules required for software development, while making software of quality, with fewer errors, and that adheres to software engineering goals and principles. The computer industry is seeking an easy way to achieve this. Many methods and techniques, such as structured programming, structured analysis and design, and an object-oriented approach, have been tried but none have achieved success.

Object-Oriented Software Reuse Crisis

Traditional methods of software development such as structured analysis and design contain functional decomposition, hierarchy charts, data flow diagrams, and state transition diagrams, but they have not addressed the crisis of continually increasing costs. Data-oriented

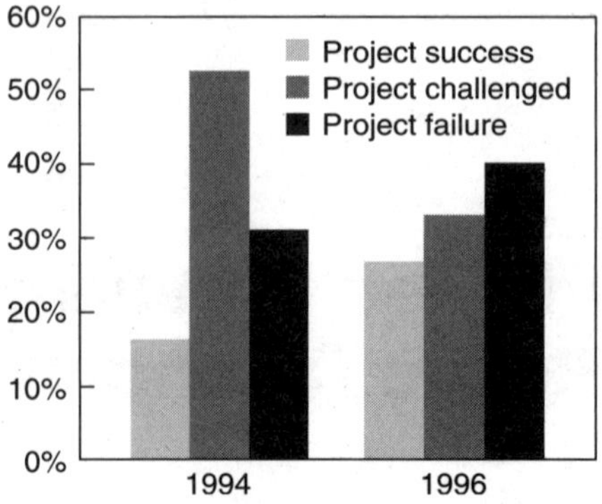

Figure 1.1 Success and failure percentages for software development projects.

analysis and design and events-oriented analysis and design and their variations deal with operations and data as distinct and loosely coupled. Operations determine the structure of the system. Data are of secondary importance. The cost of software development is growing exponentially, as shown in Fig. 1.2.

An object-oriented approach to software development is preferred because it leads to reusable classes. Objects are discrete software components and contain data and procedure together—operations and data are combined to form objects. Systems are partitioned based on objects. Data determine the structure of the software.

Benefits of an Object-Oriented Approach

The major benefit of an object-oriented approach is the ability to develop software faster and more cheaply and reliably by reusing soft-

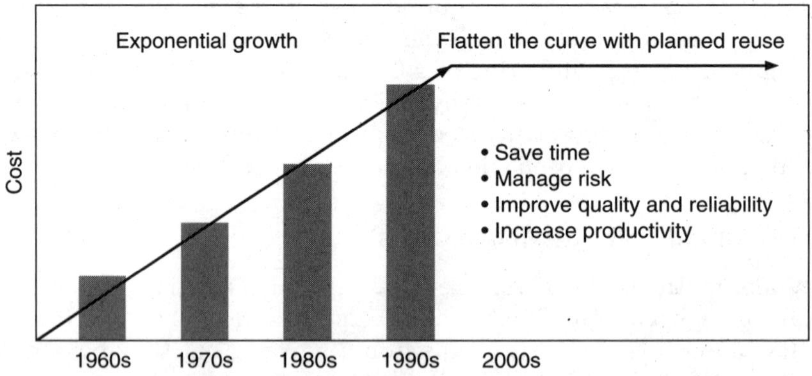

Figure 1.2 Software development crisis.

ware components. An object-oriented approach reduces both the cost and the time needed to deploy software through inheritance based on reuse. An object-oriented approach improves:

- Interoperability through standard object classes used across various software systems through inheritance
- Maintainability and reliability of software systems through object encapsulation
- Flexibility through polymorphism, as well as simplification of software development
- Availability of domain-specific objects and software reusable components repository

Importance of Software Reuse

The importance of software reuse lies in its benefits of providing quality and reliable software in a relatively short time. These factors reduce the costs of software development and maintenance. The computer industry has demonstrated that software reuse generates a significant return on investment by reducing cost, time, and effort while increasing the quality, productivity, and maintainability of software systems throughout the software life cycle. Reuse is advantageous because it:

- Increases productivity
- Enhances quality
- Saves cost
- Reduces software development schedules
- Reduces maintenance
- Enhances standardization
- Increases portability
- Contributes to the evolution of a common component warehouse
- Increases performance

Software reuse is now considered an integral principle of the software engineering process. Software reuse can be developed in a manner similar to the development of computer hardware products, as shown in Fig. 1.3.

Object-Oriented Software Engineering Goals and Principles

One goal of object-oriented software engineering is to engineer quality software that is reliable and meets the requirement specifications.

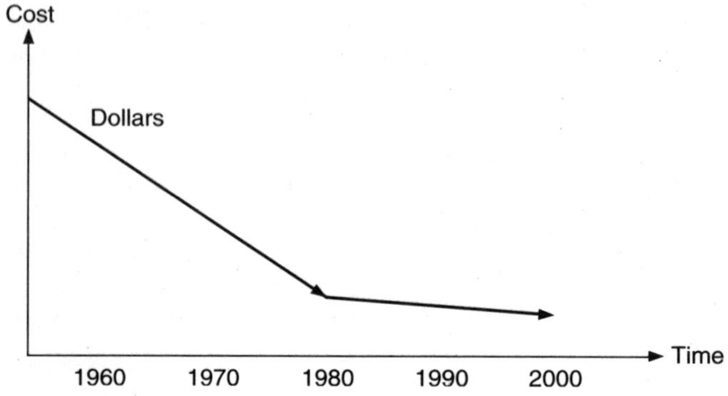

Figure 1.3 Developing cost decreases for computer hardware by incorporating reuse components and architecture.

Other goals are reliability, modifiability, maintainability, understandability, adaptability, reusability, and efficiency.

Reliability

Reliability is a system's ability to operate correctly under all conditions. Metrics are established to measure the correctness of a system. Mathematical formulas and statistical graphics are available for monitoring a system's reliability. The object-oriented approach has several features that protect data integrity and enhance reliability. With the use of exception handlers, you can validate input data and, if necessary, reprompt the user for the correct data. Software engineers can hide implementation details from users and let them see only the part of a program unit that specifies the name of the object and the form of data to be input or received from the data. Information hiding enhances reliability by protecting implementation details.

Modification

Modification allows changes to be made to a system without alteration to its original structure. Requirements change during the life cycle of a system. New versions of the system are created, with new and modification changes of requirements. The changes must be cost effective. Modifiability is achieved in a system by the design of small, meaningful modules; use of localized data in these modules; and very little use of global data or numeric literal values.

The object-oriented concept incorporates a facility that includes data values and range constraints for a given type of data in one place—the *type declaration*. A change made in a type declaration is all that is necessary to modify this data throughout the object-oriented software.

Maintainability

Maintainability keeps the system effectively live and useful throughout the life cycle. Requirements will change or modify during the postdeployment period of the system software. These changes will in turn modify the system. Modifiability and maintainability are directly related. The design of a system must be robust to enable these changes.

Maintenance of object-oriented software is eased by the fact that characteristics and behaviors are localized. When a local behavior is modified, it cannot unduly affect external entities. When a local characteristic is modified, it cannot unduly affect external entities if all accesses to it are through logical interfaces.

Understandability

Understandability helps software engineers with the management of a complex system. Remember, software design and code are written only once, but read by others many, many times. In object-oriented software, uniformity, readability, and modularity enhance understandability. The data operations that are involved are understandable. An understandable system will enhance its own maintainability. A system is understandable when it directly reflects how a problem will be solved and provides its readable solution. The real-world problem and the computer problem must be parallel at every point in the process. Well-designed object-oriented software models the problem space in an intuitive manner. Objects that exist in the problem space also exist in the solution space, along with analogous characteristics and behavior.

Adaptability

Adaptability in a system means that the system is easily adapted in a diversified environment. Object-oriented software can be easily adapted to new requirements because of the high level of reusability that is inherent in an object-oriented environment.

Reusability

Reusability is a big issue these days. Pretested software should be used so that cost and time can be saved. The development of object-oriented software means modeling a problem as a set of types or classes from which the objects are created. This set is partitioned into a hierarchical categorization that emphasizes reuse by relegating common characteristics and behaviors to the highest possible level. Once this modeling has been done, coding (translation of algorithms to program) is easier because it consists of mere creation of necessary objects from the defined classes and invokes the behavioral operations of objects. Coding can be anthropomorphized because the objects and behaviors are isomorphic with the real world.

Reusable software requires planned, analyzed, and structured design that withstands thorough testing for functionality, reliability, and modularity.

Efficiency

Efficiency is achieved by the use of available resources in an optimal manner. The factors that involve efficiency are execution speed, user time, computer memory, and computer storage. The object-oriented concept includes a large selection of efficiency-related features. They are low-level input/output (I/O), parallel programming, and error handling.

Principles of Object-Oriented Software Engineering

Object-oriented software engineering principles are formulated to achieve the established goals. These principles are abstraction, information handling, completeness, confirmability, modularity, localization, and uniformity.

Information hiding

Information hiding is the protection of implementation details within object-oriented software—the deliberate hiding of information from those who might misuse it. This differentiates the "what" from the "how." The "what" is essential information that should be available to everyone. "What" information includes specifications and interface information. The "how" information should be available only to a limited group. "How" information includes implementation details such as data structure.

Information hiding supports and enforces abstraction by the suppression of details. It increases quality and supports reusability, portability, and maintainability. It prevents confusion for the user, promotes correct data input, and enhances reliability. Information hiding also enhances localization and usually includes cohesive data; hence, good modularity is achieved and the goal of modifiability is more easily approached.

For example, it is not necessary that you know much about the electronic engineering function of your personal computer (PC). This information is hidden from you. You learn about the keyboard, how to enter your data, and how to get your desired result, although sometimes you must learn about the software so you can achieve these desired results. Another example is driving a car: it is not essential that the driver know how the car's engine functions in order to drive it. This is information hiding. The person's primary knowledge should be learning how to operate and navigate the car effectively.

Completeness

Completeness ensures that all requirements are included in the system and that every possible aspect of the problem has been considered. Software engineers must consider and plan for all possible problem and solution facets, which may include future requirement changes. Application of the principle of completeness helps achieve the goals of reliability, efficiency, and modifiability.

Confirmability

Confirmability states that a module, a group of modules, or complete system software is readily testable. A testable system implies a verifiable design: the testing of a system will confirm if it has been correctly designed. The system confirms the inclusion of the customer's requirements. Module independence is an important factor for a verifiable system. Thus, for good confirmability, modules are loosely coupled and contain cohesive data.

Modularity

Modularity is defined as the breaking down of a program into small, manageable units. Modularizing object-oriented system software breaks the solution space into smaller units. The modules are grouped around a data type and objects of that type. Only subprograms, which contain operations for objects of a certain type, are grouped together. For example, an array type may be in a package along with subprograms for calculating the average of array elements, which finds elements with the maximum positive value and elements with the most negative value.

In well-modularized system software, the top modules are generally the "what" of the process, while lower-level modules constitute the "how" of the process. This implies that the lower the module is in the module group, the more implementation details it contains. In other words, upper-level modules are the most abstract modules in the group, while lower-level modules are the most detailed.

Good modularity also implies loose coupling between modules. Coupling is a measure of dependence between modules. Global data shared by modules also increases this intermodular dependence. The passing of only required data via parameters or the localizing of data within a module decreases coupling. Loose coupling guarantees confirmability (independent module testing) and enhances the principle of modularity. Loose coupling also implies that if there are two modules—say, module A and module B—and module A gets modified, then module B will not be affected by the changes made in A. Thus, besides enhancing the modularity principle, loose coupling also brings closer the goal of modifiability.

In addition to loose coupling, there is another factor required for good modularity. This factor is called *data localization.* By localizing data in only those modules that require this data, three principles are applied: modularity, confirmability, and localization. Together these three principles facilitate easier modifiability. Only very highly related or cohesive data are localized in a module. Thus, for good modularity, loosely coupled modules must contain localized and cohesive data that are highly related.

Localization

Localization consists of placing highly related cohesive data only in modules that operate on this data. Only necessary data are passed from module to module and then only through parameters. This guarantees data integrity. Data localization implies independent modules and loose coupling. These are factors that must be present for good modularity.

Thus, important factors for good modularity are as follows:

- Data localization
- Loose coupling
- No data passing except via parameters
- Information hiding

The presence of these factors enhances reliability, efficiency, and modifiability. If data range is increased as the result of a requirements change, then only that data type statement in a particular module needs changing.

Uniformity

Uniformity includes the use of good, consistent, standardized features in all phases of object-oriented software development. Uniformity can initiate at requirement analysis and apply throughout the implementation stages. This includes testing and maintenance. This also implies that meaningful data and program names must be established. All the team players must follow the established standards throughout the software's life cycle. The result of this agreement is uniform, easily readable, and understandable software.

Objectives of Object-Oriented Software Reuse

The objectives of object-oriented software reuse are to produce software better, faster, and more cheaply by reusing existing well-tested assets. These assets are domain architecture, requirement analysis documents, prototype models, design, algorithm, coding components, test scenarios, standards, and any other related documents. The high cost of producing and maintaining software is a compelling reason to devise new ways, for example, reuse and following the successes and achievements of other branches of engineering such as computer hardware. Figure 1.4 illustrates the progress of reuse in the past, present, and future. In the past, the trend was to develop software from scratch every time a requirement was received. In the present, developers are using computer-aided software engineering (CASE) tools but are still developing new software. In the future, to reduce costs, developers will reuse software. There is enough software written and available that can be reused at a fraction of the cost of developing expensive new software from scratch.

One objective is to produce a reusable asset for independent operating systems and plug-and-play applications. Another objective is to identify common architecture, establish a repository, and integrate reuse in the software development process. In the planning phase, you collect data and refine and prepare policy, procedure, and standards for software reuse. In the domain analysis phase, you collect resources, scope the domain, conduct domain analysis, and build object models for reuse. In the repository preparation phase, you identify and procure tools, list assets, certify and validate assets, and populate the repository. In the domain-engineering phase, you integrate software, conduct domain engineering and reengineering, identify new assets, and populate the repository.

A further objective of reuse is to extract reusable assets from existing software to include in new software development. It is important to

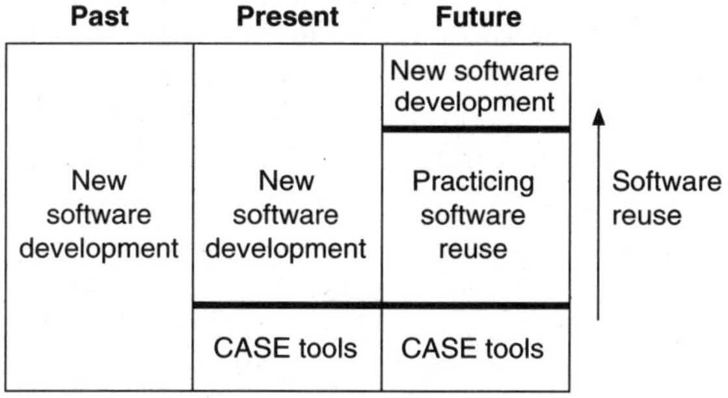

Figure 1.4 Software reuse objectives.

engineer software processes and products to achieve the objectives of reusability. Software processes define how software is developed and ensure that consistent methods are used to maintain quality and design integrity. Software product engineering focuses on the more traditional skills of architecture design, languages, platform characteristics, and application knowledge. Its importance as the basis for creating viable software systems will only grow in the new world of reuse [Kasp94]. The words *guarantee* and *warranty* are not found in software dictionaries. Maybe with the reuse of well-tested and mature software, both guarantee and warranty can be provided to customers.

Evolution of Object-Oriented Software Reuse

Software reuse is defined as the reuse of assets from existing systems to build new ones. The reuse of pretested assets improves the quality and productivity of new systems. Software reuse is the application of existing software assets to new development; thus, software reuse represents a paradigm shift in software engineering, from building a single system to building families of related systems.

Software reuse was not born yesterday or even today. Since the inception of the computer industry during the Second World War, reuse has been present in some form or another in software development. In the 1950s, 1960s, and 1970s, developers referred to *calling modules.* In the 1980s, the concept of reuse was applied in unstructured homegrown approaches. In the 1990s, structured formal approaches to software reuse are being followed. Figure 1.5 illustrates the evolution of software reuse.

Many authors have contributed to making software reuse a formal process, and many vendors and industries have shared software reuse experiences. A number of software reuse repositories are available in the industry. Computer-aided software engineering (CASE) tools are available to assist in making graphical models for reuse.

The application of an object-oriented approach makes software reuse easier. Many object-oriented methods are available, although there is no single standard for object-oriented approaches. The Object Management Group (OMG) was formed to create a standard for object-oriented approaches. The OMG is dedicated to enabling applications that are distributed over a network and written in different programming languages to work together.

The OMG is a consortium of about 750 representatives from computing-involved companies and organizations. They produce specifications, but no software, for reuse. The specifications are freely available for implementation to any member companies. The OMG members meet every six months to advance the standards process. Already the OMG has developed Common Object Request Broker Architecture (CORBA) version 2.0 for reuse (see Chapter 2). Although

1960	1970	1980	1990	2000
• Unstructured • New software development	• Structured approach • Calling modules • Ad hoc software reuse • New software development	• Software engineering • CASE tools • Standardization data • Database popularity • Object-oriented technology • Structured software reuse	• Domain engineering • Infrastructure • Repository popularity • Systematic software reuse • OMG • CORBA • Object interfaces • Client/server	• Software reuse standardization • Distributed object technology • Internet popularity • Object interfaces reuse

Figure 1.5 Evolution of software reuse.

the technology was begun independently by the World Wide Web, Netscape and others have pointed to the combination of Java and CORBA as the future of Web applications.

The OMG is planning to bolster its forthcoming CORBA 3.0 specification with a distributed object model for building components such as Microsoft's distributed common object model (DCOM). The CORBA 3.0 addition, tentatively called CORBABeans, aims to enable the creation of lightweight, reusable, graphical-based components that can be distributed across an enterprise. The OMG extends CORBA to include a component model that will be compatible with JavaBeans. The OMG is lowering the technical barrier to develop CORBA applications. The initiative follows the specification of myriad current and pending CORBA Interface Definition Language (IDL) mappings, which allow developers writing in COBOL, Java, or fourth-generation languages, such as Sybase division Powersoft's PowerBuilder, to access and generate CORBA objects without wrestling with abstruse IDL. A CORBA component model allows developers to create components visually on a project palette and access methods and properties more easily than the coding-intensive approach required by IDL. The OMG is integrating its Internet Inter-ORB Protocol (IIOP) transport with the Java Remote Method Invocation (RMI) interface for distributed object communication. The OMG's ultimate role with CORBA is to provide an integration substrate for multiple object models rather than to furnish full-blown development architecture. The OMG has been largely successful in getting its CORBA adopted as a standard by all member companies. It recently filled a gap in the architecture by adding an Object Transaction Services component, so applications that use distributed object architecture are scalable and hardy.

Chapter

2

The Object-Oriented Software Reuse Paradigm

Software reuse is receiving much attention and recognition in the commercial industry as a computer software development component. This chapter covers the software development iceberg analogy, object-oriented software development characteristics, and the importance of the software life cycle.

The Object-Oriented Software Development Iceberg Analogy

The cost of object-oriented software development is evident, but maintenance costs are hidden during the software life cycle. Figure 2.1 shows graphically in the form of an iceberg that for x dollars in system software development, about $5x$ dollars are required for its maintenance. The $5x$ dollar amount will vary depending on the length of the life of the system. The maintenance life cycle covers not only correcting the bugs in the software but the addition of new features.

Remember that requirements will change and additions and deletions will be made during the life of the system till it is retired. A good software design reduces the cost of software maintenance, but designing software with reuse in mind additionally reduces this cost.

Characteristics of Object-Oriented Software Reuse

The characteristics of the object-oriented concepts are abstraction, classification, encapsulation, inheritance, and polymorphism.

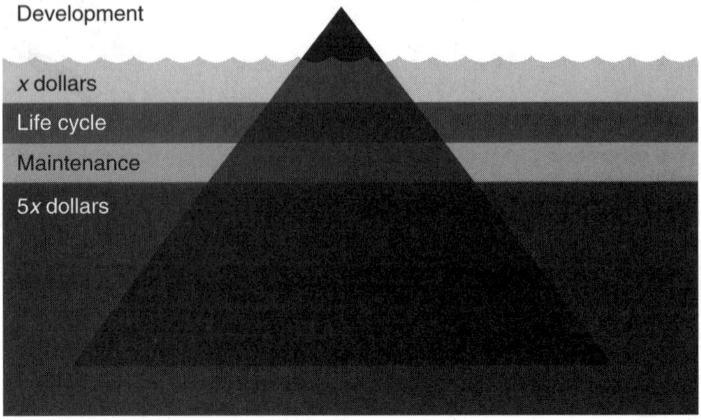

Figure 2.1 The software iceberg.

Abstraction

Abstraction means concentrating on the important essentials while the unimportant details are temporarily ignored. Good software engineering is hierarchical by an abstraction level. The hierarchy is based on functionality, process, data, and/or object considerations. This is the main technique and it is used in the management of the complexity of software engineering. In object-oriented software, the software engineers first concentrate on a design that promotes good modularity of major entities. With fewer implementation details to worry about, engineers can focus on the "what" modules in a system. These upper-level modules can be designed first. They then become less and less abstract with more implementation detailing as they approach the lower-level modules.

Abstraction aids software design in that the software engineers can disregard nonessential details and concentrate on the problem space. Abstraction is closely related to the goal of modifiability and promotes good modularity. For example, when you point to a PC on your desk, you think of the abstract word *computer* for this object and not a box that consists of memory chips, integrated electronic circuit, capacitor, resistor, inductor, and power supply. The essential details of the object *computer* to some people are visual display and keyboard, while to others they may be modem, printer, disk drive, and so on. Inessential details are integrated circuits, memory chips, capacitors, and resistors. Another example is getting your taxes done by an accountant. You give the accountant documentation of your total income, bills, deductions, and so forth, and you get a completed tax return back. To you, the abstraction, "I will have my taxes done this week," is complete. How the accountant does your taxes is unimportant. Figure 2.2 illustrates the abstraction concept.

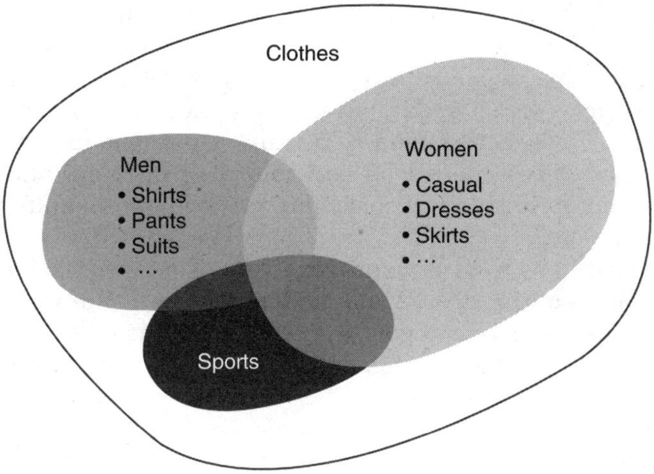

Figure 2.2 Abstraction concept.

Information hiding

Information hiding and abstraction are practically synonyms, except that information hiding includes the ability to access data. Here, only the operations on an object are visible to an application program; the data and the way the operations are implemented are hidden. Therefore, no operations can be performed other than those specified in the interface. Information hiding (and encapsulation) makes applications more flexible and extensible and provides more reusable code. They are mechanisms that hide code and data from application programs and protect them from implementation changes in a system's lower layers. Information hiding and encapsulation allow the software developer to create a clean interface between the specification and the implementation of an operation. As a result, an object-oriented application program is effectively independent from the implementation of the operations it uses.

Classification

Classification is the grouping of objects with similar behavior (methods or operations) and characteristics (data). Its class determines an object's data and methods. A class is similar to a type declaration in conventional structured programming. Here an object is an instance of a class, just as a variable is an instance of a type in structured programming. Because all objects of a specific class share the same internal structure and external behavior, they will respond to a method call in the same way.

The class of objects should define the object, the whole object, and nothing but the object. An object can be classified as an actor, a server, or an agent. Classification depends on how the object relates to surrounding objects. An *actor* object undergoes no operations, but operates only on other objects. Thus, actors tend to be fairly autonomous entities. A *server* only undergoes operations and cannot operate on other objects. An *agent* is an object that performs an operation on behalf of another object.

A class is characterized by a set of values and a set of operations that are applicable to objects of the class. Thus, constructors, selectors, and iterators apply here as a way of categorizing the operations of a class. For example, your car is a class of items with applicable operations such as:

- Starting
- Turning
- Stopping

For all instances of this class, such as your car, my car, his car, her car, and so on, these same principles apply. Thus, the car class serves as a factor for all common car operations. In some cases, the class of an object might be anonymous. A special kind of class is the *abstract class,* for which objects (instances) cannot be created. Abstract classes are primarily used as templates for other classes through the use of inheritance.

Encapsulation

Encapsulation means that an object contains both a state and an operation that can be performed on that state. This bundling of procedures and data is the foundation of the object-oriented concept. Actions on an object's state are called *methods* and are initiated by messages that are sent to the object. The encapsulated data in an object are not freely accessible from outside the object. Only an object's own methods can directly manipulate its data. Methods are invoked either by another method of the object or by a procedure call from another object (message) within the application program. With encapsulation, the user doesn't worry about how an object performs its function; the user simply knows what the object can and can't do. Users can be confident that, when an object is added to the existing code, unpredictable things will not happen to other parts of the program.

Encapsulation is the opposite of abstraction. Abstraction focuses on the observable behavior of an object, and encapsulation focuses on the implementation of the behavior. Encapsulation hides the implementation details, whereas the user of the abstraction only knows the essence of the behavior.

Inheritance

Inheritance is the ability to associate characteristics that are common to all members of a class (type) of objects. In object-oriented applications, a subclass of objects can inherit characteristics of the class (type) to which it belongs. Thus, when a new type of object is defined, a similar object already exists. In these cases you can simply define the new object type in terms of the existing object type, then new properties can be added or existing ones can be modified. When the new object type is defined in terms of an old object type, the new object type inherits properties from the older object type.

The new object type can then supplement these with its own new properties. For example, when a square or a triangle is drawn, methods are used that are inherited from the method of drawing a polygon. Different types of triangles in turn inherit characteristics from the general class of triangles.

A new type can be defined in terms of an existing object type. The newly derived type is then termed a *derived type* of the base type. The derived type normally includes new fields and methods that are not present in the base type. It redefines or overrides the implementation of a method that is defined in an underlying object type, after the override has been explicitly declared. Any methods not overridden by the derived type are automatically inherited from the nearest underlying object type. Similarly, the derived type also inherits all properties (attributes, operations) of its underlying object types. While a derived type can redefine inherited methods, it cannot redefine inherited properties. It can, however, add new properties of its own. For example, objects in a simulation often need the capability to contain a queue of other objects.

```
VehicleObj = OBJECT(QueueObj)
    ...
END OBJECT;
```

The object type VehicleObj inherits the properties of QueueObj. Here, QueueObj is a base type of VehicleObj, and VehicleObj is termed a derived type of QueueObj. Any number of new object types can be derived from a single base type.

New object types can also be defined in terms of other derived types. A hierarchy of object types occupying multiple layers is shown in Fig. 2.3. The hierarchy is modeled after the structure of an actual combat model (MODSIM II). Any object type that is either a base type of SomeObject or a type many levels below SomeObject is referred to as an *underlying type* of SomeObject, and SomeObject includes all the properties of the underlying types. Here, VehicleObj is a base type of AircraftObj as well as the underlying type of HelicopterObj and ShipObj. HelicopterObj is a derived type of AircraftObj.

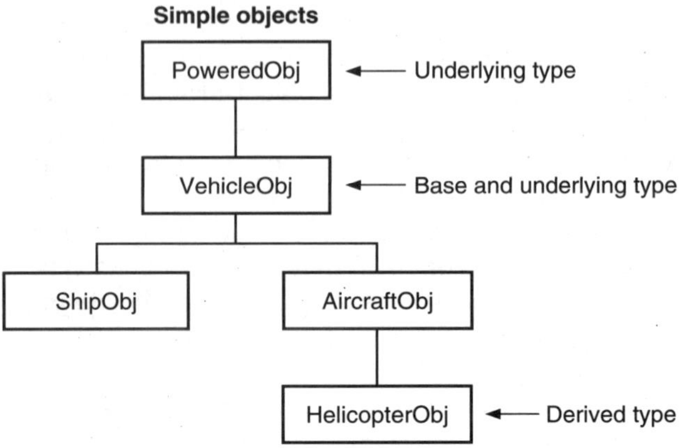

Figure 2.3 Inheritance.

A derived type can have more than one base type by means of multiple-path inheritance. This capability is called *multiple inheritance.* Figure 2.4 illustrates the multiple inheritance concepts.

```
MissileObj = OBJECT(AircraftObj, WeaponObj)
    ...
END OBJECT;
```

When a new object type is defined in this way, it has a copy of each field and each method of its base types. If the base types from which the new object type has been derived have used the same names for any of their fields or methods, then an ambiguous situation can arise. This particular situation can be avoided if the fields with matching

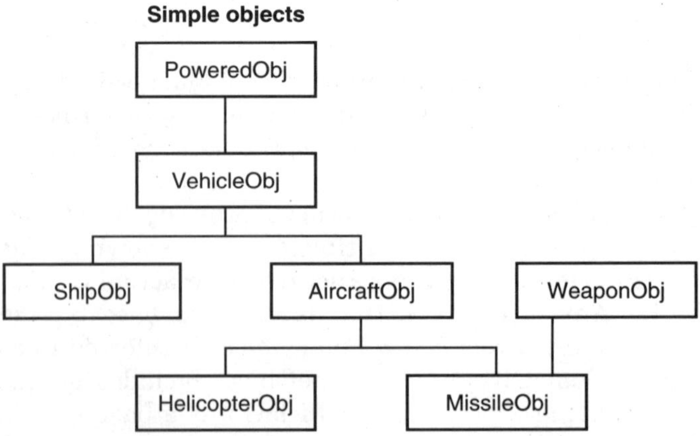

Figure 2.4 Multiple inheritance.

names have been derived from two base object types and are referenced. This is done by assigning the reference value of the type derived and then multiplying inherited objects to a reference variable of one of the base types. The desired field can then be referenced.

Inheritance allows one class to adopt the attributes (behavior and characteristics) of another class. The class that adopts the attributes is called the *subclass,* while the class whose attributes are adopted is called the *superclass* (see Fig. 2.5). The relationships between all subclasses and their superclasses are called the *class hierarchy.*

Systems that allow a class to inherit the attributes of only one other class are said to support *single inheritance,* while systems that allow inheritance from more than one superclass support multiple inheritance. The use of inheritance can easily add new classes without redefining what is common to all of them. Inheritance is a powerful modeling tool because the software developer can describe an application and its components precisely and without redundancy. Figure 2.6 illustrates inheritance. The properties of superclass Vehicle, size and speed, are inherited by the subclasses Water vehicles and Land vehicles. These properties are reused; they are not repeated in the subclasses.

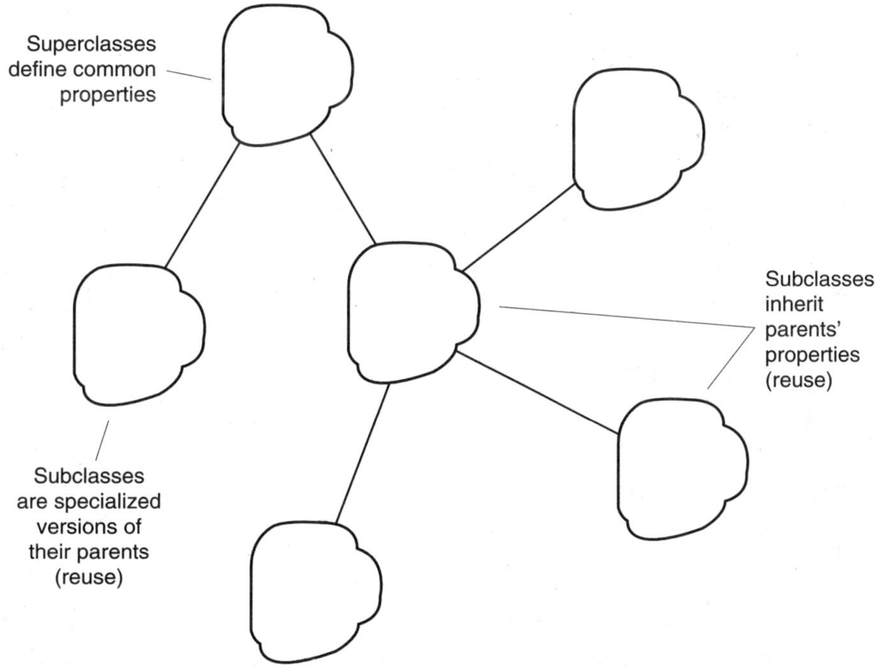

Figure 2.5 Inheritance classes.

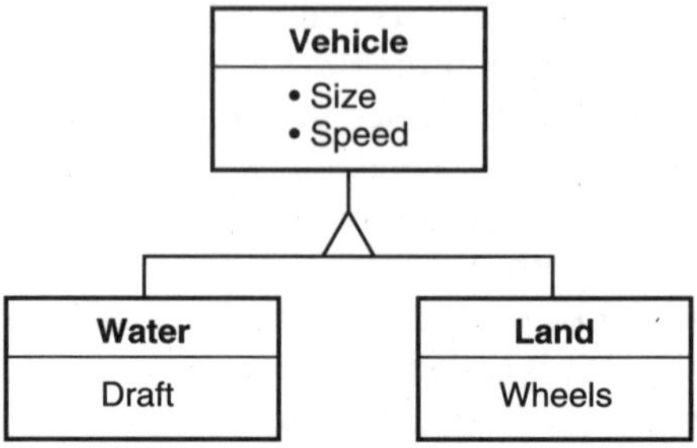

Figure 2.6 Inheritance properties are reused.

Polymorphism

Polymorphism is a Greek word that means "many forms." Thus, when an operation is performed on an object, the type of object the operation addresses determines the form of the object. The same command that would edit the text for this chapter, for example, would act differently when it was applied to the text of a generic letter because the characteristics of the two objects are different, as are the internal methods that act on them. However, the software developer and the user need only deal with the concept of *edit*.

With polymorphism, a subclass can modify or add to the attributes it inherits. A method call can cause different results. This depends on the type (class) of the object that is receiving the call. A procedure call name is overloaded when it invokes different operations to objects of different classes. For example, in Fig. 2.7 the object of classes Circle, Rectangle, and Square understands and responds to the method call Find Area but the algorithms that perform the calculations are different for each class. Thus, the call Find Area is said to be overloaded.

A class overrides the implementation of a particular method when the operation inherited from its superclass is inappropriate. In Fig 2.7,

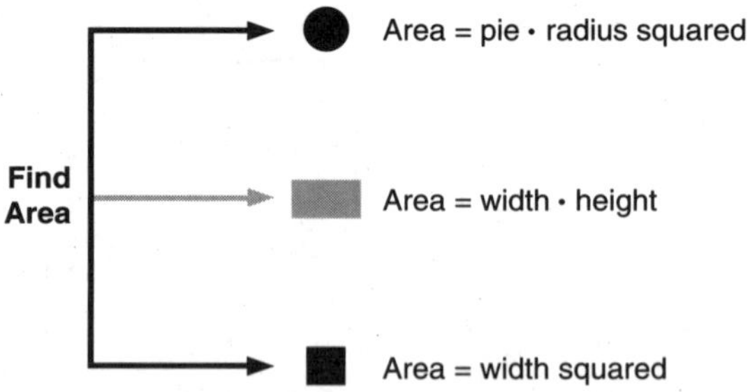

Figure 2.7 Overloading and overriding.

class Square inherited the Find Area method from Square's superclass, Rectangle. The Find Area method of class Rectangle calculates the area by the use of the height-times-width algorithm. However, since width-squared is a more efficient algorithm for calculating a square's area, class Square overrides the Find Area method it inherited from Rectangle. Inheritance applies reuse.

Figure 2.8 depicts a hypothetical graphics environment that allows various geometric shapes to be created by calling methods of specific objects. Here, R1, S1, and C1 respond to the same method call, Draw Object. The method call Draw Object allows this one call to draw the shapes, squares, or circles. The actual implementation of the method call Draw Object is redefined for each type of object. The ability to generalize behavior over many types of objects allows a higher degree of abstraction in software development because the software developer thinks about specific actions rather than the details of how they will be implemented.

Life-Cycle Importance of Object-Oriented Software Reuse

The life cycle of a system begins at the system's inception and ends at its retirement. Rather than letting a system die at retirement at a loss, some of its components should be saved for reuse in other systems if possible. Currently, retired systems are discarded without any of their parts being saved. This is a waste of effort and valuable data. These systems can be salvaged—and that is good economics.

Object-oriented software development phases are as follows:

- Statement of customer requirements
- Definition of problem
- Identification of object-oriented database
- Identification of domain

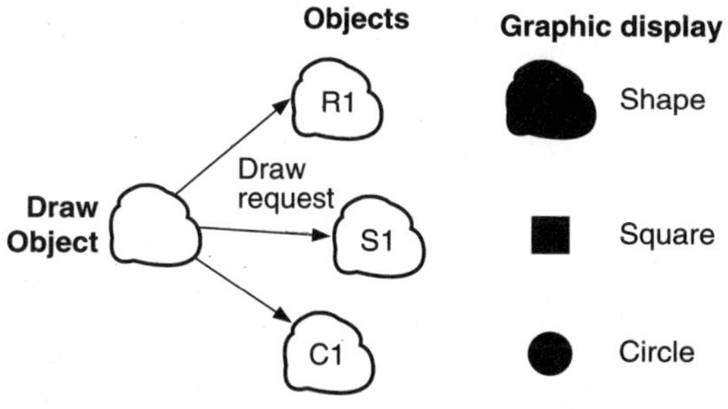

Figure 2.8 Runtime polymorphism.

- Object-oriented analysis
- Object-oriented design
- Object-oriented programming
- Object-oriented testing
- Delivery of software products

It is important that the customer be satisfied with the delivered software product. Maintenance starts after the acceptance of the software product by the customer and includes finding and solving bugs in the software, as well as adding, deleting, and changing to meet new requirements in the software. Traditional approaches involve more than 500 percent of the life-cycle expenses after the system passes acceptance testing and enters the life-cycle maintenance support environment. The cost of a system life cycle is associated with the risk and expense of eliminating errors and modifying requirements. It is a proven fact that the reuse process can reduce this cost.

The life-cycle process delineates how an organization does its work in evolving and sustaining products in a product line within a domain. Such a process involves many methods. The life cycle of a system interfaces with the systems engineering, software engineering, hardware engineering, and human-factors engineering environments. Systems engineers describe a problem space and constraints. This representation is stored in a life-cycle support environment, where iterations with software, hardware, and human-factors engineering are used to evolve a solution space.

Chapter

3

Object-Oriented Software Reuse Processes

An organization should follow a disciplined software development approach that will provide a sound basis for establishing and measuring the effectiveness of integrating software reuse. The Software Engineering Institute (SEI) has developed a *capability maturity model* (CMM) to guide computer organizations in software process improvement. This chapter covers domain, boundary, and environment definitions; software reuse classifications; and software reuse processes.

Domain

Domain is defined as a problem space for a family of applications with similar requirements. A domain is a set of related systems with commonality. A domain can be divided into subdomains to support risk mitigation and contains related assets, subdomains, and systems. A domain has a boundary and an environment. Figure 3.1 illustrates the relationship between a domain, subdomains, the domain boundary, and the domain environment.

Domain Boundary

The domain boundary separates one domain from another domain. There can be more than one domain within a domain. A domain subset is called a *subdomain,* which contains related common assets or components of a system. A subdomain is not a complete system. This implies a change of mind-set from system development to the common assets of a subdomain that will be reused in related systems.

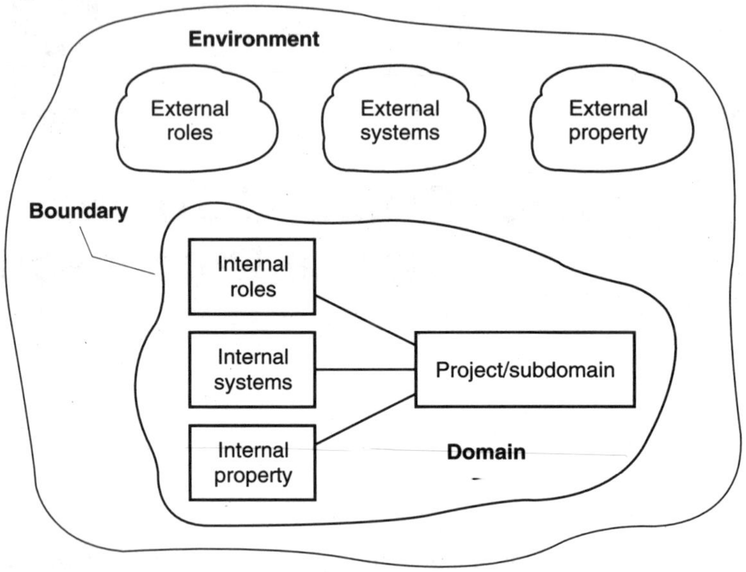

Figure 3.1 Domain, boundary, and environment relationship.

Domain Environment

The *domain environment* is where a number of correlated but independent domains exist. These domains have certain functions to perform within that environment. Computing systems are deployed and operated in a *target environment. Host environments* are where computing systems are developed and sustained. *Integration environments* are responsible for ensuring the integration of products coming from the host environments to be deployed and operated in the target environment. Figure 3.2 shows a hierarchy of domain, subdomain, and system relationships in reuse.

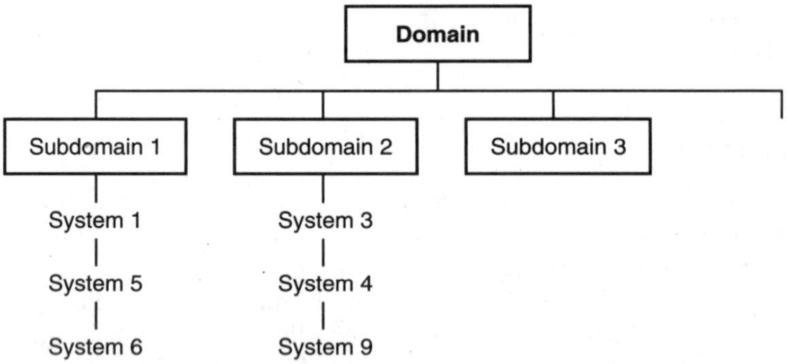

Figure 3.2 Domains, subdomains, and systems hierarchy.

Systems and applications are partitioned into classes of objects and relationship sets. The external and internal object classes that are in the context of a subdomain identify all classes that require resources or services from the subdomain or from which the subdomain requires resources or services.

Domain-Specific Architecture

A customer generates requirements and proposes a new application, product, or product line within a domain. Traditionally, the requirements are liable to change, deletion, and modification. It is vital that the requirements be frozen as soon as possible. A typical scenario is shown in Fig. 3.3. A customer continues to change requirements in all phases of software development. It is expensive to entertain changing requirements after the analysis phase, but it is even more expensive to change requirements after the design phase.

Domain-specific architecture determines the commonality and differences among the domain's concept of operations, the system requirements, and constraints.

Software Reuse Classification

Software reuse is classified as either vertical or horizontal. *Vertical reuse* classifies the reusable components from other systems within a domain. This condition exists when there are no individual components from the baseline of the acquiring system that may satisfy the new requirements or correct the fault. When this condition is true, then the reuse repository is searched for possible candidates from other systems that currently exist within the domain—for example, reuse of a mathematics package from one system in another system. This does not pre-

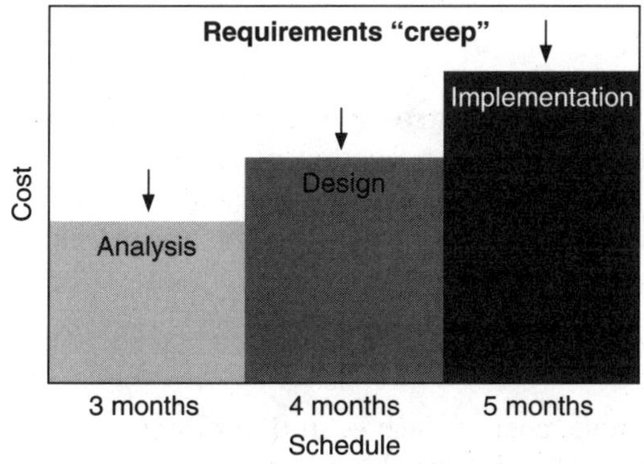

Figure 3.3 Impact of changing requirements.

clude the reuse of an entire system if such reuse is for the development of an identified separate new system. Other examples of vertical reuse are financial and health care packages.

Horizontal reuse is using the assets of existing components from domains other than the designated domain. This situation occurs when a new requirement or fault exists that cannot be satisfied with any component within the reuse repository. When this condition is true, other domain repository systems are searched in an attempt to satisfy the new requirements with components imported from external domains. Examples of horizontal reuse include the user interface and systems management.

Basic Processes

Basic processes for software reuse can be ad hoc, opportunistic, or systematic.

Ad hoc reuse

Ad hoc applies when there is no defined process for performing reuse—an individual or a small group practicing software reuse without any proper document, process, and structured formal approach. An example might be a calling routine that an individual has written for his or her personal reuse. The calling routines and modules are for printing, date conversion, mathematical calculation, and various computations.

The concept of ad hoc reuse means that during software development and maintenance phases, you can browse the repository to find an asset for reuse. This scheme does work to some extent and has limited cost-effective benefits. It is analogous to walking through a jungle without a map and a compass. You take the chance that you will find the right way to reach a destination. Ad hoc reuse is generally expensive and not productive.

Opportunistic reuse

Opportunistic reuse depends on the software developer to identify the need and browse the repository to find the needed asset. There is no standard process in place for reuse, nor is there domain architecture to provide any guidelines. Examples are a print routine for an organization letterhead or a cover letter for reports.

Systematic reuse

Systematic reuse is well-planned, cost-effective, and productive. It is introduced early in the life cycle of software development and is a formal and well-documented process, which is more domain-specific and based on a repeatable process. The intent is to reuse all the assets of a software life cycle, from requirements to implementation. Systematic reuse requires long-term management support and years of investment before it pays off. It involves changes in the mind-set of practitioners, including educating personnel, creating and managing incentives, and leading a change in culture. The following benefits were reported in the Reuse Education and Training Workshop of 1993 by organizations that have established systematic software reuse programs:

- 14% to 68% increase in productivity
- 20% reduction in customer complaints
- 25% reduction in time to repair
- 25% reduction in schedule
- 50% reduction in integration time
- 20% to 35% improvement in quality
- 20% reduction in training costs
- 400% return on investment

Formalizing the Software Reuse Process

Formalizing the software reuse process depends on informal or formal criteria. Informal reuse is an ad hoc software reuse practice that takes two forms: management-focused and practitioner-derived.

Informal reuse with a management focus normally evolves from an immediate perception of opportunity and therefore lacks a consistent application or standard across a given domain, organization, or project. Practitioner-derived informal reuse is the ad hoc, usually undocumented, code used by a particular practitioner on the same or other systems.

Formal reuse is a process-driven activity that requires common standards, procedures, and practices applied consistently and universally across a domain. All subdomains are identified and documented with attributes or characteristics. This categorization is to allow the practitioners to search and determine applicability to their problem space at a consistent and opportune time within their development processes. In addition, it allows for controlled retrieval of the selected assets at the project level.

Identifying Reusable Assets

Reusable assets should be identified from within the same system. Under this condition, individual components in the reuse repository, acquired from a system's baseline, have been identified as being able to satisfy a new requirement or correct a fault within the system. In no case is the entire baseline of the system considered reused when progressing from the baseline to the next version of the same system.

Software Development Capability Maturity Model

The SEI has developed a capability maturity model (CMM) to guide organizations in software process improvement. The SEI has defined five levels of the CMM, as shown in Fig 3.4. Level 1 is chaotic, level 2 is repeatable, level 3 is defined, level 4 is managed, and level 5 is optimized. The SEI CMM is used as the standard to assess the maturity of an organization's software development process.

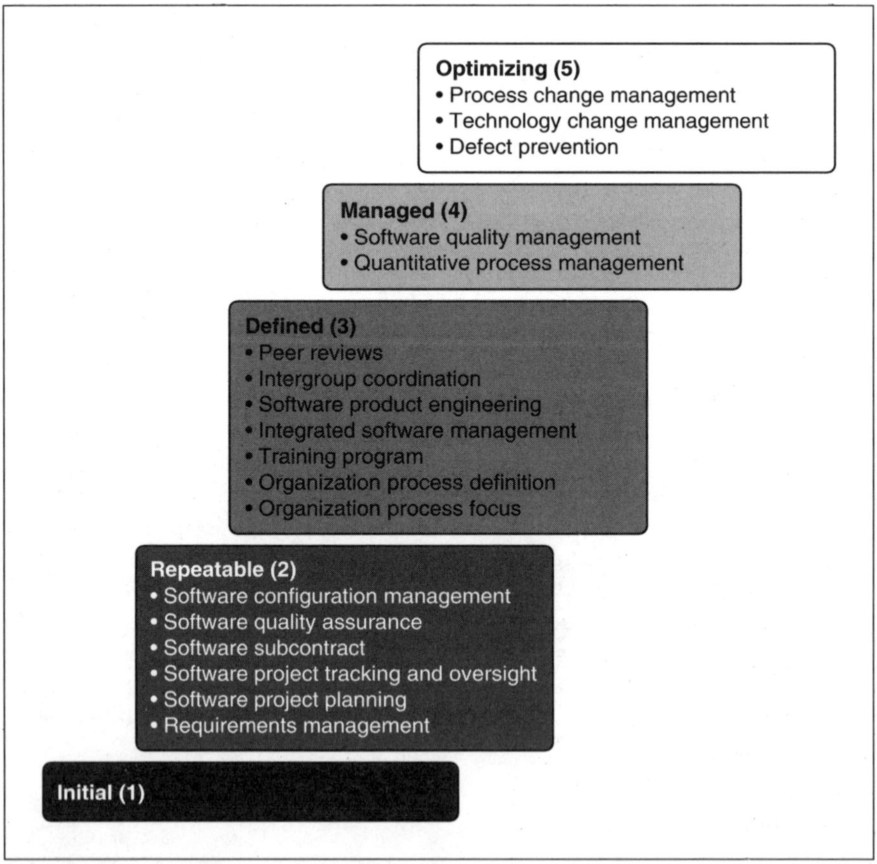

Figure 3.4 SEI capability maturity model levels.

Recently, the People Capability Maturity Model (P-CMM) by SEI, is a maturity framework that describes the key elements of managing and developing the workforce of an organization. Figure 3.5 shows a model of the P-CMM. The P-CMM indicates that, in order to improve performance, an organization must focus on people, process, and technology. The P-CMM includes practices in such areas as work environment, communication, staffing, managing performance, training, compensation, competency development, career development, team building, and culture development in an organization.

The SEI CMM has proven valuable to industry for establishing, evaluating, and improving software development processes and organizations. However, the model does not fully address issues that appear to be unique to software reuse engineering activities.

Object-Oriented Software Reuse Maturity Model

Object-oriented software reuse is the focus of considerable attention and recognition in the commercial industry as a computer software development component. As a primary benefit, software reuse promises a better, faster, and cheaper software development process. Reused software contains fewer errors than software developed by current practices because many errors will have been corrected during its prior use. An organization should follow a disciplined software development approach that provides a sound basis for establishing and measuring the effectiveness of integrating software reuse. An organization's goal is to produce the highest-quality software products with the fewest number of defects in the shortest, most cost-effective manner for the customer's satisfaction.

The current CMM does not provide sufficient details to allow an organization to completely assess, build a new, or improve upon a reuse

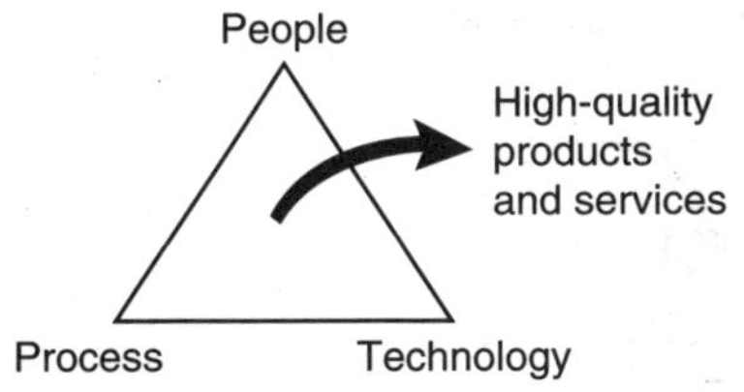

- Integrated product team (IPT)
- Integrated product and process development (IPPD)
- Integrated product and process management (IPPM)

Figure 3.5 A People Capability Maturity Model (P-CMM).

infrastructure. There are no currently known approaches or methods for measuring software reuse maturity within an organization. The following is an attempt to formulate a general framework for a software *reuse maturity model* (RMM) that could be used to augment the current SEI CMM for the purpose of guidance and evaluation of software reuse.

Software Reuse Maturity Model Concept

The concept behind software reuse within an organization is the process of drawing on suitable preassembled assets from available sources for new software system developments or enhancements. The set of available reusable assets may include requirements analysis, designs, code, and test procedures, to name a few. Figure 3.6 shows the five levels of the proposed software reuse maturity model.

Level 1 is the initial transitioning process, during which an organization may be practicing reuse, but it is ad hoc at best. The majority of the software community has been following informal practices for software reuse for a long time. Level 2 is repeatable and follows a formal software reuse approach. Level 3 is defined as the organizational implementation process. The repository is populated with the certified and validated assets. The generic architectures from the project's domain and

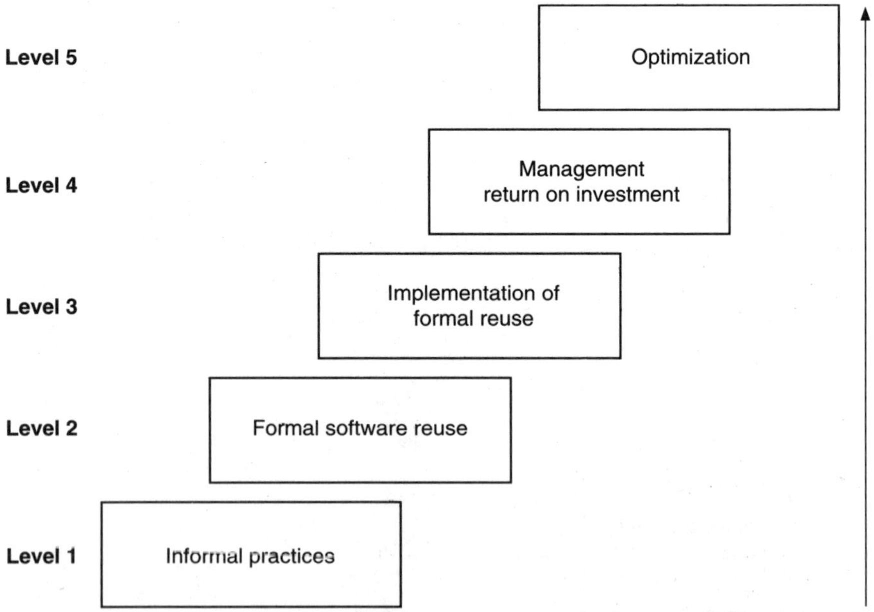

Figure 3.6 Reuse maturity model.

subdomains are further consolidated and a cohesive common organizational domain architecture is established. An initial set of reuse metrics is implemented at this time. Metrics are chosen that will show the benefits of the software reuse process in terms of higher-quality production, better profitability, and increased customer satisfaction. Common components are identified and reengineered as required. At this level, portions of the repository are to be actively in use across the organization using defined organizational processes.

Reuse technologies can be applied to all new and existing systems. The degree of reuse is determined by the amount, quality, reengineering needs, and availability of existing assets that satisfy new requirements in system development and maintenance.

Level 4 is the management of the software reuse return on investment (ROI). Metrics established in Level 3 should be used as a base to measure the success of practical use of the repository. The priority of this level is the measurement and control of the ROI. The events within this level are driven by cost, system, subdomain, domain formalization, and rate of change. From this model it can be derived that, as reuse progresses through each of the successive rings, the cost of that effort increases. It is expected that the largest cost difference will occur between steps when an organization is forced to look outside of its domain for reusable components.

Reengineering of existing components and rate of change are also cost drivers that are being considered for determining when to transition from vertical to horizontal reuse. Within a reuse repository, each component should carry with it a *reusable index*. This index could be currently defined from 1 to 4, with 4 being the most reusable and 1 being the least reusable. The determination to proceed to horizontal reuse is considered if the available assets within the reuse repository are rated at 2 or lower and the rate of change is low. If, after the search of other domain repositories, the results are similar, then the determination to reengineer an existing component versus reengineering an external component begins. If there are no components within the domain repository and all components from external domain repositories have a reusable index of 2 or lower, then the determination to reengineer the external component to fit the domain or to create a new domain component should be considered.

Level 5 is optimization. All software reuse processes are optimized. This will be a continuous process for software reuse improvement.

A sound, stepwise framework should be created to help determine the best economic progression from one level of software reuse to another. An organization should have a grasp of the impact of reengineering of existing assets to meet the needs of the domain and should construct a ruler to measure progress.

Part

2

Object-Oriented Software Reuse Initiation

One size does not fit all in software reuse. Different types of domains may require different paradigms, processes, methods, and tools.

Chapter 4

Planning for Software Reuse

An organization should establish a group to provide guidance in formalizing software reuse. One of the guidance criteria is to establish a software reuse plan and standards at early stages. The domain should be identified and a limited amount of hardware, software, and CASE tools evaluated and procured as necessary to support the software reuse activities. A software reuse dialogue should be established among the practitioners and they should continue to receive education about software reuse in order to change their mind-set from "stovepipe" developments to domain development.

Initiating Planning for Software Reuse

Planning involves the coordination of software reuse efforts in an organization. The plan should focus on integrating software reuse engineering goals and principles throughout the organization. The plan should also include the adoption of a software reuse approach to systems development and maintenance throughout the system life cycle. It is not easy to change old habits of developing software via stovepipe practices. It takes time to change the culture and the mind-set to the practice of software reuse.

Infrastructure Development

Infrastructure is defined as the architecture of a domain. *Domain architecture* is defined as the high-level graphical model that is concerned with the main assets of a domain and their roles and relationships. The architecture specifies a generic description from the user viewpoint, and the user interface, input and output operations, memory organization, and control of a system. The architecture describes the nature, configuration, and interconnection of the major players of the domain.

Architectures are needed in order to develop reusable assets that adequately meet domain-specific requirements and are properly designed to interface and interact with other domain assets. Architectures are categorized as follows:

- Domain-specific
- Process-driven
- Product-line

The domain-specific architectures capture the commonality and variance of related systems within the domain and promote the development of reusable assets to conform to those architectures. Domain-specific reuse focuses on reuse in specific domains and exploits those domains to support building of the specific architectures. Process-driven architecture is the transparent assimilation of reuse and is an integral part of the software engineering process. Product-line architecture is a set of software systems that share a common infrastructure and satisfy the requirements of one or more domains. The product-line approach is the development and application of reusable assets for system development and maintenance among systems that possess similar infrastructures.

Architecture-centric refers to the reuse-oriented architectures in high-leverage domains to spur investment in the creation of reusable assets that comply with those architectures. The infrastructure of an organization manages reuse policies, standards, processes, business practices, roles and responsibilities, technology, training, and coordination across product lines.

Preparing for a Cultural Change

Preparing for a cultural change is a continuous process in an organization. Software reuse has been practiced by almost everyone who has developed software, and its benefits have been known for many years since the dawn of the computer age. Much of that practice has been informal and ad hoc. It is now recognized that the real payoff from reuse is achieved by moving to a more systematic approach. Preparing for the culture changes involves the following:

- Paradigm change
- Process change
- Methods change

A *paradigm change* is defined as affecting the overall structure of the process and is driven by product-line characteristics, product-line life cycle, organization readiness, and constraints. A *process change* involves the activities and flows that fit into a given paradigm. A *method change* includes the detailed techniques for activities within the processes. Tools provide automated support to methods and processes. A reuse standard includes guidelines for requirements, reusability metrics, and certification.

Assessing Potential Problems

Assessing potential problems for implementing software reuse in an organization is a perpetual process. Reuse is not a stand-alone technology. Practitioners are getting close to assessing problems that only raise more questions about reuse. The practice of reuse requires that reuse considerations be built into the systems development and maintenance paradigm, together with the supporting processes, methods, and tools. It is important to note that reuse is built into the systems engineering process, especially for a product-line approach, since the architecture decisions and requirements specifications need to be greatly influenced by reuse decisions. If reuse is introduced in the later phases of software engineering, major reuse opportunities are likely to be precluded.

One size does not fit all: different types of domains may require different paradigms, processes, methods, and tools. Alternative practices and environments must be defined to accommodate different requirements.

Standards and Practices

Standards and practices establish the guidelines for use of reusable assets during software development and maintenance. These standards include the guidelines for practice during software requirement analysis, domain analysis, software design, coding, documentation, repository management, and the assets certification and validation process. An organization should establish such a software reuse standard to be followed by all its practitioners.

The requirement analysis standard establishes guidelines for reusable assets during the software requirements phase. During this phase, requirement models and documentation are created in compliance with the established software reuse standard. The main features of requirement standards are a context diagram, a requirements model, a data dictionary, a communication model, and a domain identification.

The context diagram is shown in Fig. 4.1. The context diagram establishes external interfaces with other systems and objects. This diagram is a high-level view that reflects the requirements. The requirement

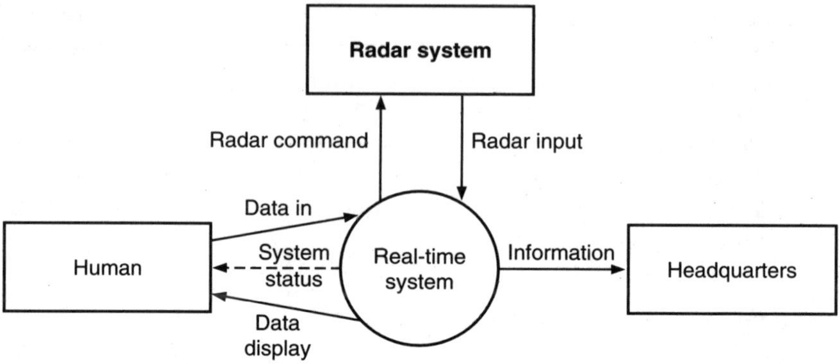

Figure 4.1 Context diagram.

model is shown in Fig. 4.2. This diagram establishes the interfaces between customers, users, and software developers. Customers are the ones who are footing the bills and providing funds, so they have a vested interest in the requirements and in software development. It is in the customers' interests to receive guarantee and warranty of the accuracy of the software. They like to see that all their requirements are being met by the software.

Customers also monitor software development to ensure that it is completed in time and within schedule. User input into the require-

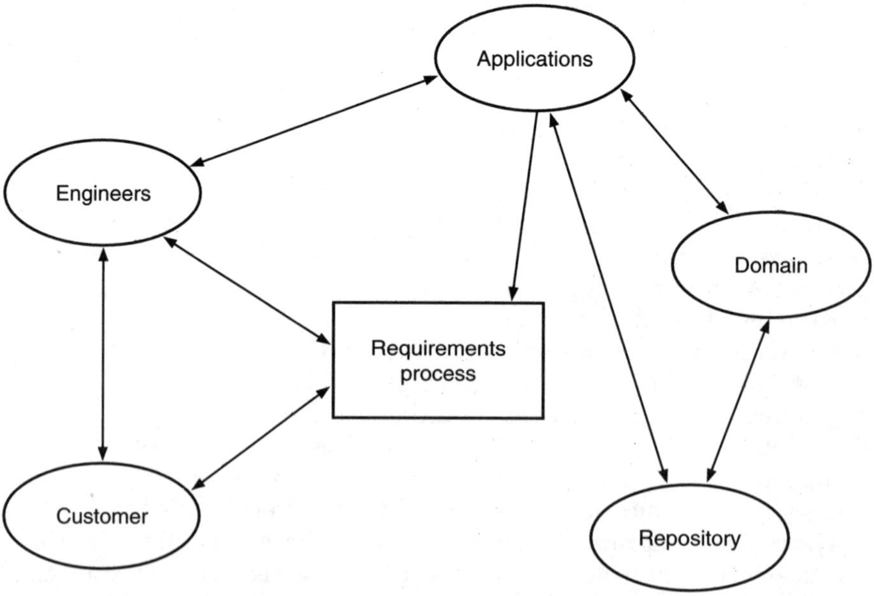

Figure 4.2 Requirement model.

ments is important because they need user-friendly software. Both customers and users form a team with software developers to generate use cases for the requirements to test the developed software. The customers and the users establish software product acceptance criteria.

The data dictionary documents in detail the elements and definitions of the interfaces, objects, classes, and data groups and data elements. This document standardizes the process, so that the software developer uses universally recognized terms and definitions throughout the software development process, which enhances the quality and efficiency.

The communication model establishes the communication between the hardware, software, objects, databases, and communication network of a system. Connecting arrows represent events crossing domain or subdomain boundaries either to other subsystems within the same domain or to entities external to the subdomain. An *object communication model* (OCM) is developed for each state model that interacts with some external entity. The OCM presents a dynamic view of the domain and subdomain, and depicts event communications between state models and external entities such as operators, physical devices, and objects.

The domain identification model establishes the domain of systems. The domain identification correlates the relationship with other domains and objects. This process facilitates the import and export of reusable assets.

The functional view of the problem space provides various levels of diagrams using the Integrated Computer-Aided Manufacturing (ICAM) Definition (IDEF) method. These levels of diagrams collectively provide a complete functional view of the domain that is being analyzed. (IDEF models will be discussed in subsequent chapters.)

The static view of the problem space includes what are collectively referred to as the domain, subdomain, and object models. A domain model consists of a domain chart, a domain mission statement, and a bridge description. In addition, object models are created for better understandability. Object models are also known as *information models* and *entity relationship diagrams.* The dynamic view of the problem space is provided to the user of the domain and consists of *state transition diagrams* (STDs), the *state transition table* (STT), the *data flow diagram* (DFD), and the data dictionary document. The STD is shown in Fig. 4.3. It consists of various states of a system, as shown in rectangles. The vertical lines are shown as transitions, events, and actions taken that depict the object's dynamic behavior. The STT is shown in Fig. 4.4. The STT maps the STD in a tabular form. Each row represents a possible state depicted on the STD. Each column represents the resulting events. The STT depicts the set of transition rules that specify what will happen if a particular event occurs while in a particular state.

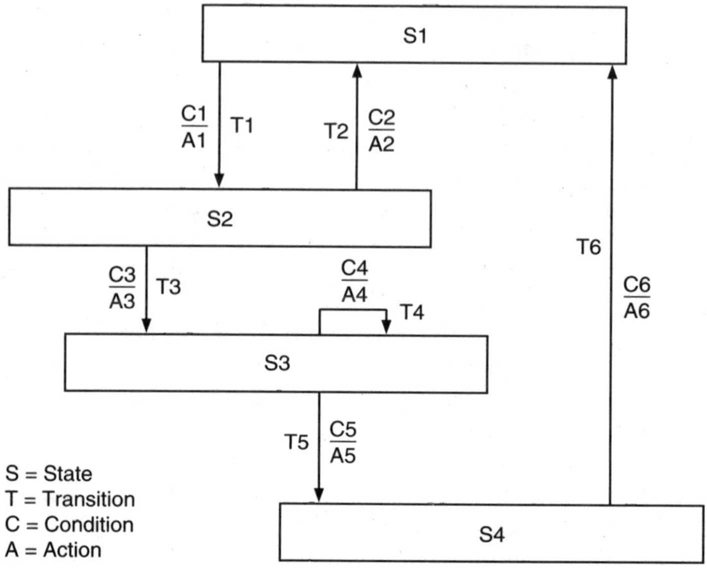

Figure 4.3 A sample STD.

The DFD is shown in Fig. 4.5. Each circle represents a requirement process and has at least one input and one output. The labels on inputs and outputs are unique names. The circles are numbered for better readability. Two horizontal lines represent a file. Databases are permanent files and are shown by a solid line.

	Event 1	Event 2	Event 3		
State 1	Effects of Event 1 in State 1				
State 2		Effects of Event 2 in State 2			
State 3	Effects of Event 1 in State 3				

Figure 4.4 A sample STT.

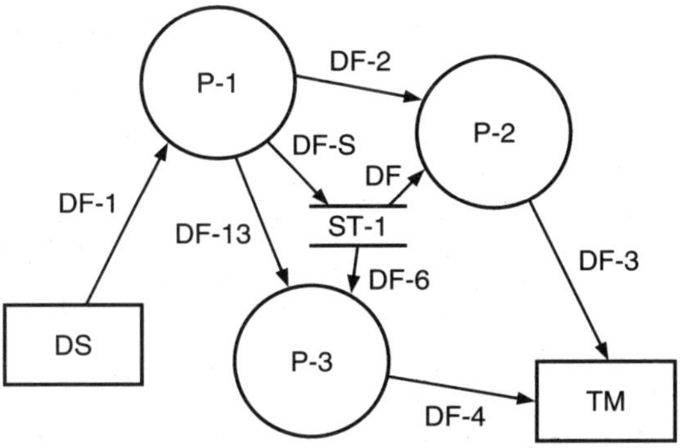

Figure 4.5 A sample DFD: requirements process model showing internal interfaces.

An action DFD can be created for each state modeled in an STD. The actions identified for that state are broken down into a series of processes. These processes depict all data and control flows, accessing of stored data, and data exchanges with external entities. The process description document describes all processing and data conversions, and how input data generates the output data or control flows.

Design Standard

The design standard establishes guidelines for preliminary and detailed design. The design phase ensures that the result of requirement analysis and domain analysis is in conformance with the software requirement. The object-oriented design consists of a class diagram, class structure charts, dependency diagrams, and inheritance diagrams.

The class diagram is shown in Fig. 4.6. Each class diagram indicates the class that is represented, all encapsulated data, inputs/outputs, and operations. The diagrams include the data type of all inputs/outputs.

A class structure chart is shown in Fig. 4.7 and is based on the concept of a *module,* which is a piece of code that is invoked and, when complete, returns control to the caller. Each module is represented by a rectangle on the class structure chart. The order of invocation as well as all inputs and outputs are depicted on the chart. The data types of all inputs and outputs are shown on the chart.

The dependency diagram is shown in Fig. 4.8. The dependency diagram is a road map to the program, repository, and environment as a whole. Each class is represented on the dependency diagram by a class box minus the operations, encapsulated data, and input/output. Lines are drawn between the class boxes to illustrate the dependencies between them. The inheritance diagram shows the inheritance relation-

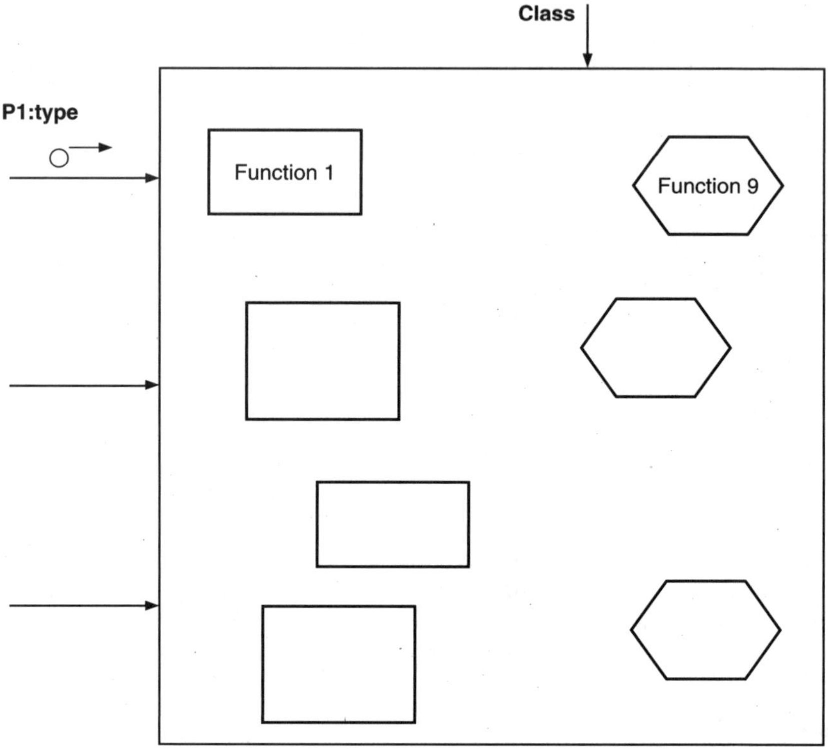

Figure 4.6 A sample class diagram.

ship between classes. At present a standard for software reuse assets is lacking in the industry. Few well-defined reuse policies and procedures are available.

Policy and Procedure Development

Policy and procedure development is a process associated with the software development life cycle. Policies and procedures provide guidance and structure and, in some cases, constraints on the practice of software reuse.

Policy and procedure development includes the mechanism of collection, identification, and implementation of reusable assets. Policy and procedure development also includes refinement of identified potential reuse assets and a process for reporting anomalies against the existing reuse assets. In addition, policy and procedure cover reengineering of assets to incorporate necessary changes. Policy and procedure development also includes a mechanism for populating the repository and configuration management of reusable assets.

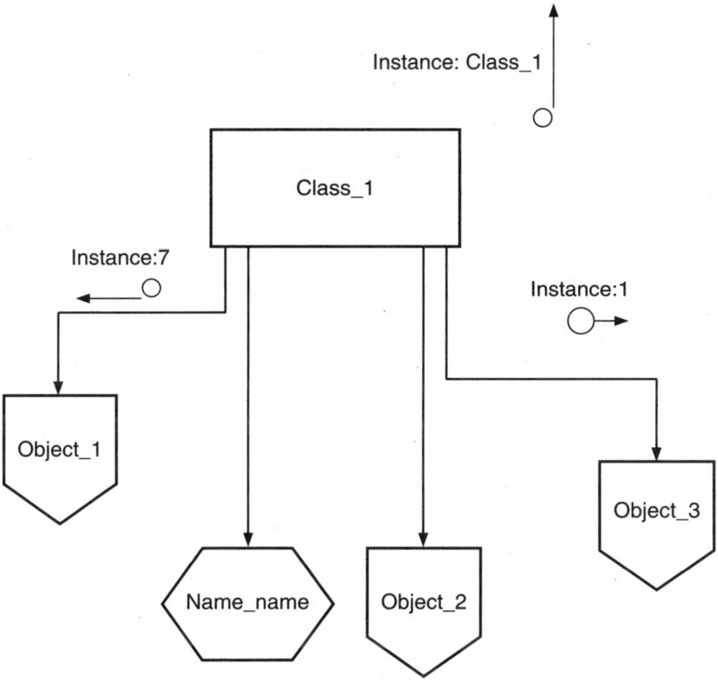

Figure 4.7 A class structure chart.

The objective of policy and procedure development is to provide a central receiving point for accepting and processing assets. Policy and procedure development provides a mechanism to buffer and control the flow of assets to potential reuse asset refinement and further to the repository preparation process. This separates collected assets from inappropriate submission. The policy and procedure development process places assets under product engineering configuration management for further processing. The policy assists the gathering of raw data on the collection of potential reuse assets for inclusion in the reuse repository.

An organization should prepare and establish policies and procedures for managing formal software reuse processes. A sample outline of a policy and procedure document is shown in Table 4.1. The minimal list of policies and procedures would include potential reuse asset collection, potential reuse asset refinement and preparation for repository population, reuse asset anomaly processing, reuse asset reengineering, reuse asset certification and repository population, and use of the reuse repository system. This document places assets under product engineering configuration management and also provides a road map of the reuse management process.

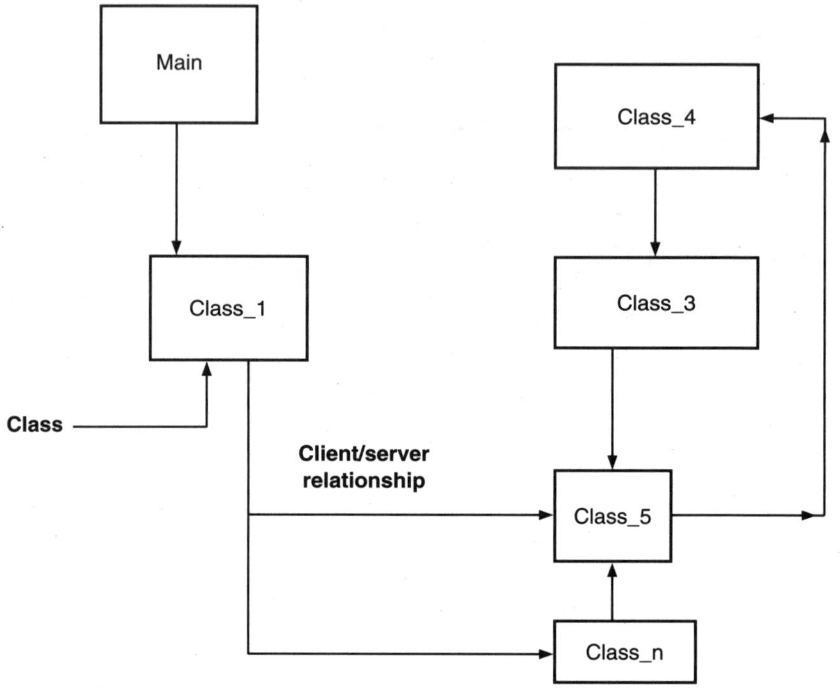

Figure 4.8 A sample dependency diagram.

The potential reuse asset refinement and preparation for repository population policy and procedure document determines whether the asset requires reengineering. This document prepares assets for inclusion in the reuse repository system. It classifies assets by assigning appropriate keywords, key phrases, and facets. This document details how to collect and record specific information pertinent to the asset. This document categorizes each asset according to its completeness and merit. A number assigned to the asset indicates that this asset has that number of associated products, which include requirements, design, code, test, documentation, and training documents.

TABLE 4.1 Policy and Procedure Outline

1. Policy
2. Purpose
3. Scope
4. Objective
5. Responsibilities
6. Procedures
7. References
8. Definitions
9. Acronyms

The reuse asset reengineering policy and procedure document identifies reuse changes to reuse assets. Reengineering is a method for updating and changing assets and associated products in the repository system, and domain models and architecture. This provides improved reuse assets that have well-defined interfaces, cohesive functionality, increased reusability, and better domain functions. This ensures consolidation of reuse assets into a single reuse asset that performs a common function. Reengineering assists in creating the required associated products that are not present in the repository system—for example, test procedures, design specifications, and necessary documentation that do not exist for an existing source code asset. Reengineering also creates assets that meet identified domain requirements that are not present in the repository.

The reuse repository system population policy and procedure document ensures that changes to the modified and reengineered asset are properly processed. The document guides the placement of the potential, modified, and reengineered asset under configuration management. These assets are also being populated into the repository. The reuse repository system policy and procedure document enables user access to the repository by providing proper accounts. The document provides a road map for searching and extracting reuse assets from the repository system. This document provides guidelines for maintaining metrics, status, and management reports regarding the reuse process. It also functions as a guide for the maintenance and handling of any problem with the repository system.

In addition, these policies and procedures provide training that will help to eradicate ignorance among practitioners.

Education and Training

An organization should provide education and training courses to the core software reuse group. These courses teach domain analysis and the design process and they are available from a variety of sources. This knowledge can help software reuse groups in doing domain analysis using, for example, IDEF models or object models. An organization could invite vendors to demonstrate their software reuse tools. Management needs to provide the necessary funding to purchase a limited amount of the tools required to facilitate software reuse and to perform the initial domain parsing. Education and training are the instruments for the development and presenting of reuse courses and courseware.

Reuse Issues

Reuse issues are open questions in many organizations. Everyone considers reuse to be important but they want quick results. Many of these issues are the result of a lack of management encouragement of incentives for software developers to incorporate reuse processes. There are no incentives for applying the principles of reuse. There is no trade-off mechanism, or reciprocal arrangement, between requirements and reuse. Only limited reuse cost models and metrics exist in the industry, which indicates a lack of vision on the part of industry leadership as well as a lack of knowledge about data rights and licensing. Other reuse issues include resistance to increased organizational interdependency and management concern about minimal payback in the near term. The perception among software developers seems to be that if a component was not invented within their own organization it is no good.

Legal Issues

There are no financial incentives for software developers to create reusable assets. There are more questions than answers regarding legal issues: Does anyone own data rights? Is anyone responsible for reusable software components? Who is liable if a reusable component crashes a system? Who vouches for the correctness of a reusable component? Is there any guarantee or warranty for a reusable component?

Chapter

5

Object-Oriented Software Reuse Management

Management is an art for some professionals and a science for others. Management is a technique that varies from person to person and is used in dealing with practitioners, systems, and projects. A good management technique facilitates the successful completion of a project within both budget and schedule. This chapter covers some of the management techniques applied to software reuse projects.

Establish Domain

Establish your domain: A good manager identifies the domain in the early stages of the project. Conducting a thorough analysis of existing systems in the organization can identify the organization's domain (or domains). Some systems may be unique and others interrelated. A domain may be made up of subsets, referred to as *subdomains,* so you should scope the domain and identify a whole domain and its subsets.

A domain is a group or family of related systems. All systems in that domain share a set of capabilities and/or data. The domain's identification for a system is an important issue; the domain should be within the system's environment and boundary. The software developer selects a domain expert, an individual who has thorough knowledge of the domain and its subdomains. The domain expert explores candidates for software reuse components (i.e., subdomains) as he or she progresses in all phases of the object-oriented software development. The selection of a domain and its subdomains successfully leads to the identification of software reuse components during the domain analysis.

Case Study 5.1

The purpose of this case study is to identify the domain and subdomains associated with maintaining a personal checkbook. The domain is Financial Accounting, as shown in the Fig. 5.1. Existing subdomains must now be identified that are relevant to the task of maintaining a checkbook. Applicable subdomains include functions such as bookkeeping, accounts payable, accounts receivable, and taxable items. (Figure 5.1 depicts this domain and subdomain relationship.) Each subcomponent may be reused, possibly resulting in savings of both money and time. In terms of software code, interfaces may have to be written, if they are not yet available to connect those reusable assets.

Writing a Software Reuse Plan

Writing a software reuse plan (SRP) is important in order to identify various phases, activities, and roles; the schedule; and project organization. The purpose of an SRP is to provide guidelines and a road map to conduct day-to-day business, which consists of events, actions, and processes necessary to operate a software reuse center in an organization. This includes the responsibilities of various sections, the practitioners, and management. The plan should be considered only as a guideline to follow during the development life cycle. It should not be considered as untouchable—as the saying goes, "Plans are made to be changed."

An outline of an SRP is shown in Table 5.1.

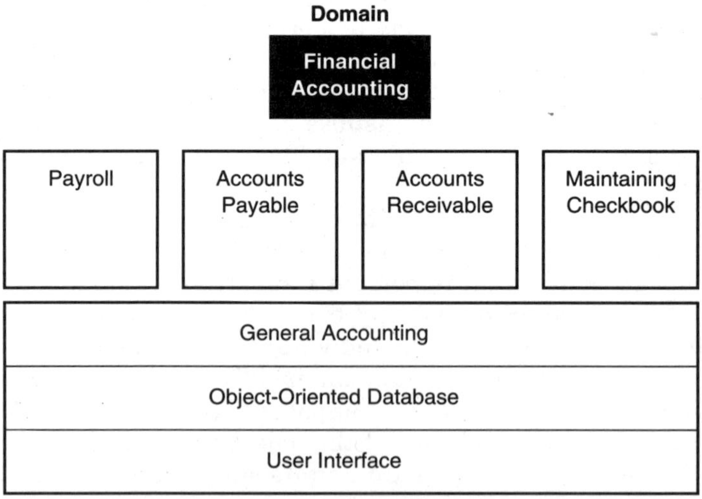

Figure 5.1 Financial Accounting domain and subdomains.

TABLE 5.1 Software Reuse Outline

- SRP purpose
- Various responsibilities and duties
- Operation and maintenance of reuse center
- Customer and user participation
- Configuration management
- Quality assurance and control
- Training
- Establishment and maintenance of repository system
- Reuse Life-Cycle Phases

Responsibilities and Duties

Various responsibilities and duties relate to domain architecture, domain analysis and design, establishing and maintaining a repository, networking, training, and managing a data review board. Select an experienced manager to form a team of domain engineers, domain asset engineers, domain repository administrators, domain system integrators, domain assets quality administrators, domain assets testers, domain assets configuration managers, and support groups. A sample organization is shown in Fig. 5.2. The domain manager is an expert in the domain and in management and is responsible for managing the team. He or she ensures that the repository is functional and that assets are tested in

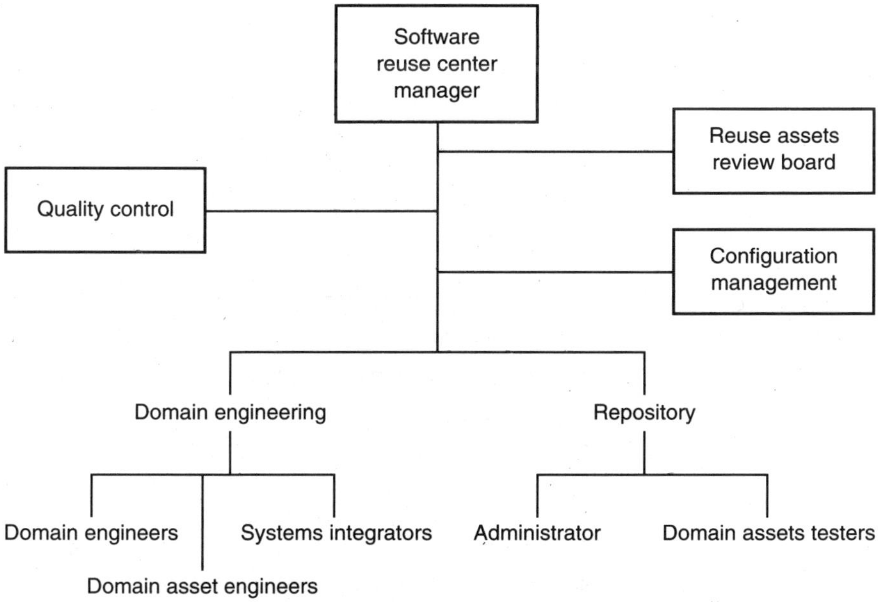

Figure 5.2 Software reuse center organization.

accordance with the software reuse plan. The domain manager is an expert in designing and maintaining the domain infrastructure architecture, as shown in Fig. 5.3. He or she is responsible for reporting the progress of the reuse project to higher management. Management's commitment is important for the success of the reuse center.

Domain engineer

A domain engineer, the domain expert, conducts domain analysis and identifies and builds assets for reuse. He or she uses customer requirements to analyze and identify desirable reusable assets. The domain engineer explores other repositories on the Internet and selects, from a range of available assets, for his or her domain. The role of the domain engineer is to support and satisfy the client's needs, as well as to maintain the domain infrastructure architecture.

Domain analyst

The domain analyst performs domain analysis and identifies, collects, organizes, and represents all relevant information in a domain. This information is based on the existing systems in the domain; knowledge collected from domain experts; underlying policies, procedures, and standards; and emerging state-of-the-art technologies.

Domain designer

The domain designer identifies a reusable asset that is suitable for its domain. The designer has access to other repositories via the Internet

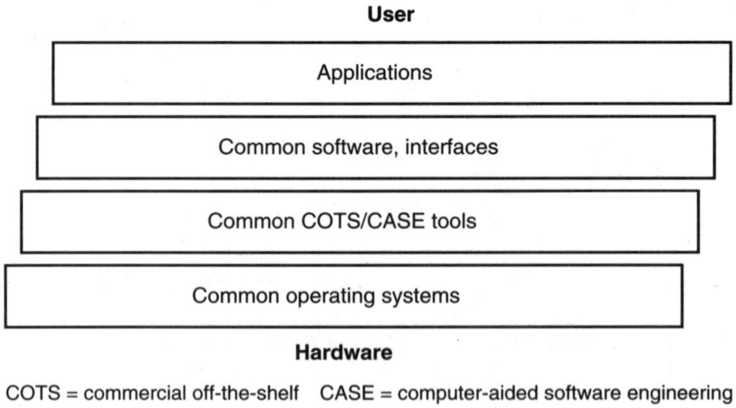

Figure 5.3 Domain infrastructure.

and intranets, and explores and researches for the right asset at the right time. The designer maintains a description of the available assets in the repository to be accessed by developers.

Each asset has a unique identifier. Each interface is documented in the repository with a proper description, protocol, constraints, and the names of systems that are reusing it. The description covers hardware, design, and programming. It also includes the processing resources and its utilization characteristics, which include the following parameters:

- Memory size—the amount of internal memory (absolute, spare, or both) of the computer
- Word size—the number of bits in each computer word
- Processing speed—the computer processor capacity (absolute, spare, or both)
- Character set standard
- Instruction set architecture
- Interrupt capabilities of the hardware
- Direct memory access
- Channel requirements
- Auxiliary storage
- Growth capabilities of any part of the processing resource
- Diagnostic capabilities
- Allocation of pertinent processing resources to each computer software configuration item (CSCI)

Configuration management

Configuration management (CM) is the process of managing the configuration assets with a proper unique number schema. These assets, under CM's control, are accessible by practitioners for reuse. Configuration management is responsible for processing and validating submitted information regarding the potential, modified, or reengineered assets. All reusable assets are configuration managed. The CM personnel are the only ones with write privileges to the CM database.

Once a candidate asset is accepted and adapted for reuse, it is placed under CM control. The CM-controlled assets are changeable only if either an anomaly has been discovered or the asset has been modified in use. Any asset anomalies that are discovered are identified with a fault report and submitted for proper analysis and disposition. The Data Review Board for asset reuse consists of representatives from various diversified fields and systems who decide the course of action for the identified anomaly. The corrected asset is certified and submitted to CM for update in the CM database. The process of building systems identifies reusable assets and retrieves them from the CM database. Configuration management tracks the assets that are modified and incorporated into systems via a *software change order.*

Quality management

Quality management ensures that the reuse processes and the policy, procedures, and standards are implemented and followed. The quality section is responsible for monitoring, auditing, and checking the correctness of various reuse documents, models, functions, and activities. Quality management verifies and validates the reuse assets.

Operation and maintenance of the reuse center

The domain manager and the staff are responsible for operation and maintenance of the reuse center. The manager delegates duties and responsibilities to each member of the staff to perform certain tasks. The manager supervises the performance of the staff.

Customer and user participation

Customer and user participation is an important factor in the success of the reuse effort, because practitioners generally like to be involved in all reuse activities. Their input is important because they are the ones who will apply the reuse assets. They should be informed on a regular basis about the progress of the reuse center, and they should have proper access to it, as well as to services provided by it. A fee may be required for certain services.

Training

Training may be provided by the reuse center as a service to customers and users. This training may cover topics such as repository usage, reuse assets management, reuse basics, software development with reuse, domain analysis, and design processes. It also should include the operation and reuse of the repository. The reuse center should develop and maintain a repository user's manual.

Establishment and maintenance of the repository system

This is the responsibility of the software reuse center team. One of the team's major tasks is to select the best repository system suitable to the domain's needs. The team maintains the repository to ensure that it is functional and operational at all times. The repository should be easily accessible to customers and users.

Reuse Life-Cycle Phases

Reuse life-cycle phases encompass the selection and certification of reusable assets. The repository should be populated with certified reusable assets and their respective descriptions and identifications. Customers and users should be informed about any new asset. All reuse assets that are accepted must undergo the adaptation and certification process before submission to CM. These phases are as follows:

- *Delineation* indicates how well the reusable asset is described in terms of documentation, comments, and conformance to the policies, procedures, and standards (PPS).
- *Relevance* describes how well the reusable asset matches the requirements of the functional and application domain.
- *Coherence* indicates the overall design quality.
- *Connectivity* indicates how well the reusable asset connects to other reusable assets comprising the functional and application domain.
- *Inerrancy* indicates how error free the asset is and how well it has been tested.
- *Mobility* indicates how easily the reusable asset can be ported to new platforms and environments.

Integration of Reuse into Software Development and Maintenance

The process of building systems is accomplished by the integration of reuse assets from the repository. Figure 5.4 shows a schema for the integration of systems with reuse assets. For example, the software development team receives new requirements for a system. These requirements are analyzed. The domain engineer also examines the requirements and confirms whether the requirement is already present in any domain repository. The software developers get the reusable, well-tested assets and save time and money in the integration of the system.

Checklist: Preventing Reuse Project Failure

This checklist describes why a reuse project might fail, which can help participants to turn around a failing one. Experience shows that most reuse project failures are the result of one or more of the following.

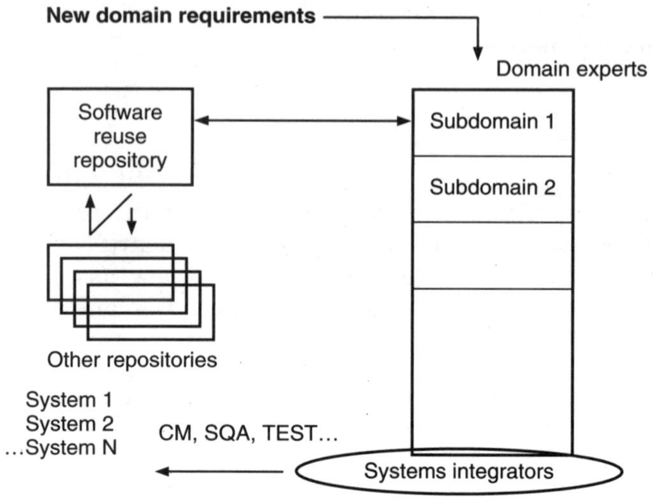

CM = configuration management SQA = software quality assurance

Figure 5.4 Integration of systems with reuse assets.

1. The software reuse team does not understand the requirements of the customers and users.
2. The scope of the reuse project is not well-defined.
3. The chosen reuse and repository technology changes.
4. Senior management support and commitment is lacking.
5. The return on investment is not realistic.
6. The schedule for completing the project is not realistic.
7. Users are resistant because of proprietorship of assets.
8. The reuse project lacks professionals with appropriate skills.
9. Cooperation and enthusiasm among the practitioners is lacking.
10. Fear exists that the success of the reuse project might hurt future business.
11. Best practices and lessons learned are ignored.
12. Frequent changes occur in labor and management.
13. Ego and pride interfere.
14. Representation to senior management is incorrect.
15. Management holds prejudiced and dogmatic views.
16. Customers and users are not involved in the progress of the reuse project, which creates a vacuum, as well as resistance.

17. Professionals are not paid for completing the project but are paid based on hours billed.
18. An unseasoned manager is assigned to manage a highly visible reuse project.
19. Miscommunication exists among the key players, management, customers, and users.
20. Reuse benefits are not properly communicated among the practitioners.
21. The budget dries up.
22. Milestones are not achieved on schedule.
23. The reuse project is not advertised properly.

Any of these points can doom a reuse project to failure. A reuse project can be successful by avoiding such pitfalls. Therefore, reuse projects should be monitored on the basis of these checkpoints and necessary precautions should be taken to prevent failure.

Part

3

Domain Engineering

If you do not know where you are going, any road will lead you there.

EASTERN SAYING

Chapter

6

Domain Engineering Basics

Object-oriented system software is usually part of a domain that consists of other related systems software. This chapter presents the basics of domain engineering, application engineering, and object-oriented software life-cycle models. This chapter also covers domain architecture for software reuse to be used in object-oriented software.

Domain Engineering

Domain engineering is a process of creating an asset that can be managed and reused. Basically, domain engineering consists of domain analysis, domain design, and domain implementation. Domain engineering activities are analogous to application activities. Domain engineering activities include analyzing and documenting existing systems and preparing the domain generic architecture. Any requirement received for the domain in the future is analyzed with respect to the generic architecture. Based on the analysis, the domain engineer suggests an architecture that meets the majority of the application requirements within the domain. The integrator implements the reusable assets that satisfy the architecture.

Domain engineering is a process for building reusable assets, which includes activities for analyzing the domain, identifying common reusable assets, and populating them in the repository, as illustrated in Fig. 6.1.

Domain engineering is an iterative process for the design and development of a product in a family and an application engineering process for producing members of that family. The domain engineering life cycle addresses domain analysis and architecture engineering, as well as the creation and evolution of a particular asset or components. The

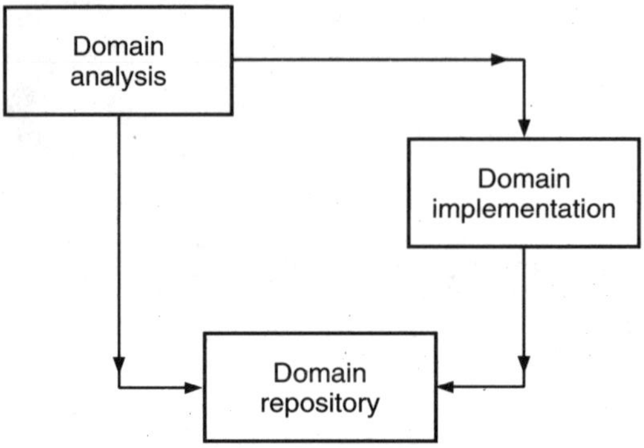

Figure 6.1 Domain engineering model.

major components of domain engineering are domain analysis, the domain repository, and domain implementation. The domain engineering goals are to identify, derive, organize, abstract, and represent the commonality and differences among assets within a particular domain. This further facilitates the reusability of life-cycle work products within an organization's body of domain knowledge.

Figure 6.2 further illustrates the concepts of domain engineering. Domain engineering is not a part of any one project—it cuts across all projects.

Application Engineering

Application engineering is the process that generates the life cycle of a system. This process organizes and directs resources for producing and supporting a system by applying the reuse paradigm. The process

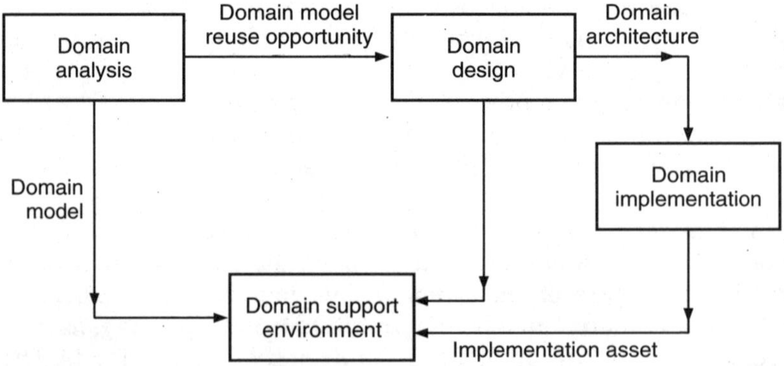

Figure 6.2 Domain engineering components.

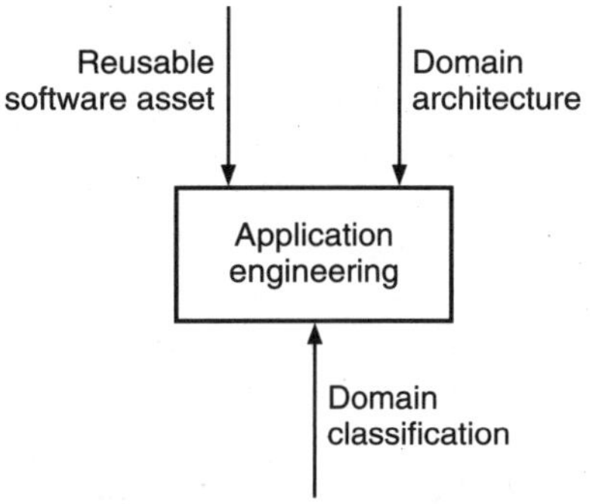

Figure 6.3 Application engineering.

includes activities for employing reusable assets from a repository, as shown in Fig. 6.3.

Application engineering makes use of the products of domain engineering, as illustrated in Fig. 6.4. The application engineering life cycle addresses the construction of new or reengineered systems using the generic requirements, domain architecture, and components. Figure 6.4 distinguishes between domain engineering and application engineering, treating them as separate life cycles. The top row of processes shows a series of domain engineering activities, starting with domain analysis and producing a domain model. The next step is the software architecture development activity that produces domain software architecture.

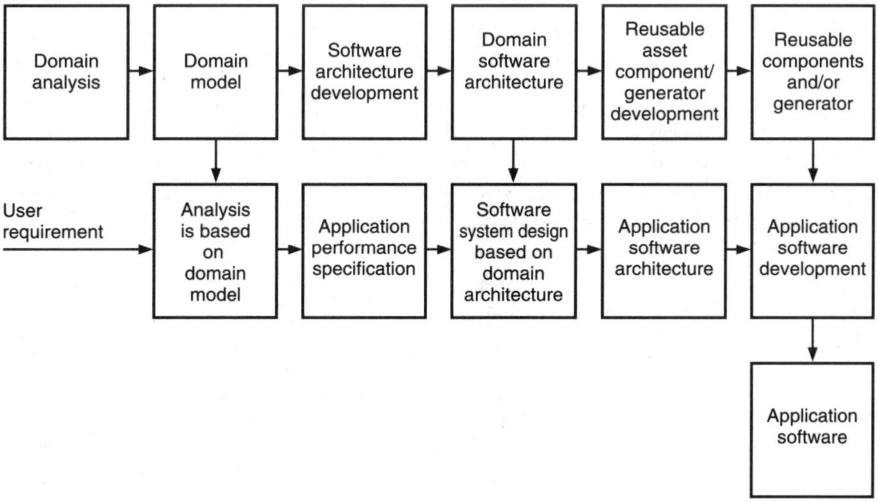

Figure 6.4 Domain engineering and application engineering approaches.

Finally, the reusable asset component generator development activity produces the components and/or generators. The bottom row of processes, which can produce a family of application systems, is a series of application engineering activities, involving analysis based on the domain model that produces application requirements. The next step is the design based on a domain architecture that produces an application architecture/design. Finally, implementation is based on the set of available implementation assets that produces an application system. At each stage there is feedback from application engineering to domain engineering to assist in the evolution of the reusable domain products. Sitting between the domain engineers and the application engineers is a reuse repository that would house all the domain assets to be shared across applications. Figure 6.4 implies that reuse must be integrated throughout the application engineering process. The domain model provides generic domain requirements that must be considered as part of the system requirement analysis. The application architecture should be derived from the domain software architecture or generic architecture.

System Life-Cycle Models

A system life-cycle model is a process for studying the system from its inception to its retirement. A system life-cycle model consists of reuse activities and phases. An activity is a process that is completed by reusing a particular method. Phases are imposed on a process as a way of controlling them. Phases produce products for review, walk-through, and inspection. There are many models available and it is up to the system analyst and management to select the one suitable to the system requirements.

Models are abstractions that assist the conceptualizing of the object-oriented software development process. A software model represents components of the development process. The finite phases of a model are not realistic. Models are constructed with the builder's idea of what is important. This idea necessarily dictates the greater visibility of a certain set of concerns, some of which are not clearly defined. Models can be made for the object-oriented software development process, the software itself, or the software management process. Models ensure that the object-oriented software product matches the customer's requirements. Such assurances correlate to other considerations as follows:

- Type of system that will be developed
- Technical orientation of people that are involved in the development effort
- Tools that are used in the effort

The customer can validate the system. A model can incorporate the concept through a structured formalism that ties requirements to the end product.

Models reflect various ways of viewing the object-oriented software development process. These viewpoints contribute to the formulation of other models, as in a chain reaction. Models can assist in management of the object-oriented software, testing, maintenance, and retirement of a system. Some of the popular models are briefly discussed.

Waterfall life-cycle model

The waterfall model partitions the software process into a sequence of distinct phases. Each of these phases is well-defined for a specific project in terms of its inputs, outputs, activities, resources, and criteria before the transition to the next phase. The waterfall model assumes that each phase will be completed before the next one is started—a top-down concept, as shown in Fig. 6.5. This model is well suited for well-defined and -understood requirements. In practice, the model is not so clean and has many iterations of feedback from other phases in each phase. Thus, the drawback is that the distinct phases are unrealistic in practice.

The waterfall model was first introduced in 1970. This software evolves in an orderly, linear sequence of transitions from one phase to the next. The model divides the software process into the following phases:

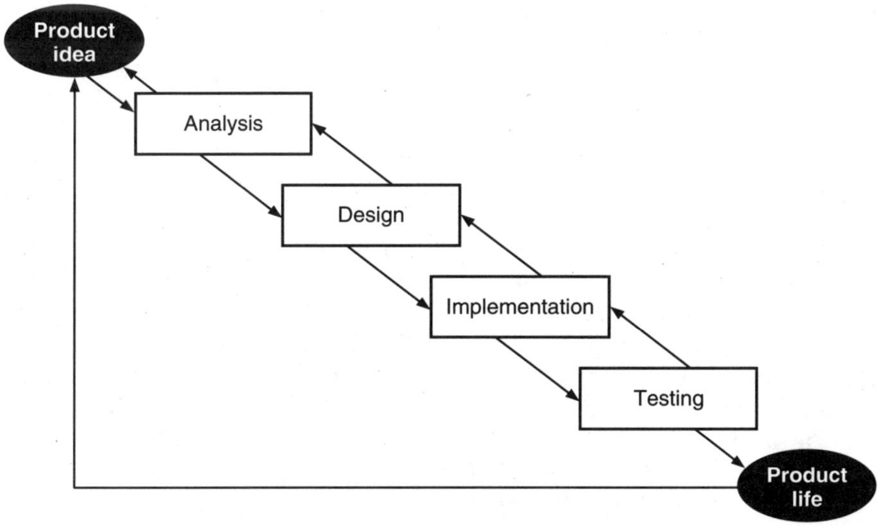

Figure 6.5 A sample of the waterfall model.

- System requirements
- Software requirements
- Analysis
- Design
- Coding
- Testing
- Operations

Each phase is conceived in terms of input, process, and output. The software process proceeds through a sequence of steps, with iterative interaction between phases that are confined to successive steps. The deliverable software is usually produced and then is used as input into the next phase.

In reality, system or software development is never so clean. As shown in Fig. 6.5, feedback loops exist between phases. Because of these feedback loops, the deliverable products at each phase need review and revision before their acceptance. The design phase may be subdivided into many phases, involving an increase in detail.

The model derives its strength from its classic steps that are taken successively. It provides a structured template for software development. This model is not popular among object-oriented software developers because of its weakness, which is that more interactions between nonsuccessive steps are needed. Identification of all the requirements for object-oriented software is not an easy job.

The model has been most useful in helping to structure and manage large, medium, and small software development projects in organizational settings. Opportunistic software reuse can be achieved by following this model.

Incremental model

In the incremental model, an initial subset of the system is fully developed. Then, in successive steps, more elaborate versions are built upon the previous ones. The architectural design of the total system is envisioned in the first step, but the system is implemented by successive elaboration. The object-oriented software is developed in small, manageable increments that represent degrees of functional capability, as shown in Fig. 6.6.

The strength of incremental development is that the increments of functional capability are easier to understand and test. Use of the increments is a means of incorporating user experience into a refined product in a much less expensive way. This model combines the classic

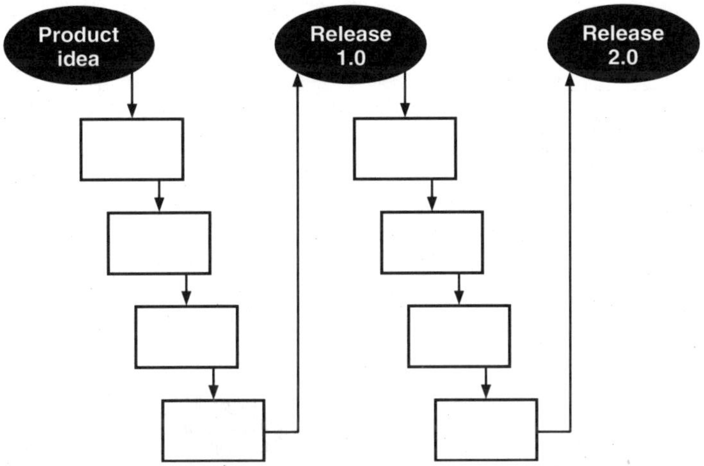

Figure 6.6 A sample of the incremental model.

software life cycle with iterative enhancement at the level of system development organization. It also provides a way to periodically distribute object-oriented software maintenance updates and services to geographically dispersed users. This model of object-oriented software evolution is popular in the computer industry. The baseline of the previous iteration can be reused for the next iteration.

Prototyping life-cycle model

One of the variations on the waterfall model is prototyping, as shown in Fig. 6.7. This model is useful for quick results and without documents to show the concept of proof for the system requirements.

The prototyping model advocates the early development of components representing the eventual system. Often these components represent the user interface to the system. A skeletal implementation of this interface is developed with the intent that it would provide an opportunity for feedback from the object-oriented software user before the final system is specified and designed. While the clarification of the user interface is one goal, prototyping may also be employed as a concept within the context of another model. In this case, the second model of the object-oriented software process may regard prototyping as but one component of the process that will be used for clarification of the behavior of the system at an early point in the development. Prototyping technologies usually accept some form of software functional specifications as input, which in turn are simulated, analyzed, or directly executed. As such, these technologies allow software object-oriented

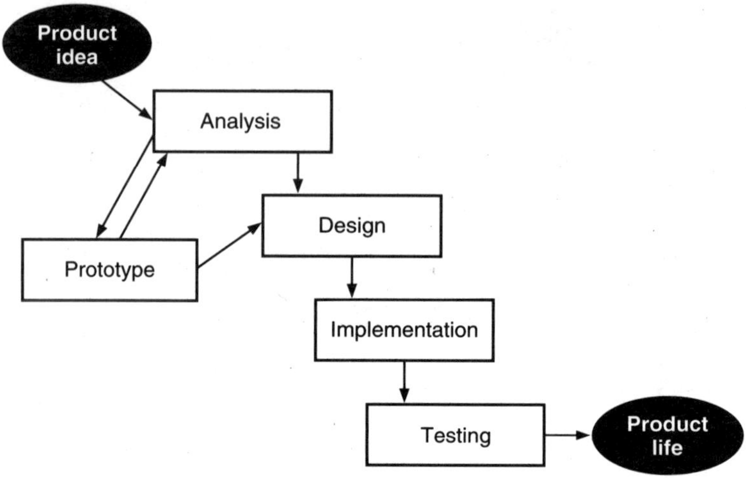

Figure 6.7 A sample of the rapid prototyping model.

design activities to be initially skipped or glossed over. In turn, these technologies can allow rapid construction of primitive versions of software systems that users can evaluate. These user evaluations can then be incorporated as feedback that refines the emerging system specifications and designs. Depending on the prototyping technology, the complete working system can be developed through a continual process of revising and refining the input specifications.

This model has the advantage of always providing a working version of the developing system, while redefining object-oriented software design and testing activities for input of specification refinement and execution.

Assembling reusable components model

The basic approach of reusability is to configure and reuse preexisting object-oriented software components in viable application systems. However, the suitability of the components for a particular system depends on their size, complexity, and functional capability. Most approaches attempt to utilize components similar to the common data structure, with algorithms as their manipulation. Other approaches attempt to utilize components resembling functionally complete systems or subsystems that are user-interface management systems. There are probably many ways to utilize reusable software components in evolving software systems. However, cited studies suggest that their initial use during architectural or component design specification is a way to speed implementation. They might also be used for prototyping purposes if a suitable software prototyping technology is available.

Spiral life-cycle model

The spiral life-cycle model is also a variation of the classic waterfall model, as shown in Fig. 6.8. Each of the development phases is carried out in one or more cycles. Each cycle begins with a risk assessment and includes a prototype to provide insight into the risk issues.

The spiral model was developed at TRW in 1988. The model involves multiple iteration through cycles, with the intent of analyzing the results of prior phases by determining risk estimates for future phases. At each phase, alternatives are evaluated with respect to the objectives and constraints forming the basis for the next cycle of the spiral. Each cycle is completed with a review involving parties with vested interests. Boehm [Boeh88] states, "The model reflects the underlying concept that each cycle involves a progression that addresses the same sequence of steps for each portion of the product and for each of its levels of elaboration from an overall concept-of-operation document down to the coding of each individual program."

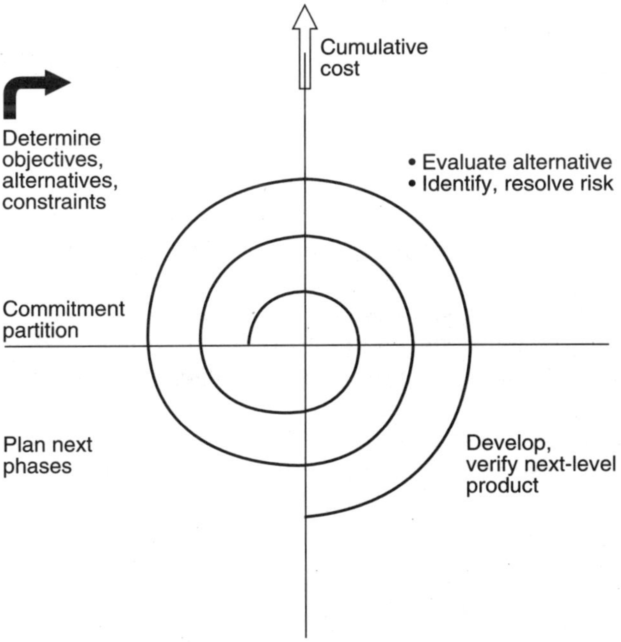

Figure 6.8 A sample of the spiral life-cycle model.

The radial dimension represents the added incremental cost incurred in completing the developmental steps. The angular dimension represents the progress made in completing each cycle of the spiral. The basic premise of the model is that a certain sequence of steps is repeated while developing or maintaining software. The steps are first done at a very high level of abstraction, and then each loop of the spiral represents a repeat of the steps at successively lower levels of abstraction.

The strength of the model lies in its flexibility for managing a system's object-oriented software development life cycle. An examination of risk can be planned at each major abstraction. The model accommodates any mixture of specification-oriented, process-oriented, object-oriented, or other approaches to software development. This model is favored by object-oriented software developers because of its aforementioned strengths. The weakness of the model is a lack of matching with any existing standards. The model depends on identifying and managing sources at project risk. The model needs more uniformity and consistency; however, it does assist in the systematic reuse process.

Star process model

The star process model is nonphased. This model is useful for user-interface activities. User-interface development occurs in bottom-up and top-down activities. The star model is based on empirical evidence from observations of software development. The star model allows for small, localized minicycles that are important to user-interface development.

Operational model

Behaviors particular to the problem domain are modeled and simulated in the beginning stages of the operational model in order to explore with the software customer the manner and sequence in which events happen. This exploration is made possible with the construction of an operational specification for the system. Concern at the specification level with *how* the system behaves is in contrast to other models whose specifications define the system in terms of a black box mapping the inputs to the outputs.

While the behavior of the problem domain is emulated in the specification, the object-oriented software structures that will eventually be used in the actual system that produces this behavior are determined later in the development process.

Transformational model

The transformational model starts with a program specification and ends with a program. The transformational model's progress between the two points is made through an automated series of transformations. According to Partsch and Steinbruggen [Part83], "Transformation rules are partial mappings from one program scheme to another so that an element of the domain and its image under the mapping constitute a correct transformation. Transformational programming is a software process of program construction where successive applications of transformation rule. Usually, this process starts with a (formal) specification of a formal statement with a problem or its solution and ends with an executable program."

The benefit associated with the transformational model is the reduction of the labor intensity of software production through the automated transformation. This model assists in preserving correctness through the application of formal transformations and replaces the final product testing by verification of the program specifications. One of the abilities of this model is to produce desired transformations through a combination of small units from specialized programming knowledge.

Developing a Domain Architectural Model

A domain architectural model is a generic picture of related systems in the domain. The architectural model is plug-and-play, an open architecture designed around a client/server model. Figure 6.9 shows a sample of a generic domain architectural model. The model consists of a standard reusable environment, a set of standard off-the-shelf reusable components, and a set of reusable programming standards that describe how to add new functionality to the environment. The model is designed to run on hardware platforms such as PCs and workstations. It extends the Windows paradigm, which allows applications to coexist, by providing the capability of applications to share data, services, and functions at the server level.

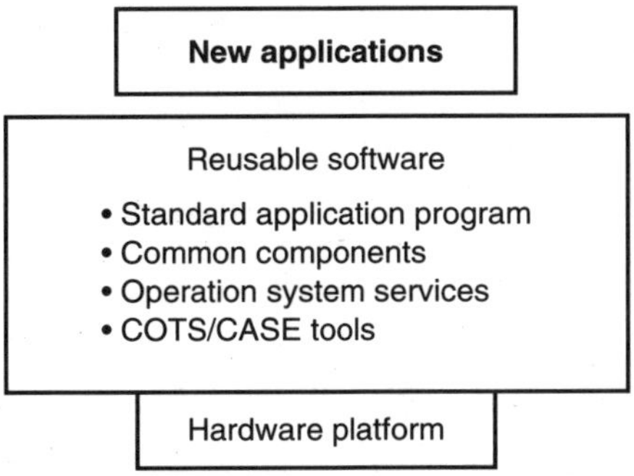

Figure 6.9 A sample of the generic domain architecture model.

Conventionally, software developers build common functions from scratch for every system. Each developer implements the functions differently, which leads to incompatibility between related systems. Thus, while most of the production systems have similar functions, they cannot easily interoperate. Surprisingly, organizations invest a great deal of time and money to rebuild the same functions.

The concept is to construct an architecture model for building interoperable systems, an infrastructure for supporting related applications. The model facilitates an automated process for software integration and tools and provides a collection of reusable software components. This architecture model provides both an approach and a methodology for software reuse.

Chapter

7

The Reusability Process

The reusability process entails finding ways that existing software can be reused in new software development. Software standards such as IEEE 1498 clearly emphasize reusability. The object-oriented approach provides convenient ways that pretested software can be reused. Software reusability results in increased adherence to object-oriented software engineering goals and principles and reduces costs and improves the schedules of new software development during the maintenance life cycle. This chapter covers software reusability, processes and activities, and repositories.

Software Reusability

Software reusability is the process whereby new software systems are implemented from preexisting software, as illustrated in Fig. 7.1. The reusability process captures commonality and differences from the models of systems. This includes the development and acquisition of reusable resources, management, and the use of those resources. Reusability can be applied at any scale and any level of abstraction. Software reusability is identified during domain analysis, requirement analysis, design, implementation, and testing phases. Reusability enhances compliance with object-oriented software engineering goals and principles. Reliability is also enhanced by the reuse of software that is seasoned and pretested. New software development schedules are reduced by not having to rewrite the reusable code or redesign detailed components. The size and performance requirements of reused components are also known, which includes processor time and memory. Software readability is improved if shared components are well designed. Examples of reuse situations are as follows:

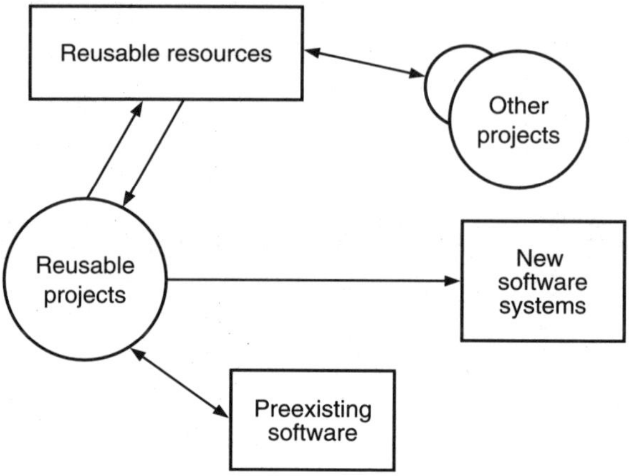

Figure 7.1 The reusability process.

- Requirements analysis models and documents
- Use cases
- Classes
- Inheritance
- Reuse objects
- Design models and documents
- Code components
- Structure charts
- Test cases
- Test scenarios
- Modules
- Functions

There are always limitations on the reuse of existing software. This depends on customer requirements, which may prevent reuse. Limitations may occur because the software design is not clear enough and does not provide any guidelines for reuse. They also can occur when documentation is not clear enough for effective reuse in particular software. It is then more economical to write new software than to reuse the existing software.

The Software Reusability Process

The software reusability process steps are:

- Construct
- Collect
- Catalog
- Classify
- Comprehend
- Customize

To *construct* means to reuse existing methods and products. To *collect* means to reuse the existing library and continue building it. To *catalog* is to reuse descriptive information. To *classify* is to reuse semantic and functional information. To *comprehend* means to reuse resources identification and analysis. To *customize* is to develop applications from reusable resources.

Software Reusability Process Activities

Software reusability process activities are listed in Fig. 7.2. The process model consists of adaptive, parameterized, and engineered components. The adaptive model for reuse is the process of modifying a system or component so it will perform its function in a different manner or on different data from what was originally intended. In an adaptive model, *construct* in this context means that modular software is built while software engineering techniques, such as information hiding and data encapsulation, are applied. Here, *collect* means that the database is organized in terms of projects and project software. In this case, the *catalog* is the description of projects and software modules, and *classifying* uses architecture models and applies reverse engineering. *Comprehend* means maintenance of benchmark and other performance information that also includes test data. *Customizing* means the use of CASE tools and reengineering support for maintenance.

Constructing in the parameterized process model for software reuse means building software as standard products and continually refining them, just as in a software factory. Here, *collecting* means establishing inventory for the software factory. In this case, *cataloging* gives descriptive information about standard products. *Classifying* is semantic and functional, and tailors information on products. In this model, *comprehending* has rapid prototyping capability; *customizing* is automated customization and system generation. The engineered process for software reuse is shown in Fig. 7.3.

Basically, three activities occur in the reuse process as they are shown in Fig. 7.4: domain engineering, applications engineering, and reuse management [U.S. DOD94]. Domain engineering, as discussed before, identifies and develops reusable assets within a domain—for

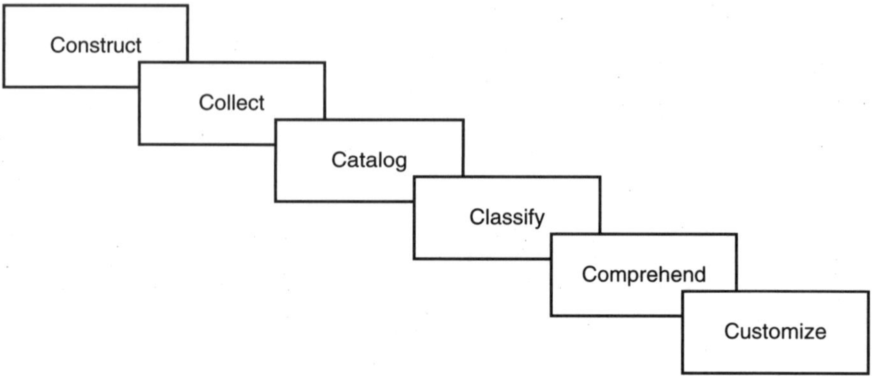

Figure 7.2 Major activities in the reusability process.

example, requirements, design, and coding. Application engineering then uses the assets from domain engineering when new applications are developed within the domain. Application engineering also identifies assets for reuse after they have been used and modified for new applications. These assets are then transferred into the domain engineering mode. Domain engineering can be categorized as engineering-for-reuse, as it represents the supply side of reuse, whereas application engineering is the demand side. These two processes are linked by the reusable asset management process that serves as the intermediary (or supplier) of reuse. This includes one or more of the repositories, the tools, and the procedures required so that reusable assets can be managed.

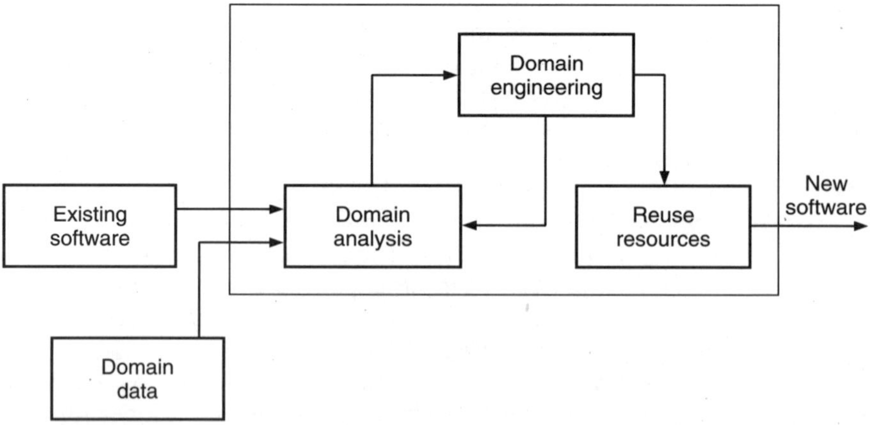

Figure 7.3 Software reuse engineering process.

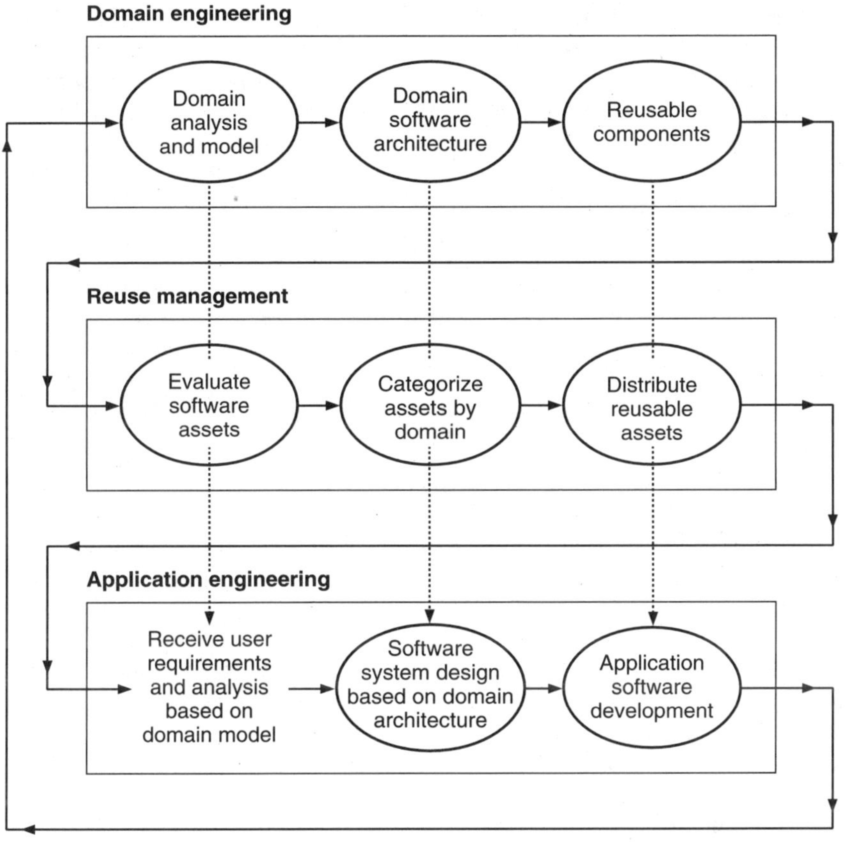

Figure 7.4 Software reuse activities.

Domain Repositories

A domain repository is a mechanism for defining, storing, and managing reusable assets. The repository concept is identical to a library mechanism. A database is the core of a repository, which consists of integrated computer-aided software engineering (CASE) tools.

A good repository is easy to access and operate—that is, a repository is user-friendly. Repositories are available via the Internet and PCs. The repository provides formal representation for reuse assets. A repository is a common place for creating, maintaining, and retrieving reusable assets—it is a mechanism for sharing and reusing assets for developing software systems.

A repository is populated once with reusable assets, and this information is used and reused many times. The reusable assets are updated regularly in the repository. The repository holds and manages the information needed to create, modify, evolve, execute, and maintain a software system. Internet capabilities assist in making this information available throughout the world. There are many repositories available in the computer industries, and some of them are discussed here.

Establishing a Reusable Repository

Establishing a reusable repository is the right approach in an organization. A repository contains workable software components that are free of defects and that meet the organization's software reuse needs. Believe it or not, every possible line of code that could be written has been written in a given language; however, only a domain and software engineer's experience and knowledge can determine whether that particular code is in existence. Many organizations have established centralized reusable software repositories. The repository evaluates, accepts, maintains, and makes reusable assets available for specific software projects. As the primary support tool for software reuse, the repository supplies reusable software assets in a fashion similar to a retail outlet store. Thus, it is a software reuse facilitator. The items for consumption can be based on vertical domains, horizontal domains, the types of components it contains, or the software language used. At present, there are many software reuse repositories and some of them are listed in App. C.

Advanced Application Partitioning Toolkit (AdAPT)

AdAPT is a library of object-oriented software tools that enables software developers to create robust partitioned applications. AdAPT is a solution designed to work in PowerBuilder and can be tailored to fit other object-oriented development environments, such as Java and C++.

Ada Math Advantage

Ada Math Advantage 2.0 consists of 106 frequently used mathematical and utility components distributed across 16 packages. Applications include signal processing, image processing, linear algebra, interpolation, statistics, and basic math operations. Source code is provided as well as testing data and installation scripts. Software is warranted and supported. This software has been successfully ported to platforms ranging from PCs to Cray supercomputers, using a large number of different compilers.

AdaSAGE

AdaSAGE is an application development and integration environment with a proven history of success. It provides numerous capabilities that include one of the world's fastest database systems, as well as query language, multiuser development, graphics, both character and Windows-based user interfaces, text retrieval, and WIN32 support. AdaSAGE professional users claim that it is an ideal product for integrating original source code with commercial off-the-shelf (COTS) objects and other language libraries into a seamless final system.

Comprehensive Approach to Reusable Defense Software (CARDS)

CARDS is a Department of Defense (DOD) program, sponsored by the U.S. Air Force Electronic Systems Center, dedicated to reducing the cost and time required to deliver high-quality, software-intensive systems. CARDS helps to maximize today's scarce resources by investigating, developing, and integrating systematic software reuse techniques and products. Systematic software reuse relies on defining product lines, establishing architectures that address the requirements of the components of the product lines, and developing and managing the reusable components that populate the product-line architecture.

Asset Source for Software Engineering Technology (ASSET)

The ASSET library is funded under the Defense Advanced Research Program Agency's Software Technology for Adaptable Reliable Systems (STARS) programs. IBM, the library's primary contractor, and its subcontractor SAIC will gather, categorize, safeguard, and disseminate defense-related software products, design, and specifications. ASSET contains several collections of information or assets and groups of related files or elements.

Booch components

The Booch components consist of several dozen domain-independent data structures and tools, each with multiple implementations so that a client can select the representation that provides the most suitable time and space characteristics. The Booch components are available in Ada, C++, and Smalltalk.

Computer Software Management and Information Center (COSMIC)

COSMIC is NASA's Software Technology Transfer Center. It is the central repository for software development under NASA funding. Program source code is made available for commercial development, for university research, and for reuse by other government agencies through NASA's Technology Utilization Program. Subject areas for programs developed under NASA funding include computer graphics, structural mechanics, aerodynamics, thermal analysis, control system design, trajectory determination, CAD/CAM, and artificial intelligence.

CORBAplus for C++

CORBAplus for C++ is a CORBA 2.0–compliant object request broker for developing enterprise-class distributed object applications. CORBAplus achieves full CORBA 2.0 compliance with IDL to C++ mapping; interoperable and standard communication (IIOP); CORBA services (naming, event, and relationship); and static and dynamic interfaces.

Energy Science and Technology Software Center (ESTSC)

The ESTSC is the centralized software management facility for the U.S. Department of Energy (DOE). Operated by the DOE office of Scientific and Technical Information, the ESTSC licenses and distributes federally funded software developed by the national laboratories, other facilities and contractors for DOE, and the U.S. Nuclear Regulatory Commission. This software represents the latest in federal technology. In addition, the collection contains selected software from the Nuclear Energy Agency of the Organization for Economic Cooperation and Development [ACM97, p. 73].

The software packages in the collection can be used for many different applications. Software packages are designed to run on personal computers, workstations, mainframes, and supercomputers. In many cases, the packages are available in several environments to allow the software to be used on various computers and operating systems.

Generic Reusable Ada Components for Engineering (GRACE)

GRACE is a library of 275 Ada software components based on commonly used data structures such as strings, matrices, lists, stacks, queues, trees, and graphs. Each component includes complete requirement specifications, design documentation, source code, and one or two test programs. GRACE is completely portable and fully warranted [ACM92, p. 87].

Object Text

Object Text is an object-oriented text parser. This 32-bit ActiveX server is designed to allow Windows developers to search for specific segments of text in much the same way as words, sentences, and paragraphs are read. It cuts coding time, simplifies debugging, and increases the flexibility of the search-and-replace process.

Orbix

The Orbix object request broker allows developers to create distributed applications based on the OMG's CORBA standard. Orbix integrates heterogeneous network environments, is CORBA 2.0–compliant, and includes many beneficial extensions.

Domain-Specific Repository (DSR)

A domain-specific repository consists of the basically reusable assets of one domain in an organization. The DSR assists in the work by facilitating reuse of existing and pretested software rather than having to reinvent it. It is important that this repository be structured in such a way that it will be useful and easily accessible. Table 7.1 provides a checklist of guidelines for the software reuse repository. It is expensive to establish an effective software reuse repository.

The challenge of reusability is to provide software engineers with the capability to find what they want, when they want it. Time and cost are of the greatest importance. Such information should be available in

TABLE 7.1 Software Reuse Repository Guidelines

- A separate repository should be established for each computer language.
- Only necessary and reusable software components should be included.
- Software components should be small, with less than 100 lines of code.
- Software components should be robust and standardized.
- The repository should be properly cataloged.
- Selection criteria should be properly structured so that the components are easily accessible.
- Software components should be indexed.
- Software components should contain a minimum amount of comments in the code for explanation. (Detailed explanation should be included in the design documents.)
- Identifiers for the software components should be self-explanatory.
- An easy-to-use electronic search capability for the reuse components should be available and included in the repository.

catalog form, where it can be easily found and is accessible, eliminating the need to rewrite lines of code. Keywords and key phrases should be used so users can identify the software components that might meet their needs. Many repositories include various kinds of software components. It is equally important to provide the necessary training to the software engineers who look for such information.

It is the design effort that builds reusable software. The reuse repository should be properly built, and it is a software engineering effort that will continue building such repositories. The custodian of the repository should be expert enough to provide a proper index and catalog, and to update the repository with the latest versions of the software components. The data included with such reusable software components should contain the date of creation, the author's name, any proprietorship information, comments, and the date of test, and it should reference tested data with any modification. This information is needed before a particular component can be reused. Selecting of components that can be reused readily is not an easy job.

Software engineers should be trained in reuse capability, and necessary training should be provided so the best use of the repository can be made. Management should establish goals for utilization of the reuse repository. Incentives should be provided for reusing software. It needs to be a management commitment that all areas of an organization should be involved in the reuse software repository.

Domain Repository and Application Development

The domain repository is a mechanism for defining, storing, and managing information about reusable assets. A basic form of a repository is a library mechanism. The repository provides one central place for creating, maintaining, and retrieving assets. The repository supports application development life-cycle activities. These activities hold and manage the information needed to create, modify, evolve, execute, and maintain a software system.

The domain repository permits software system components, assets, and information about software systems to be shared and reused across software systems, life cycles, and domains, and on the Internet to other domains and systems. The domain repository supports an open architecture environment and allows for the use of plug-and-play CASE tools from various vendors, as well as use across multiple platforms.

The primary objective of the portability strategy is to reduce the difficulty in identifying and changing the necessary parts of the software program for acceptance on the target computer. When sound object-oriented software engineering practices are followed during the design and coding phases, the result is software that is easier to port and reuse.

Selection Criteria for Suitable Reusable Software

Selection criteria for suitable reusable software initiate in the early stages of software development during the domain analysis, software requirement analysis, and design phases. Significant savings can be realized if the products of these phases can be reused. Software reuse is considered to have great potential to enhance productivity in software development. Object-oriented analysis and design make the reuse of isolated architectural elements more practical in the long run. Many COTS packages are available for such purposes. Table 7.2 is a checklist of the selection criteria for suitable reusable software.

At the lowest granularity level, a typical subroutine library of mathematical functions or subroutines code is available for reuse. The choice of granularity involves a trade-off. A large granule of code can yield a very high productivity gain when it is reused, but a close fit is generally not easily found between a user's requirements and a large aggregation of code. On the other hand, a library of many small granules generally provides chunks of code that match a user's requirements, but the productivity gain is smaller and the problems of indexing and searching are greater. Mathematical subroutines have been used for a long time and they yield benefits despite their generally fine granularity because they are relatively easy to comprehend, standardize, and index.

Object-oriented languages center around the creation of abstract data types. Ada95, Smalltalk, C++, and Java are software languages that are particularly suited to and will take advantage of code reuse.

TABLE 7.2 Selection Criteria for Suitable Reusable Software

- Reusable software should belong to a reputable repository library.
- Reusable software should be of the highest possible quality.
- Reusable software should be correct, reliable, and robust.
- Reusable software should be easily portable.
- Reusable software should be clear enough that it is easily understood.
- Reusable software should be well documented.
- Reusable software should be adaptable.
- Reusable software should be easily modifiable and fit the requirements of current applications.
- Reusable software should be easily maintainable.
- Reusable software should conform to well-established design principles, such as information hiding.

These languages and other object-oriented languages have features, generics, and packages that make it easier to design code for reuse. One of the design goals of these languages is to facilitate the creation and exploitation of reusable parts in recognition of the potential productivity improvements that reuse can bring.

Packages, visibility control, and separate compilation support modularity and information hiding. This allows the separation of specific application parts of the code, which will maximize the general-purpose parts that are suitable for reuse and allow the isolation of design decisions within modules, which facilitates change. Systems in these languages types support localization of data definitions so that consistent changes can be made easily. Generic units directly support the development of general-purpose and adaptable code and can be instantiated so specific functions can be performed. The careful use of these features will produce code that will more likely be reused. Some common examples of reuse involve classes, functions, and modules.

Chapter

8

Distributed Object Technology

Distributed object technology provides the mechanism for linking objects in a network. With distributed objects, users concentrate more on what they need rather than on how to get it. This chapter covers distributed object technology, environments, and Common Object Request Broker Architecture (CORBA).

Distributed Object Environment (DOE)

The distributed object environment is a mechanism for objects to access each other's public state and export functionality. CORBA is technically superior, but many vendors claim that the distributed object environment based on Java is superior. The DOE is useful in client/server development and Internet applications. The developers put together complex client/server systems simply by assembling and extending reusable distributed objects. Distributed objects can be altered without changing their core functionality. They allow you to specify cell-defined and strongly typed entities. Thus, developers can mix and match reusable assets, even if the assets reside across the network.

Intranets, extranets, and the Internet have contributed to the growth of object technology by requiring better management of object distribution throughout the enterprise. An *intranet* is an electronic business application within an organization. An *extranet* is an electronic business application deployed within the larger community of an organization and includes its supplier, vendors, and contractors. Connecting either one to the Internet makes the information it contains accessible from anywhere in the world using ubiquitous browser software. Intranets, extranets, and the Internet require the management of distributed transactions regardless of platform, language, and scalability. The World Wide Web is a highly advanced distributed object system. Figure 8.1 shows a graphic view of the distributed object environment.

The integration of the Web with CORBA or the common object model (COM) provides an excellent opportunity for distributed object technology. CORBA and COM are server-centric architectures that place the state and behavior of objects in server processes called as shared libraries or repositories. Clients can send requests to objects that logically reside elsewhere. Thus, the DOE is an environment that allows objects to be distributed across a heterogeneous network and allows each of the computing components to interoperate as a unified whole. When objects are distributed across a network, clients can be servers and, conversely, servers can be clients.

Distributed Computing Environment (DCE)

The distributed computing environment combines object-oriented concepts with client/server technology to produce a framework for building modular and scalable distributed applications at a relatively high level of abstraction. Distributed object technology provides the means to do so by enabling access to applications and data wherever servers are located. The DCE provides a standardized environment for distributed applications across platforms, but it is only a foundation.

In the DCE, hardware, software, and networking work together in a system. In the DCE, a graphical model of a system is prepared, well-

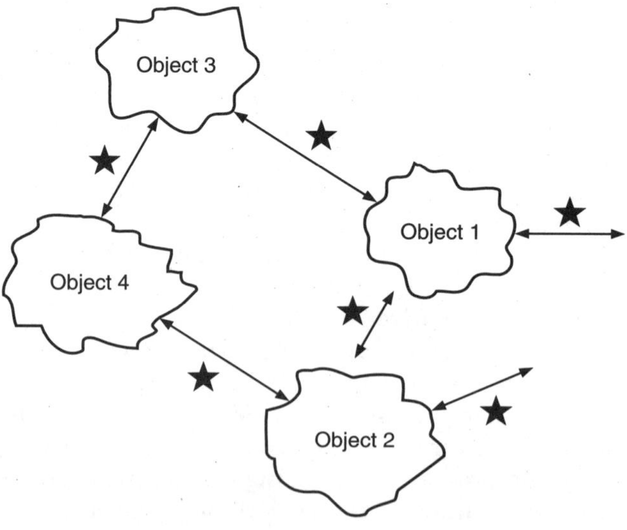

Figure 8.1 A sample of the distributed object environment.

tested components are reused, and interfaces are identified. The integration of a system saves money and time. The DCE is more cost effective in multiple applications than in a single application. DCE products are compatible, as most of the core services are standardized by and licensed from the Open Software Foundation. Two users can standardize on disparate platforms and still work together.

Common Object Request Broker Architecture (CORBA)

The Common Object Request Broker Architecture is an object-oriented standard produced by the Object Management Group. The standard has defined many key areas of distributed computing. The CORBA standard includes mapping between an Interface Definition Language (IDL) and C++, Java, Smalltalk, and Ada95. The OMG is working with Microsoft to enable CORBA and COM to provide standard architecture for distributed object computing. Figure 8.2 shows a graphic view of the structure of CORBA.

CORBA solves the interoperability problem. Each node is an object with a well-defined interface that is identified by a unique handling technique. The messages are passed between a sending object and a target object. The target object is also identified by its unique handling technique. The message format is defined in an interface known to the

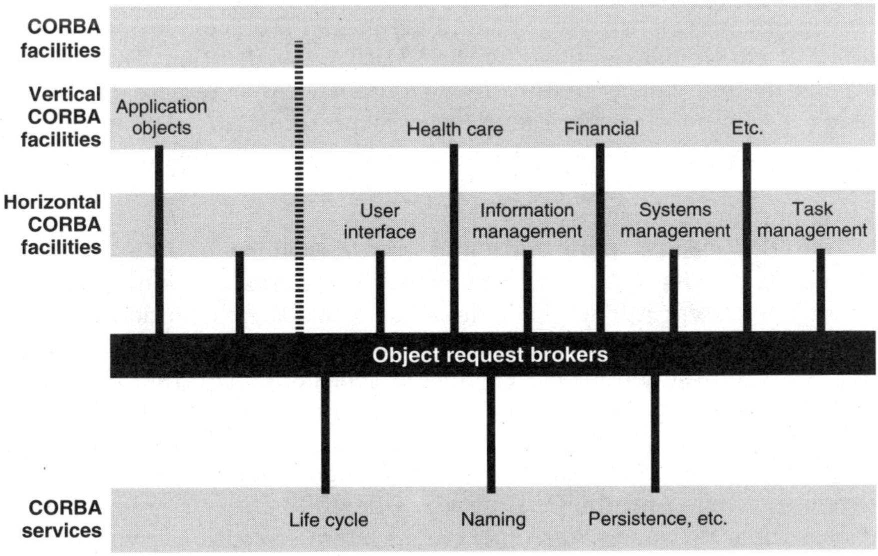

Figure 8.2 An overview of CORBA. *(Source: OMG)*

system. CORBA connects objects only and not applications. The OMG provides enterprise integration in Object Management Architecture (OMA). OMA describes the overall architecture for distributed object computing based on the object request broker (ORB). CORBA specifies a messaging facility for the DOE. CORBA consists of four major parts, as follows:

1. The *application objects* are the objects that you create specific to your applications. These are the objects that exist in support of a particular application. You define these objects using the Interface Definition Language so that the objects can communicate with other CORBA-compliant object request brokers.
2. The *object request broker* (ORB) is the center of all activities. The ORB is middleware that establishes the client/server relationships between objects. Using an ORB, a client can transparently invoke a method on a server object, which can be on the same machine or across a network. The ORB intercepts the call and is responsible for finding an object that can implement the request, pass it the parameters, invoke its method, and return the result. The client does not have to be aware of where the object is located, its programming language, its operating system, or any other system aspects that are not part of an object's interface. In so doing, the ORB provides interoperability between applications on different machines in heterogeneous distributed environments and seamlessly interconnects multiple-object systems.

The ORB is a piece of infrastructure technology that helps in the development of CORBA objects and arranges for objects to access each other at runtime, as defined by the CORBA specification. The ORB is an engine that can communicate with other local or remote objects by using a common interface and network protocol. An ORB can make requests to other ORBs and they can also process responses. All of these processes happen behind the scenes, hidden from the user and the client/server applications.

The ORB assures portability and interoperability of all application objects that exist on various connected computers. In fielding typical client and server applications, developers use their own designs or a recognized standard to define the protocol to be used between the devices. Protocol definition depends on the implementation language, network transport, and a dozen other factors. The ORB simplifies this process. With an ORB, the protocol is defined through the application interfaces via a single-implementation, language-independent specification, the IDL. And the ORB provides flexibility. It lets programmers choose the most appropriate operating system, execution environment, and even programming language to use for each component of a system under construction. The ORB allows the integration of existing components. In an ORB-based solution, developers simply model the legacy component using the same IDL they use for creating new objects, then write wrapper code that translates between the standardized bus and the legacy interfaces.

3. The *CORBA facilities* provide services to applications and consist of two subparts, vertical and horizontal. These are a collection of services that relate more to clients than to the server. The vertical CORBA facilities define higher-level objects and interfaces that include domain-specific vertical services. The horizontal CORBA facilities are domain-independent horizontal services.

4. The *CORBA services* provide a group of services that use object interfaces. They define interfaces for general-purpose supporting services. They provide a base set of services encapsulated within the ORB. The object services augment the base functionality of the ORB.

CORBA benefits

CORBA offers many benefits. It allows applications to communicate with one another no matter where they are located or who has designed them. The entire system is self-describing. The specification of a service is always separated from the implementation. CORBA 2.0 provides enough detail, especially considering the object-to-object communications links, to enable two ORBs from two or more vendors to work together. You discover objects and reuse them. The CORBA concept relates to domain and subdomain relationships. The CORBA specification includes how objects are defined, created, dispatched, invoked, and how they communicate with each other.

Interface Definition Language

The Interface Definition Language defines interfaces to objects. The interface of each object is defined in a unified way by the IDL. The ORB interfaces are defined via an IDL. The interface definition specifies the operations the object is prepared to perform, the input and output parameters it requires, and any exceptions that may be generated along the way. Remote objects view a CORBA object purely in terms of this interface. The IDL is accessible to objects written in any language and across platform communications architecture. The CORBA architecture separates the interface, written in OMG IDL, from the implementation, which must be written in some programming language.

To the client or user, the interface represents a promise that when the client sends a proper message to the interface, the response will come back. To the object implement, the interface represents an obligation that all of the operations specified in the interface must be implemented, in some programming language.

Architecture

The major components of CORBA are the ORB, the IDL, the interface repository, the basic object adapter (BOA), the Static Invocation Interface (SII), the Dynamic Invocation Interface (DII), and the object reference. We have already discussed the ORB and IDL.

The interface repository contains all IDL definitions that describe the attributes, operations, user-defined types, and exceptions of the server objects. The BOA represents the interface between the ORB and the server applications. It dispatches objects that the server applications maintain and exchanges messages with the server. The SII is a stub-based interface used by client programs in order to invoke service on application objects. The DII is a generic interface that does not require stubs, but rather supports dynamic construction of object invocations by the client program at runtime. The object reference is the value that unambiguously identifies an object. Object references are never reused to identify another object.

Common Object Model

The common object model is a part of the Microsoft Windows family of operating systems. The COM defines a set of base classes and a mechanism for constructing and dynamically linking objects. The COM provides the underlying object model for components. All COM objects are required to implement behavior that allows software components to plug and play. Microsoft engineered the COM with distribution in mind and it initially supported communications on a single machine.

The COM provides a framework for developing and deploying software components. The developers capture abstractions as component interfaces and then provide binary classes that implement those interfaces. The COM includes an IDL, derived from the open group DCE IDL.

Both the COM and CORBA provide encapsulation by allowing a client access to an object only through the object's interface. Both the COM and CORBA provide polymorphism, the ability for different kinds of objects to respond approximately to the same message. Both the COM and CORBA support inheritance theoretically. In reality, the COM does not directly implement inheritance. It is a part of the framework of Object Linking and Embedding (OLE) and ActiveX.

Distributed Common Object Model (DCOM)

The distributed common object model is Microsoft's object broker. The DCOM is an extension of the COM and extends the programming model introduced by COM to work across the network. The DCOM provides communication across networks using the remote procedures call

(RPC). Future versions of the DCOM will support other protocols. These extensions will include improved location and packaging transparency, additional threading modeling, new security options, and additional administration capabilities.

Clients can access DCOM objects on remote machines without specific coding for the network. Alternatively, clients can specify the remote host that should be accessed when creating a new DCOM object.

The DCOM is part of Microsoft Windows NT 4.0. It uses the same mechanism as the CORBA IDL, but with a different name and object definition language (ODL). The DCOM supports distributed application development and provides directory, security, transaction, and processing support. With its mechanisms for placement of parameters, client proxies, and server stubs, the DCOM distributes COM object infrastructure to support client requests made to objects on remote computers, as shown in Fig. 8.3.

The DCOM is an OLE-enabled infrastructure for distributed development. It provides developers as well as users with access to data from other OLE-enabled applications. While linked applications can share data, embedded applications actually commit their data to applications that access them. The basic OLE concept formed the foundation of the COM, which specifies how to build COM and OLE components and distributed objects, including the application programming interfaces (APIs) and protocols that link COM/OLE components and distributed objects. The COM also specifies naming conventions and

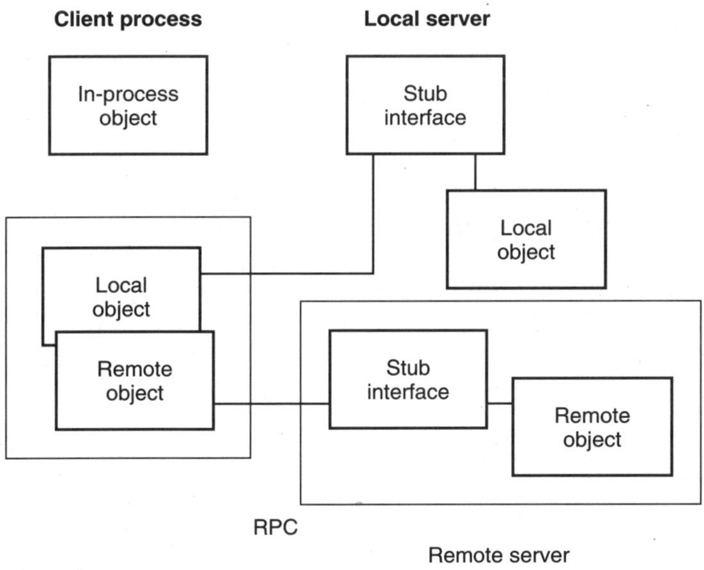

Figure 8.3 DCOM client server application overview.

security and directory services for object-to-object communications. The COM defines how components are built and how they interact. The DCOM defines distribution and communications with COM-enabled objects on the network.

The DCOM itself is not a development environment. It is simply a means of distributing application services. Developers can build servers for distribution using any COM-enabled development tool for ActiveX. Once the ActiveX exists, the DCOM takes over. A DCOM server can reside anywhere. Developers need only reference the server in the client applications, and the DCOM can find the correct resource for the client.

ActiveX

ActiveX is compatible with 3.0 or the latest versions of Internet Explorer that Microsoft offers free of charge. ActiveX was designed by Microsoft as a simplification of the COM to support linking of objects and applications across the network. ActiveX is widely discussed as a means of dynamically loading applets across the network, but it actually supports client- or server-side objects. ActiveX can be used interchangeably with browsers or with stand-alone applications. The most widely used ActiveX objects are so-called controls that implement user-interface components; however, an ActiveX object need not have a user interface.

An ActiveX control is an in-process COM server. ActiveX components exist as precompiled binary objects suitable only for a specific platform.

All CORBA 2.0–compliant products provide interoperability with each other using the IIOP. The CORBA 2.0 Internet Inter-ORB Protocol provides a standardized protocol for all CORBA-compliant ORBs. This enables objects developed using ORBs from different vendors to interoperate transparently. The IIOP communication reduces network traffic while expanding the services that can be offered by a Web browser. The OMG has adopted a formal specification for COM/CORBA interworking. The term *interworking* was created by the OMG COM/CORBA committee to distinguish interoperability between technologies from inter-ORB interoperability.

Building distributed applications requires a proven infrastructure—one that scales to handle the diversity of the enterprise or the Internet for that matter. CORBA provides that infrastructure, allowing you to build standards-based systems from components implemented in a variety of languages and running on a myriad of different platforms. CORBA guarantees interoperability between these components through use of a standardized wire protocol—the IIOP. The IIOP defines a common data representation and a set of request and reply messages. The ORB from a single vendor has no problem communicating from a client to servers across a network. An ORB from different vendors can also interoperate with the IIOP. On the Active platform, the DCOM is the plumbing and wiring that connects COM objects into distributed applications. The DCOM acts as part of the operating system's infrastructure, allowing ActiveX and Active Server objects to find each other over a network.

Distributed System Object Model (DSOM)

The DSOM is an IBM product and is an extension of the system object model (SOM). The SOM is an object-oriented technology for building packaging and manipulating binary class libraries. The SOM is language-neutral. The SOM preserves the object-oriented characteristics of encapsulation, inheritance, and polymorphism. Major benefits of the SOM are that the changes to the SOM class do not require source code changes in client programs. Then those client programs need not to be recompiled.

The SOM conforms to the OMG CORBA standard. With the SOM, class implementers describe the interface for a class of objects in the CORBA IDL.

CORBA 3.0

In the future, CORBA 3.0 will include IDL mappings for developers writing in COBOL, Java, or fourth-generation language, such as Sybase division Powersoft's PowerBuilder, to access and generate CORBA objects without wrestling with the abstruse IDL. A CORBA component model would allow developers to create components visually on a project palette and access methods and properties more easily than the coding-intensive approach required by the IDL. The component model will be based largely on JavaBeans. JavaScript will be among the scripting languages considered, according to the chairman of the OMG.

The OMG plans to bolster its forthcoming CORBA 3.0 specification with a distributed object model for building components that is designed to head off the DCOM. The CORBA 3.0 addition, tentatively called CORBABeans, aims to enable the creation of lightweight, reusable, graphical-based components that can be distributed across an enterprise. The CORBA 3.0 specification will provide mapping from Java to C++ objects and hide the CORBA IDL to ease programming. The OMG has proposed three stipulations to the CORBABeans specification:

1. The specification should equally address the needs of the Java community and the C++ community.
2. The Java-related features should be pertinent and not brought into CORBA just for the sake of it.

3. The CORBA 3.0 must be backward-compatible with earlier versions of CORBA.

Case Study 8.1: International Trading

Advanced Trading Corporation (ATC), in New York, is interested in buying a special type of sugar, brown sugar, from the international market. To gain the competitive edge, the company used distributed object technology, as shown in Fig. 8.4. The ATC has many branch offices throughout the world.

Discussion. The ATC is using C++ as the object-oriented language for its inventory system at the headquarters in New York. The system runs on a UNIX environment. The ATC shipping agent in Singapore developed the shipping system in COBOL language and it runs on a mainframe. From its branch office in Los Angeles the ATC is monitoring current pricing on the Internet from all over the world and maintains this information on an EXCEL spreadsheet. The new order processing has been developed in Smalltalk and runs on a powerful workstation operated by the purchasing agent at the ATC's New York office.

This application combines different hardware and software technology. However, neither application developers nor users care about machines, locations, or programming languages. They view the world simply as distributed objects.

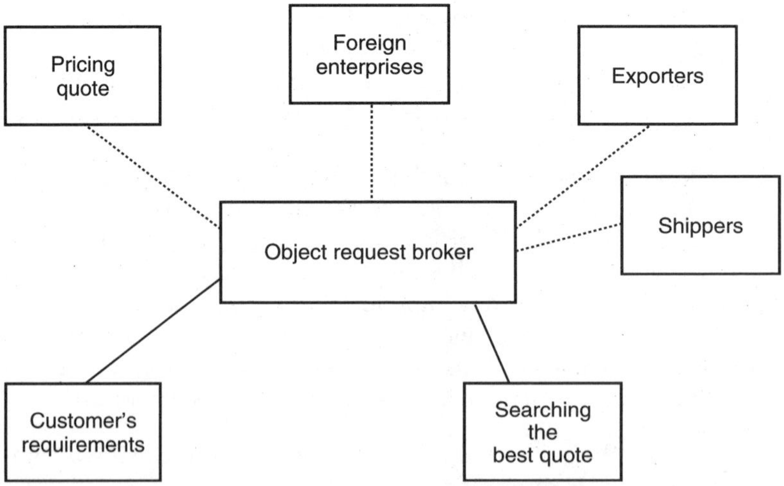

Figure 8.4 A logical flow with distributed object technology.

Chapter

9

The CORBA Framework

This chapter covers CORBA products that are available from various vendors. Some of the vendor products, such as Orbix, ObjectBroker, CORBAplus, and VisiBroker, as well as examples, will be discussed.

Orbix

Orbix is a complete implementation of the OMG's Common Object Request Broker Architecture. With Orbix, programmers can develop distributed applications using object-oriented client/server technology and use object technology to compose new applications from existing components and subsystems. Orbix is a CORBA-compliant object request broker.

The standard implementation of Orbix for C++ is available on a range of UNIX platforms, including Solaris, HP-UX, SunOS, AIX, and Digital UNIX. (Orbix is a product of IONA Technologies.)

OrbixWeb

OrbixWeb brings CORBA to Java—it allows Java applets and applications to be plugged into the CORBA infrastructure and thereby allows them to interoperate seamlessly with both Java and non-Java applications and components across the enterprise. A full and complete development and runtime environment is provided to allow you to build both client and server Java CORBA components.

The OrbixWeb-generated code and runtime classes are pure Java, which means that any Java development environment can be used to build OrbixWeb applets and applications. To run an OrbixWeb applet requires only a Java-enabled browser on the client machine. OrbixWeb has no dependencies on preinstalled browser components or classes—

the same applet will run on any Java-enabled browser including Netscape Navigator (3.x, 4.x) and Microsoft Internet Explorer (3.x, 4.x). As OrbixWeb applets are regular Java, they can be downloaded, signed, and cached just like any other set of Java classes. OrbixWeb can, of course, be used to build Java server applications.

OrbixWeb is at the leading edge of Java: it is the first Java ORB for JDK 1.1 (1.0.2 is also fully supported) and is fully compatible with Sun's Javastation.

OrbixTalk

OrbixTalk brings leading-edge messaging technology to the CORBA environment. The OMG's CORBA Event Service specifies a model of distributed messaging involving the notion of (push or pull) suppliers delivering (typed or nontyped) messages to (push or pull) consumers via a named event channel.

OrbixTalk is an implementation of the OMG's CORBA Events Service standard. It uses Internet Protocol (IP) multicast as the underlying transport to ensure high levels of performance and scalability. This efficient messaging scheme conserves network bandwidth and optimizes server and network performance. OrbixTalk enables CORBA developers to build and deploy massively scalable mission-critical applications in distributed environments. It provides for typed and nontyped communication, extended APIs for ease of use, and different qualities of message delivery service, including those that are reliable (out-of-the-box) and guaranteed (via the MessageStore™ persistent extensions). OrbixTalk 1.1 ST/MT is available on Solaris 2.x, HP-UX10.x, AIX 4.1, and Windows NT 4.0. OrbixTalk MessageStore 1.0 is also available on these three platforms.

Additional Orbix products

OrbixEvents is an IIOP-based implementation of the CORBA Event Service. OrbixNames applies a federated naming structure to objects with the implementation of the CORBA Naming Service. OrbixTrader finds objects by relevant criteria—an object search engine implements the CORBA Trader Service. OrbixSecurity provides a selection of security implementations for distributed applications. OrbixManager monitors the system administration tools for distributed applications.

Orbix for Windows closely integrates Microsoft OLE and ActiveX technology with the OMG's Common Object Request Broker Architecture. Orbix provides interworking between the common object model (COM) and CORBA. Orbix for Windows is the leading solution for three-tier application developers working in the Windows environment.

Orbix for Windows allows applications to make CORBA objects available to OLE-based desktop applications and vice versa. Orbix provides integration for Windows and allows a high degree of transparency so that a client working with Microsoft's COM can view CORBA objects as if they were COM objects, and a client working with the CORBA object model can view COM objects as if they were CORBA objects.

The primary benefit of Orbix for Windows is that it allows application integration across multiple operating system platforms from Windows NT and Windows 95 to a range of UNIX and other platforms and across multiple programming languages. However, Orbix for Windows can also be viewed as a means to provide distributed processing between existing OLE clients and servers. The current COM product is designed for single-machine applications. Only Orbix for Windows can fully integrate COM with CORBA in order to provide the distribution infrastructure.

Case Study 9.1: Manage Your Bank Account

A user of an account object will want to make deposits and withdrawals. The account object will also need to hold the balance amount of the account and perhaps the name of the account's owner. An example interface is:

```
//IDL
interface Account {
     // Attributes to hold the balance and the name
     // of the account's owner.
     Attribute float balance;
     Readyonly attribute string owner;

     // The operations defined on the interface.
     Void makeDeposit (in float amount,
               Out float newBalance);
     Void makeWithdrawal (in float amount,
               Out float newBalance);
};
```

Discussion. The "account" interface defines attributes "balance" and "owner"; these are properties of an "account" object. The attribute "balance" may take values of type "float," which is one of the basic types of IDL and represents a floating-point type. The attribute "owner" is of type "string" and is defined to be "readyonly."

Two operations, "makeDeposit ()" and "makeWithdrawal ()," are provided. Each has two parameters of type "float." Each parameter must specify the direction in which the parameters are passed. The possible parameter modes are:

In: The parameter is passed from the caller (client) to the called object.

Out: The parameter is passed from the called object to the caller.

Inout: The parameter is passed in both directions. Here, "amount" is passed as an *in* parameter to both functions and the new balance is returned as an *out* parameter. The parameter-passing mode must be specified for each parameter, and it is used to improve the self-documentation of an interface and to help guide the code that the IDL is subsequently translated to. Line comments are introduced with the character // as shown. Comments spanning more than one line are delimited by /* and */.

Multiple IDL interfaces may be defined in a single source file, but it is common to define each interface in its own file (*Source:* Orbix by IONA).

ObjectBroker

ObjectBroker lets programmers develop new object-oriented applications from scratch or integrate existing applications without rewriting them, in a distributed, multivendor environment. This simplifies the task of creating distributed client/server solutions, by allowing the integration of existing applications as well as the deployment of new applications in a mixed environment. Application processes on different platforms work together seamlessly, interoperating and exchanging data. Employing object-oriented technology, ObjectBroker shields developers from having to learn platform-specific detail, networking protocols, and operating systems, while isolating clients and servers from changes to network software and topology. The ObjectBroker increases the enterprise-level integration and at the same time improves scalability, ease of use, and performance.

Now a remote CORBA object can be dragged and dropped and linked among unmodified Microsoft desktop applications. ObjectBroker automatically provides OLE Automation access to a CORBA object's methods, as well as a local desktop rendering of the object for drag-and-drop and embedding operations, as shown in Fig. 9.1.

Case Study 9.2: A-Bank Information System

To remain competitive, A-Bank began offering products such as mutual funds and brokerage accounts. The customers expected to receive a single, unified statement listing the balance and transactions for all of their accounts, ranging from checking and savings accounts to mort-

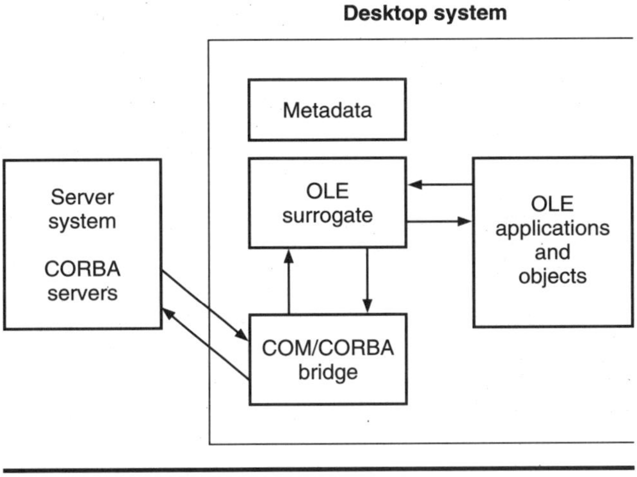

Figure 9.1 ObjectBroker overview.

gages to credit cards to brokerages and retirement accounts. A-Bank realized that to meet customers' demands, the bank needed to change from an account focus to a customer focus, whereby customers would expect their banking activities to be structured in terms of their overall relationship with the bank, rather than in terms of a single account they might own.

Like most banks, however, A-Bank computer systems were optimized for account processing rather than providing integrated customer data. Direct-deposit accounts were managed by mainframe computers, while mutual funds were tracked by a Digital VAX/VMS system. Meanwhile, brokerage account processing was outsourcing to a vendor who used a Tandem system. As a result, bank employees were required to log in to several different computer systems, all with character-cell user interfaces. What should have been routine transactions for customers required bank employees to navigate three or more disparate information systems, as shown in Fig. 9.2. A simple question from a customer, such as "How much money do I have in all of my accounts combined?," could require an employee to go to several separate systems of record, none of which offered a graphical user interface (GUI). This became an impediment to efficient customer service.

A-Bank began to seek out remedies to this problem. It was clear that reengineering all of the bank's systems of record to embrace client/server or any other technology would be neither practical nor cost effective. Too much was already invested in the legacy systems. A-Bank needed a way to overcome the inherent disparity among the existing systems. It needed to seamlessly integrate these systems' functionality

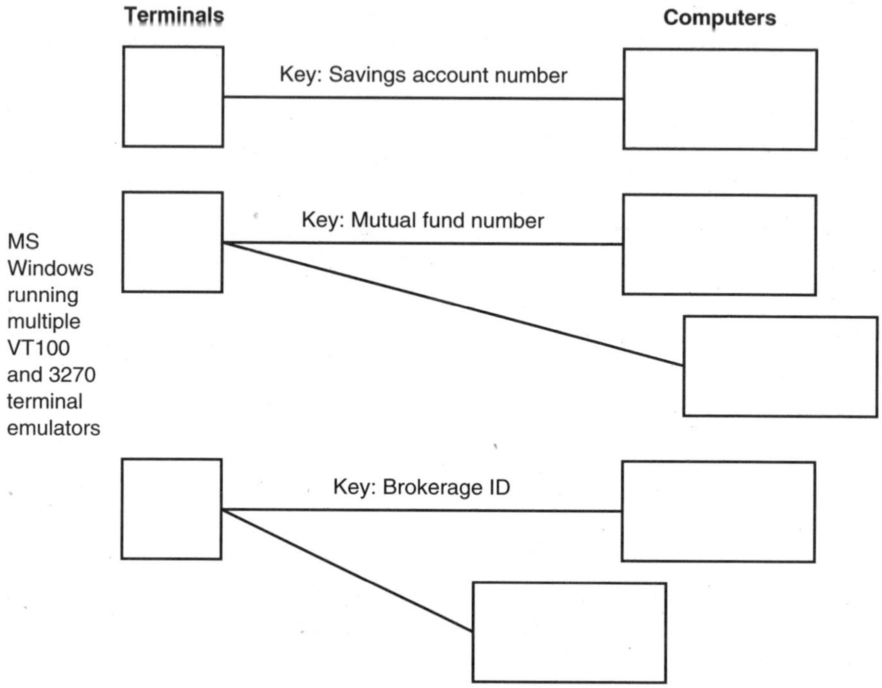

Figure 9.2 Information access before.

and preferably deliver the integrated result through a graphical user interface. A key objective was to deliver the integrated functionality through a native Microsoft Windows user interface.

A-Bank consulted Digital Equipment Corporation. The Digital/Cushing Group Team recommended three-tier client/server architecture to deliver a rapid solution that was production-grade quality. The Digital/Cushing Group Team also recommended the use of Digital's ORB technology to meet the goals. The object request brokering offers a way to construct distributed application systems using object-oriented semantics to define an application-level communication protocol between client and server programs. The selection of Digital's ORB set the direction for the effort within A-Bank that would evolve to become what is now almost certainly the success story of the CORBA-based application development effort, as shown in Fig. 9.3. This technology enabled A-Bank to become the first bank to offer Internet-based access to account balances, not to mention several other innovations (*Source:* Digital/Cushing Group Team; A-Bank is actually the Wells Fargo bank).

CORBAplus

CORBAplus is a line of CORBA 2.0–compliant object request broker products that turn a heterogeneous network into a unified network environment. With a unique patterns-based architecture, CORBAplus delivers superior performance, scalability, reliability, adaptability, and extensibility. In addition, CORBAplus simplifies the development and management of distributed object applications by supplying high-level services and GUI tools. The CORBAplus product line includes the following features:

- CORBAplus for C++
- CORBAplus, Java Edition
- CORBAplus, ActiveX

Standards compliance

CORBAplus fully complies with the CORBA 2.0 specification. This includes the IIOP, the standard IDL-to-C++ mapping, and the preliminary IDL-to-Java mapping. CORBAplus also supports all IDL types, the interface repository, both static and dynamic interfaces (SII and DII), initialization, the basic object adapter (BOA), all activation policies, typecodes, and the standard CORBA/COM mapping.

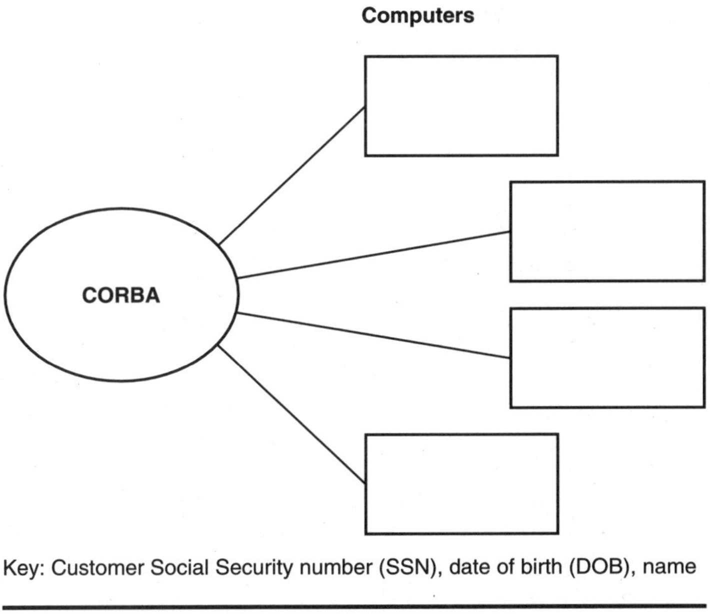

Figure 9.3 Information access after.

Interoperability

CORBAplus natively uses the IIOP for communication and can communicate with any other CORBA 2.0–compliant ORB. There are no switches or environment variables for this feature.

CORBAservices

CORBAplus provides three CORBAservices: Naming, Event, and Relationship.

CORBAplus COM/CORBA bridge

The CORBAplus-ActiveX bridge is fully compliant with the COM-CORBA Interworking Specification of the OMG. It provides complete, bidirectional interoperability between ActiveX (COM, DCOM, Automation, Dual Interface) and CORBA object systems and also supports the OMG IIOP for communication across the network.

Asynchronous messaging

CORBAplus is the first CORBA ORB to provide direct support for asynchronous object requests. CORBAplus's asynchronous messaging implementation includes a simple programming paradigm (extensions to the IDL and an SII call) and a callback handler. It allows programmers to write single-threaded applications that issue multiple requests and are then interrupted when the responses are available. This capability is vital for business applications that require time-efficient operation, need to simultaneously manage multiple activities, want to avoid blocking, or must respond to multiple concurrent events.

Multithreaded support

CORBAplus ships with a portable thread class library that sits on top of the native system threads. Threads, thread pools, and mutexes are supported with a high-level OO abstraction. With CORBAplus, you can simply and quickly write portable, multithreaded distributed applications.

Dynamic Type Manager

The Dynamic Type Manager (DTM) provides maximum flexibility when using the Dynamic Invocation Interface (DII). It allows new object types to be added to the distributed system at runtime. Without the DTM, use of the DII would be limited to types known at compile time. In other words, you could only add services that used previously known types, which is not a real-world scenario. The DTM gives you the flexibility to dynamically add any distributed object service.

URL object addressing

CORBAplus enhances the CORBA specification that allows you to connect CORBA objects in a straightforward and simple way. CORBAplus uses the Internet uniform resource locator (URL) format for object addressing, making it easier to locate and work with your objects. Instead of trying to understand unwieldy string field object references, you can use a URL reference to connect to a remote CORBA 2.0 object.

IFR Explorer

CORBAplus provides a visual tool for interacting with the CORBA interface repository (IFR). The CORBAplus IFR Explorer is an easy-to-use tool that allows you to browse, select, and edit components of the interface repository and then generate CORBA stubs and skeletons, as well as a standard COM/CORBA bridge.

Graphical IDL compiler

CORBAplus provides an IDL compiler tool that allows you to open IDL files, set compile options, and compile files from a convenient Windows interface.

Configuration tool

CORBAplus provides you with a tool to configure and run the CORBAplus infrastructure on Windows NT. This tool allows you to configure your CORBAplus environment, environment variables, and CORBAplus-specific NT services.

Command-line tools

CORBAplus also has command-line tools as follows:

- *Name utility* Provides an interactive way to create, explore, and delete contexts and objects from the CORBA Naming Service.
- *Executable repository utility* Provides the ability to list and remove executables from the executable repository.

Unified network computing environment support for heterogeneous systems

With CORBAplus, you program to one application program interface (API) and use one set of classes. These are portable over Windows 95, Windows NT, Sun Solaris, HP HP-UX, and IBM AIX.

Support for multiple languages

CORBAplus provides support for C++, Java, and Visual Basic through CORBAplus for C++; CORBAplus, Java Edition; and CORBAplus, ActiveX. By using the CORBAplus suite of products, you can mix and match your favorite object languages.

Support for multiple object models

CORBAplus provides support for both the CORBA object model and COM. With the CORBAplus suite of products, you can use CORBA to write your distributed object services and COM for the front-end client. (CORBAplus is a product of Expersoft Corporation. Expersoft is a registered trademark of and PowerBroker is a trademark of Expersoft Corporation. Java is a trademark of Sun Microsystems, Inc.)

VisiBroker

VisiBroker introduces for Java a complete implementation of the CORBA 2.0 specification for developing distributed object–based applets. The CORBA specification was developed by the OMG to address the complexity and high cost of developing software applications. CORBA defines an object-oriented approach to creating software components that can be reused and shared between applications. Each object encapsulates the details of its inner workings and presents a well-defined interface, which reduces application complexity. The cost of developing applications is also reduced because, once an object is implemented and tested, it may be used over and over again.

VisiBroker's ORB connects a client applet, running in a Java interpreter or Java-enabled browser, with the objects it wishes to use. The client applet does not need to know whether the object resides on the same computer or is located on a remote computer somewhere on the network. The client applet only needs to know the object's name and understand how to use the object's interface. The ORB takes care of the details of locating the object, routing the request, and returning the result. A client application may also provide object implementations for other clients.

The ORB is not a separate process. It is a collection of libraries and other resources that client applications and object servers use to communicate.

Accessing distributed objects

To use an object, your applet must first bind itself to the object, specifying the object's interface name. The ORB locates the host that offers an object with the requested interface name. After the bind is completed, the client application can invoke operations on the object. The client's method invocations are translated into requests that are sent to the object server.

VisiBroker is an ORB that offers a complete implementation of the CORBA specification. VisiBroker makes it easy for you to develop distributed, object-based client applets and servers. VisiBroker offers the following features:

- Support for the Java programming language
- Object lookup by name or by URL
- Ability to distribute objects across a network
- Support for persistent object references
- Interoperability with other ORB implementations

Developing applets with VisiBroker

The first step in creating an applet with VisiBroker is to specify all of your object interfaces using CORBA's IDL. The IDL mappings for the Java language are covered in the *VisiBroker for Java Reference Guide.* VisiBroker uses the interface specification you create and the Id12java compiler to generate stub routines for the client applet and skeleton code for the object implementation. The stub routines are used by the client applet for all method invocations. You use the skeleton code, along with code you write, to create the server that implements the object. The code for the client and object, once completed, is used as input to your Java compiler to produce a Java applet and an object server.

Interoperability with VisiBroker for C++

Java applets created with VisiBroker for Java can communicate with object implementations developed with VisiBroker for C++, which is sold separately. Simply use the same IDL you used to develop your Java applet as input to the orbline compiler, supplied with VisiBroker for C++. You may then use the resulting C++ skeletons to develop the object implementation.

VisiBroker features

In addition to providing the features defined in the CORBA specification, VisiBroker offers enhancements that increase application performance and reliability.

Fault tolerance

VisiBroker can determine whether the connection between your client application and an object server has been lost as the result of a server crash or network failure. When a failure is detected, an attempt is made to restart the server or to connect your client to a suitable server on a different host.

IIOP gateway

The IIOP gatekeeper allows Java clients and servers running within any Java 1.0–compatible browser to be transparently available to other CORBA objects, even when a firewall is in place. The gatekeeper can simultaneously be used as an HTTP daemon, thereby eliminating the requirement for a separate HTTP server during the application development phase.

Optimized binding

When your application binds to an object, VisiBroker selects and establishes the efficient communication mechanism. Depending on the platform and the location of the requested object, the bind may be established through a pointer reference or a TCP/IP socket.

Dynamic Invocation Interface

VisiBroker maintains an interface repository that contains the IDL specifications for the object that have been activated. This repository can be used by client applications to discover a recently added object, obtain the object's interface, and dynamically construct requests to act on the object. (VisiBroker is a product of Visigenic.)

Chapter

10

Domain Models

Domain models represent graphical presentation for object-oriented software development. The first step in the reuse process is to understand the customer's requirements and then graphically show the customer requirements in the form of logical models. The domain model determines objects and establishes the relationships between objects within the domain infrastructure.

Domain Prototype Model

The domain prototype model (DPM) captures in detail the domain-specific knowledge of the application in a form that lends itself to careful, point-by-point verification by the domain engineer. The DPM provides, through formal models of the problem domain, a detailed and documented foundation from which requirement decisions are made. The DPM transfers the domain knowledge accurately to the software engineers and communicates the requirement analysis in a form that is easily understood and mapped into an object-oriented design.

The DPM concepts comprehend the customer's requirements, graphically show the logic to the customers, and interpret the stated requirements within the domain boundary and environment. Then they determine objects, establish relationships between objects within the domain infrastructure, determine instantiation criteria for objects and their relationships, and develop functional processes, as shown in Fig. 10.1. The domain engineer receives requirements, analyzes, and looks around by accessing domains to determine available assets that can be reused within the framework.

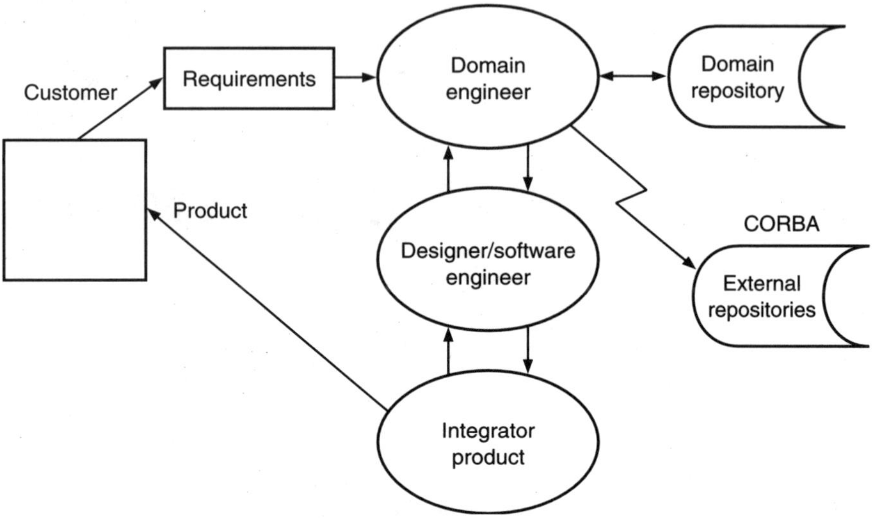

Figure 10.1 A sample of a domain prototype model.

Domain Functional Model

The domain functional model (DFM) makes use of data flow diagrams and develops the required processes that drive the objects through their event chains. The principle of data flow diagrams is discussed in *Software Engineering Methods, Management, and CASE Tools* [Sodh91]. Only a few concerns about objects will be discussed here. The following is a list of suggested processes for the development of a data flow diagram of a single object.

- Develop an object behavior model (OBM) that formalizes the behavior of an object over time.
- Analyze the action that is performed when the state is entered.
- Break the action down into a sequence of processes.
- Depict each process as a data flow diagram.
- Place each action data flow diagram on a separate page.

The data of an object are represented as a data store in the data flow diagram. The data store will be recorded in the *domain data dictionary* (DDD). The data store for the object contains all the attributes of the object. The instances of the object are created and stored in the data store. The data store holds all data and all attributes of all instances of the object. The data store is shared by all action data flow diagrams. The data flow diagram involves data stores that are made up of attributes of

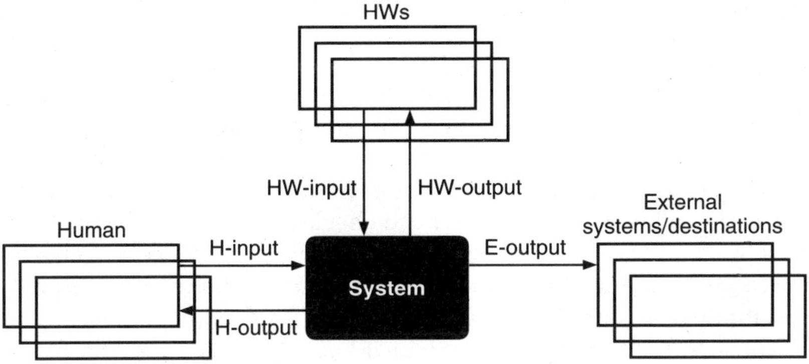

Figure 10.2 A sample context diagram.

that data. These processes are discrete. Data flow diagrams are the offspring of a *context diagram,* as shown in Fig. 10.2. The context diagram establishes the external interfaces of the system. The data flow diagrams identify the internal interfaces of the system as shown in Figure 10.3. The data flow diagram consists of rectangles that are the source or destination of data outside the system. A data flow symbol (arrow) represents a path by which data moves into, around, and out of the system. A process symbol (circle) represents a function of the system that logically transforms data. A data store is a symbol (open-ended rectangle) that shows a place in the system where data is stored.

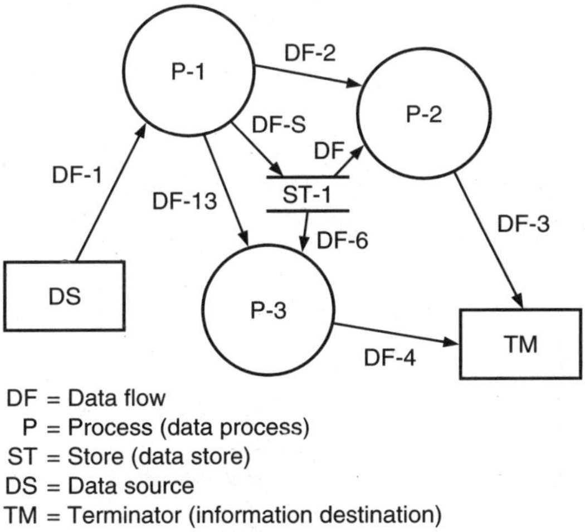

Figure 10.3 A sample data flow diagram.

Case Study 10.1

This is an extension of Case Study 5.1 in Chapter 5. You have a checking account in the "Universe Bank." You are free to write as many checks as you want, as long as you have enough money in the account to cover them. The bank has a good reputation, and there is a $25 charge for every check that is drawn on insufficient funds. The bank does not want to keep customers whose checks bounce regularly.

Once a month, the bank's bookkeeper sends your cancelled checks along with a computerized financial statement and balance sheet, and other documents, which the bank processes on its computer, "Data Universe." You need to reconcile your checkbook for any error made by either the bank or you (while entering the transaction in your checkbook). Also, you need to record any annual tax-deductible expenses in your yearly journal that will finally be recorded on a 1040 form for income tax. You may automate the system that balances your checkbook in the most economical way.

Discussion. You want to identify reusable components that meet the requirement. You explore the organization's domain repository for any reusable assets with characteristics to meet a similar requirement. You access other repositories including CORBA to see if you can reuse any available assets.

It is interesting to note that almost all people do maintain their checkbooks. There must be some reusable assets for this purpose sitting somewhere in a repository. A sample solution is provided in Figure 10.4, which shows a context diagram and identifies external interfaces, and in Figure 10.5, which partitions the system and identifies internal interfaces. The model can easily be further partitioned to create a reusable asset in a future system, as shown in Fig. 10.6.

Domain Dynamic Model

The domain dynamic model (DDM) formalizes the life or event histories of objects and relationships within the domain boundary. The life

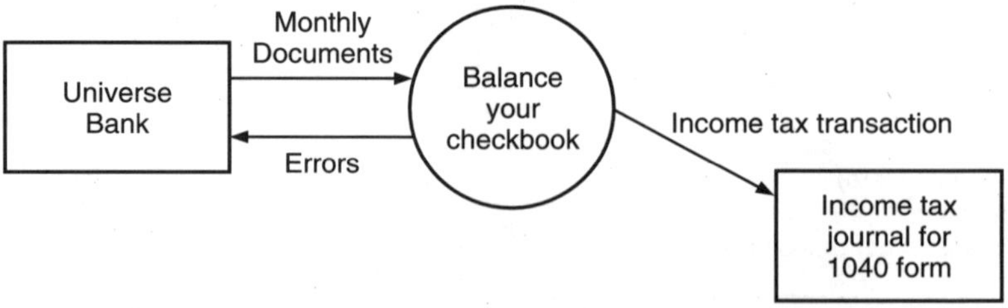

Figure 10.4 A context diagram.

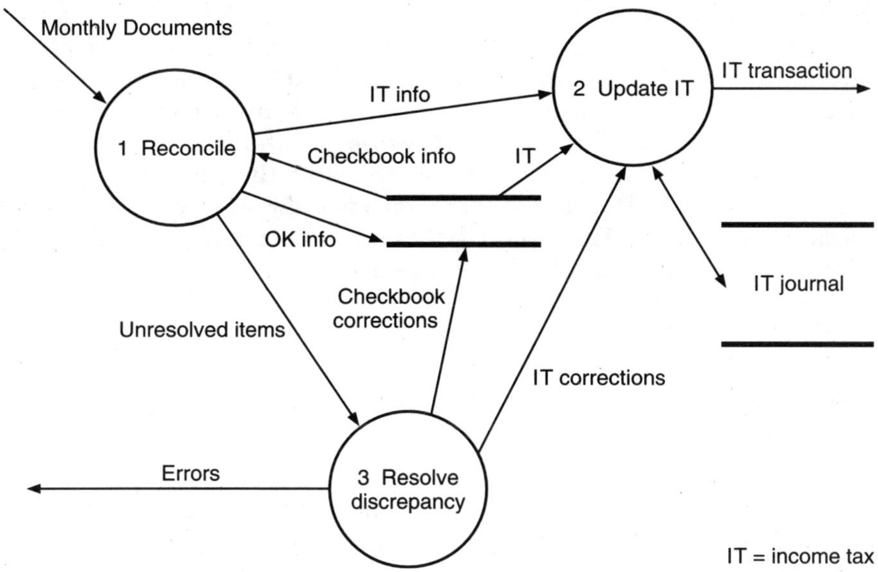

Figure 10.5 Level 1 partitioning of the system.

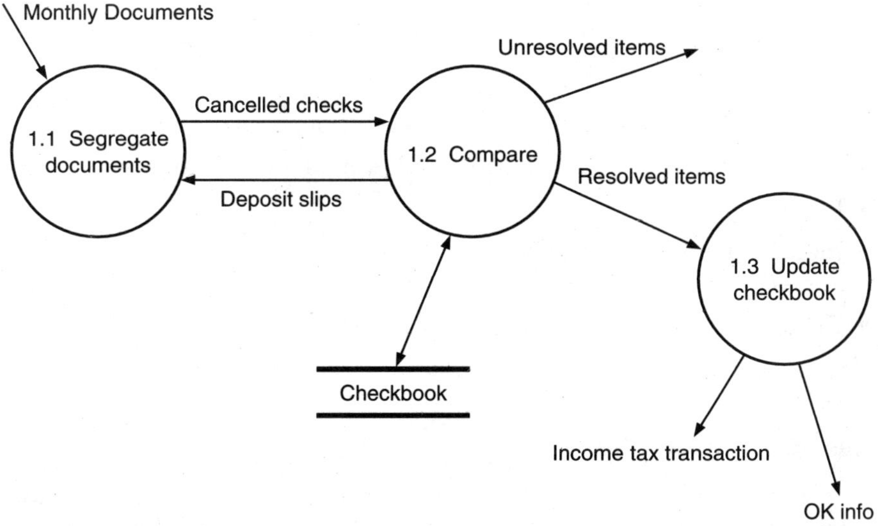

Figure 10.6 Level 2 partitioning.

cycle of an object is therefore the behavior of an object during its lifetime. An object may be in only *one* state at a time. The states are mutually exclusive. These states are discrete, and transitions can occur instantaneously. Transitions from any state to any other state are not always allowed. Incidents cause transition of things between states. Some incidents cause a progression only when the thing is in certain stages of its life cycle. Similar characteristics of real-world *things* have a common life cycle. Thus, the DDM is a formalization of the life cycle of an object in regard to the following parts:

- States
- Events
- Transitions
- Actions

The *state* of the DDM corresponds to the state of an object's life cycle. An *event* is an incident or action that causes a progression to another state or to the same state. The *transition* is the new state of an object if a particular event occurs while the object is in a particular state. The *action* is the function that is performed immediately when entering a new state. Each state can have only one action, but that action might consist of many processes.

A sample DDM is shown in Fig. 10.7. The boxes represent the states. The lines represent the events. The event causes the transition to the new state. A DDM is built for each dynamic object. The following are suggested guidelines for constructing a DDM.

- Analyze and record the life cycle of one instance of the model.
- Record the various states for that instance.
- Identify the states that consider all relationships of the object.
- Define the action that will be executed upon entry into a state.
- Identify nonfinal states.
- Identify events that the object must generate so it can exit nonfinal states.
- Expand actions that generate these events.
- Complete the state transition diagram (STD).

Case Study 10.2

A message-processing system is to be developed to provide user communication with a central host computer. The user can compose a mes-

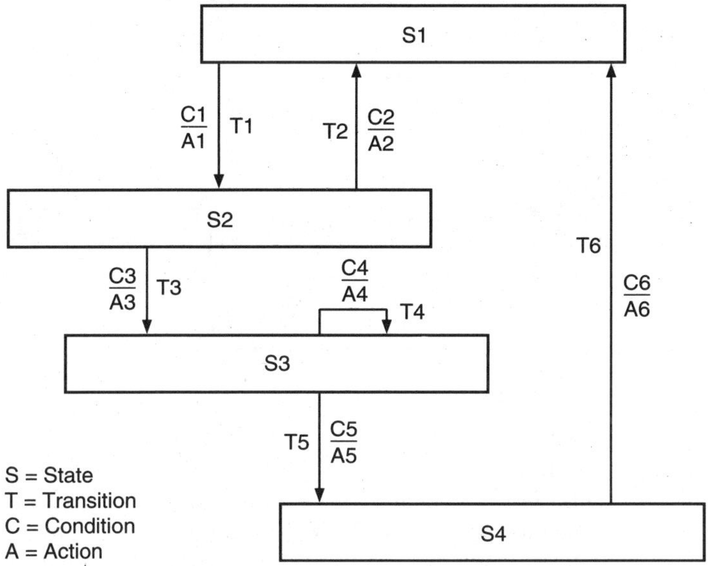

Figure 10.7 A sample domain dynamic model (state transition diagram).

sage, print the message on a local printer, send the message to the host, read a message from the host, and log the message sent to the host in a local floppy-disk file.

A *message* is a free-format group of characters up to 1024 bytes long. A *message buffer* is circular and if the message length exceeds 1024 bytes, then the first character will be overwritten.

Commands from a user are single-keystroke control codes:

CRTL-P prints a message.

CTRL-S sends a message.

CTRL-R reads a message received from the host.

CTRL-L invokes the logging control submenu.

As messages are received from the host, they are stored in a buffer. Each message received overwrites the message previously stored in the buffer, so only the latest message received may be read at any particular time. Messages can be read as many times as the user wishes. If the user is reading a host message, then the ESC key must be pressed to resume message composition. Messages that are sent can be logged to a local floppy disk. This is controlled through a submenu, activated by the CTRL-L command.

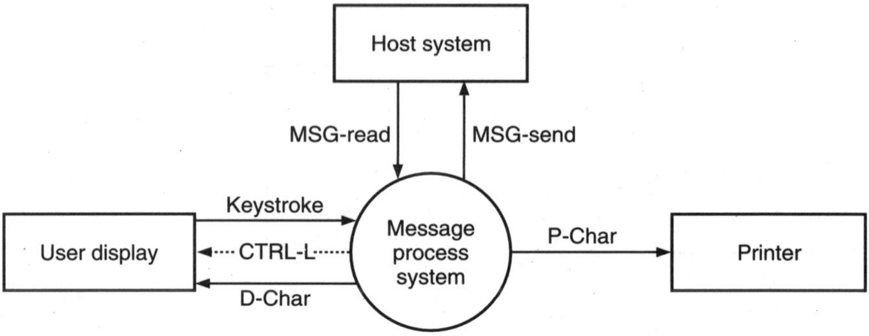

Figure 10.8 Functional model (context diagram).

Discussion. This case study is a typical example of a real-time system. A sample solution is shown in Figs. 10.8, 10.9, and 10.10. In Fig. 10.8, a dotted line indicates one bit of information and is represented by the label "CTRL-L." In Fig. 10.9, the storage "Buffer" is shown a few times to avoid confusion. Each duplicate "Buffer" is noted by "*." The dotted circle (number 5) will be further transformed into an STD, as shown in Fig. 10.10.

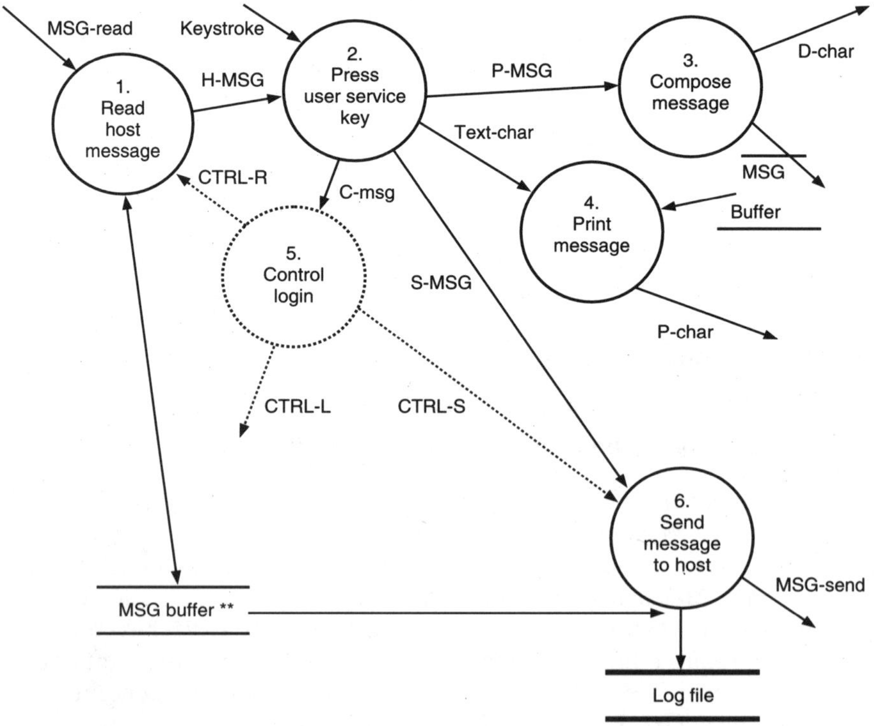

Figure 10.9 Functional model (data flow diagram).

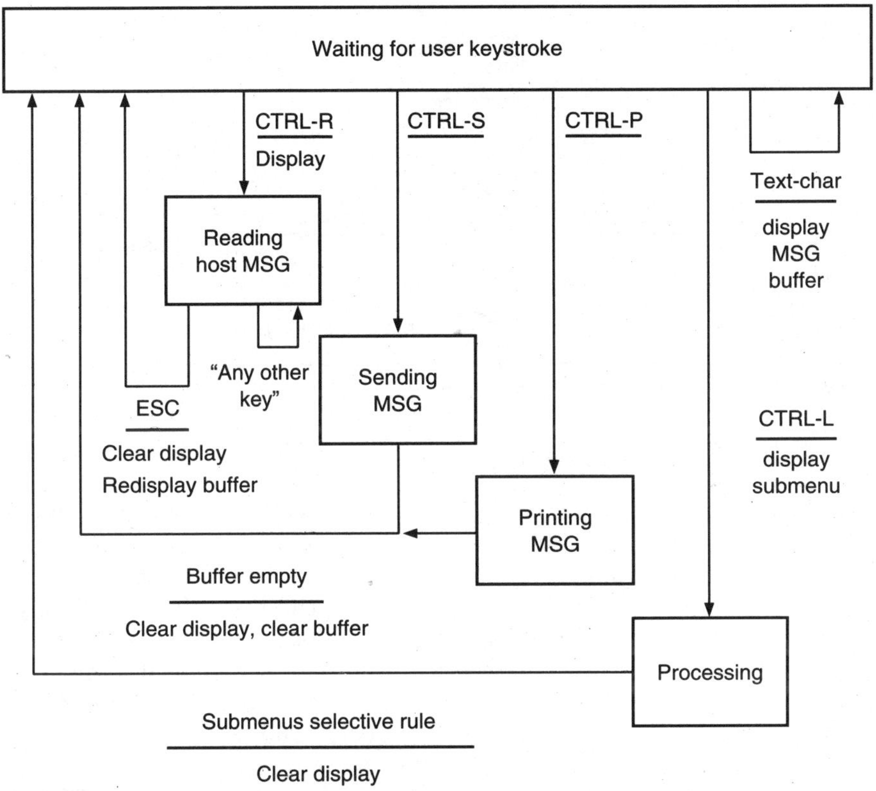

Figure 10.10 STD sample solution.

Domain Object Model

An object is a mental abstraction of a set of real-world things. The domain object model (DOM) uses concepts from object-oriented and structured approaches that include abstract data types, inheritance, and modules with coupling and cohesion. The DOM uses graphical models with proper documentation that transfers the requirements from one phase to another for implementations. The DOM assists in the software requirement object-oriented analysis and object-oriented design (OOD). The OOD is implemented in any suitable object-oriented programming language. The DOM contains all the analysis needed to understand a customer's requirements. The model contains information with regard to all the external interfaces. These interfaces are linked with external systems, as illustrated in Fig. 10.11. The idea behind drawing this graphic is that the customer's requirements are understood in an unambiguous way and that the customer understands his or her own stated requirements.

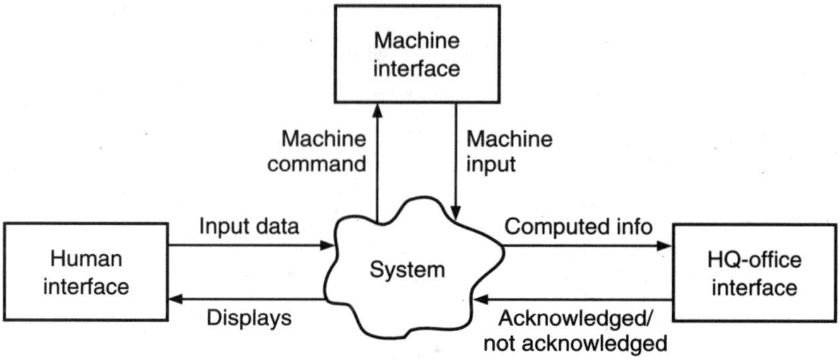

Figure 10.11 A sample domain object model.

Domain Information Model

The domain information model (DIM) identifies the conceptual entities of the problem and formalizes them as objects and attributes. A complete and unambiguous understanding of the problem is the goal. The DIM identifies things about the problem and their relationship. Things and associations are modeled here. The model is simple enough to be easily read and understood. Significant emphasis is placed on formalization of the relationships between objects. A model is developed and depicted graphically, as shown in Fig. 10.12. The textual descriptions are used in the definition of the model's semantics.

The abstractions of like *things* are grouped together into sets. *Things* are alike if they behave in the same way and can be described by the same characteristics. The first priority is to name an *object.* The char-

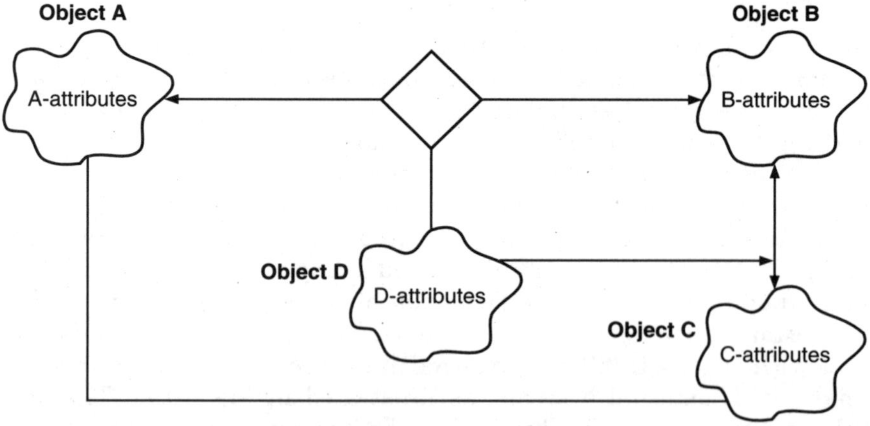

Figure 10.12 A sample domain information model.

acteristics that all elements of the set have in common are called *attributes* of the object. An attribute is the abstraction of a single characteristic that is possessed by all entities and was abstracted as an object. The set of attributes must be complete, fully factored, and mutually independent. Attributes use a dot notation. For example:

```
Object.Attribute
```

Attributes can be of three types: descriptive, naming, and referential. *Descriptive* attributes provide facts that are intrinsic to each instance of the object. A *naming* attribute provides a fact about the arbitrary name carried by each instance of the object. A *referential* attribute links an instance of one object to an instance of another object.

Tables are used for defining the types of questions that can be answered by inspection of the objects. The table name is the name of the object. Each column of the table is an attribute of the object, and each row is an instance of the object. The instance is the specific element of the set and is denoted by that object name. Every box in a table contains exactly one value. Attributes of an object should not contain internal structure. Tables are the basic formal structure of the DIM because they are simple and adequate. The object representation by table assists in the identification of the objects and attributes. The table also helps in the representation of instances of objects.

Associations exist between things in the real world. These associations must be formalized in this model. These can be recognized by verb phrases in the descriptions. For example:

The car *has* tires.

Thus, a relationship is named by the verb phrase. It can be phrased in both directions of the relation. For example:

A class *is composed* of students.

and

Students *compose* a class.

The same two objects may have more than one relationship between them. This depends on their type of relationship. An object may be related to itself. There can also be a relationship between multiple objects. For example:

The floppy disk *was formatted* on the disk drive.

The floppy disk *is owned* by a student.

The floppy disk *contains* disk files.

TABLE 10.1 Multiplicity Forms

Multiplicity	Notation	Notation	Example
One-to-one	◄——►	(1:1)	A husband *has* a wife.
One-to-many	◄——►►	(1:M)	A student *owns* books.
Many-to-many	◄◄——►►	(M:M)	A capacitor *is* a component of a computer.

This type of relationship, involving two objects, can be classified into three fundamental forms and called *multiplicity,* as shown in Table 10.1.

Case Study 10.3

The town of Fort Cobb, in the middle of Oklahoma, needs a traffic light (TL) on the main street. There are about 3000 residents in this town, most of whom travel to nearby cities for jobs. The main street intersects with another road.

The object TL establishes a proper relationship with other objects such as clock, traffic sensor, traffic, intersection, and control panel.

The traffic light attributes are manufacturer, model, serial number, and road intersection name. The clock attributes are manufacturer, model, serial number, TL manufacturer, TL model, and TL serial number. The traffic sensor attributes are manufacturer, model, serial number, TL manufacturer, TL model, TL serial number, and road name. The traffic attributes are road name, TL manufacturer, TL model, and TL serial number. The intersection attribute is road name. The control panel attributes are manufacturer, model, serial number, button selected, TL manufacturer, TL model, and TL serial number.

Discussion. This case study and others discussed here are common scenarios in the industry. A good question to ask is why these scenarios have to be designed from scratch when there is enough information available to reuse assets, saving money and time by not having to redo work. A sample partial solution is shown in Fig. 10.13.

Domain Data Dictionary

The object, attributes, and their relationships are documented in a data dictionary. This document consists of a written description of the objects, formalizes the identification of the objects, forms part of the formal system specification, and separates descriptions that are written for each object. This is a live document and should start at the beginning of the software engineering and be enhanced throughout the software development and maintenance phases.

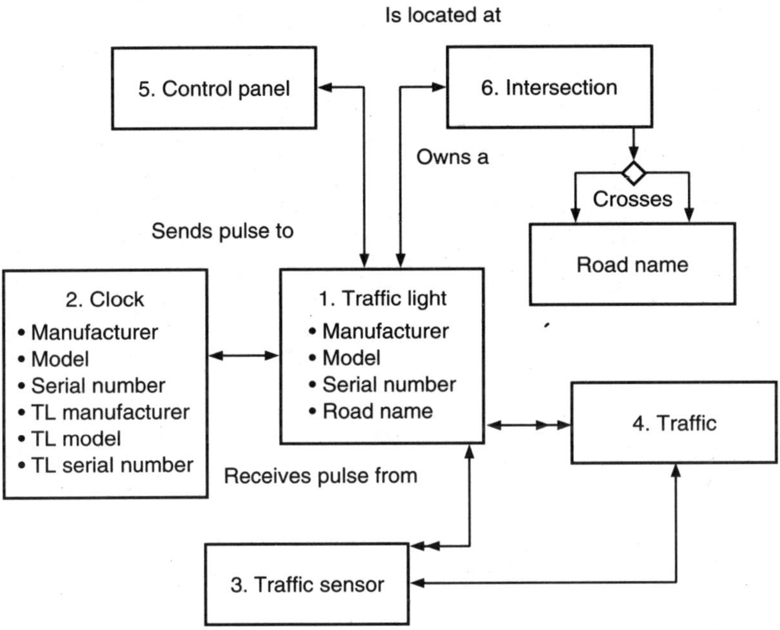

Figure 10.13 A sample solution.

The goal is that the requirements are mutually understood and recorded in the proper document before proceeding to any further analysis or design activity. The definition of the notations that are used in the graphic should be clear and properly recorded in the document for understandability. The object data dictionary can be initiated at this level by the recording of this essential information.

Part

4

Domain Analysis Process

You have talked and talked. You have listened and you have communicated. Now you understand each other, but you still do not agree. WHY?

Chapter

11

Domain Analysis Methods

Domain analysis is a technique to systematically find commonality across related software systems for achieving software reuse. This chapter covers current methods for domain analysis: KAPTUR, DESIRE, Genesis, and IDEFo.

The Domain Analysis Concept

Domain analysis involves analyzing a portion of the domain engineering process to identify reuse components. The process of domain analysis consists of collecting, organizing, analyzing, and presenting information to identify reuse opportunities within the domain. Traditionally, problems are formulated and defined as requirements for specific software systems or parts of systems. In contrast, domain analysis identifies and models problems for a group of related systems in a domain and develops generic requirements to address recurring problems in the domain and to ensure that domain capabilities will remain viable throughout changes in technology, time, needs, people, and budget.

Domain analysis is conducted as an iterative process that consists of four logical processes: identifying the domain, scoping the domain, analyzing the problem space, and designing the solution space. Each logical process can be further partitioned to describe its associated responsibilities and activities. This method of structuring the problem and solution is called *abstraction*. Abstraction helps manage complexity by hiding details until they are relevant and necessary for understanding.

Benefits of Domain Analysis

There are many benefits of domain analysis: it minimizes redundant object-oriented software development efforts, improves process productivity, and improves product quality during system/object-oriented software development and the maintenance life cycle. Domain analysis reduces costs, risks, and schedules, while increasing user suitability and opportunities for competition by lowering domain knowledge–based barriers.

Domain Analysis for Reusability

Domain analysis for reusability is the systematic exploration of related software systems to discover and exploit commonality. Domain analysis reveals a set of features that are common to a class of systems and represents them in an exploitable form. It also provides a method that maps commonality to specific instances. The objectives are to help develop domain analysis products and support the implementation of new applications through an understanding of the domain, by supporting user-developer communication, and by providing reuse requirements, as illustrated in Fig. 11.1.

Domain analysis consists of the following:

- Context analysis
- Domain modeling
- Architecture modeling

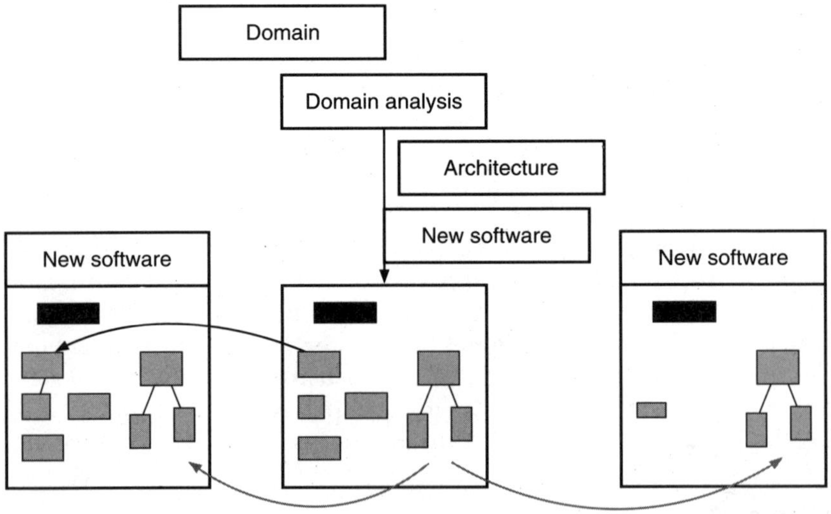

Figure 11.1 Domain analysis product.

The methods used in domain analysis are reused in the software development process. The domain analysis products can be further used in software implementation. Figure 11.2 shows the major features of the domain analysis method.

Context modeling

Context modeling involves the domain scope and requires analyzing the variables of external conditions. *Context analysis* consists of structure diagramming and context diagramming. The *context model* is a structure diagram that shows how the domain is placed in relation to other domains. It is a top-level data flow diagram that shows external entities and data flows between the domain and the external entities. The context diagram provides an end user's perspective of the capabilities.

Domain modeling

Domain modeling is the analysis and modeling of domain problems. Domain modeling consists of an entity relationship (ER) model, a feature model, a functional model, and a domain terminology dictionary. The ER model is the combination of Chen's entity relationship model notation and the semantic data model. The semantic data model comprises "is-a" and "consists-of" notations. A sample ER model is shown in Fig. 11.3.

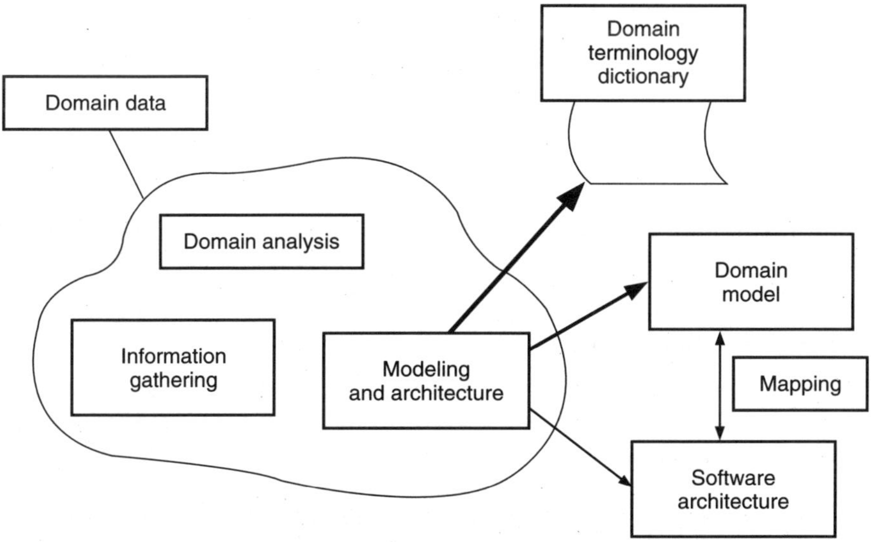

Figure 11.2 Domain analysis method.

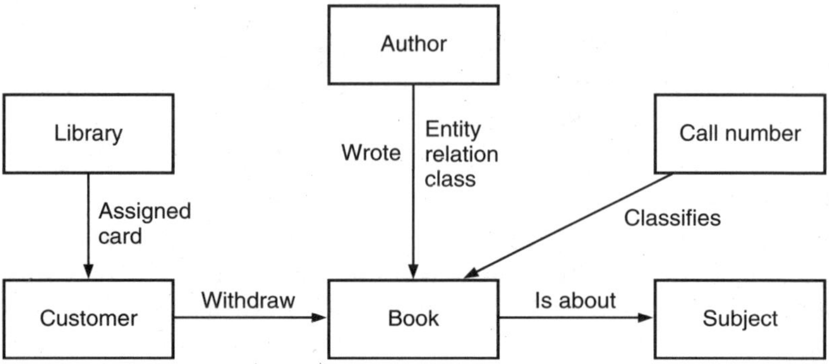

Figure 11.3 A sample ER model.

The feature model provides an end user's perspective on the capabilities of applications in a domain. These capabilities can be mandatory, optional, or alternative. The capabilities of an application are defined as an instantiation of the feature model. This model is used for parameterizing other models. The major components of the feature model are the features diagram, composition rules, issues and decisions, and a record of system features.

Data flow models show the logical flow of data among the processors and data stores. The data flow model describes the internal interfaces among the components of the software system. The domain terminology dictionary standardizes baseline terminology. It provides the result from information gathering in all phases and is essential in an evolving domain.

Architecture modeling

Architecture modeling is the analysis and modeling of application architectures for domain problems. Architecture modeling is a process that involves an interaction model and a module structure chart.

Current Methods

There is no single method that can be claimed as the standard for domain analysis. The necessary information for domain analysis is collected from diversified resources. A good domain analysis method is evaluated by its process, product, and CASE tools.

The *process aspect* considers how the domain analysis method affects an organization; how to manage and maintain the product; how the producer gathers, organizes, validates, and maintains information; and how the users can effectively apply the products in the software development. The *product aspect* considers the types of products that are generated by the method, how they are represented, and how applicable they are in applications development. The *CASE tools support aspect* considers the availability of CASE tools and the extent to which the CASE tools support the method, how well the support CASE tools are integrated, their ease of use, robustness, and the vendor's support.

KAPTUR

Knowledge Acquisition for the Preservation of Tradeoffs and Underlying Rationales (KAPTUR) is a tool for knowledge representation and domain analysis. The KAPTUR domain analysis provides a baseline structure. Any deviations from the baseline are stored as distinctive features of the domain, along with a rationale for the new features. One of the major concepts behind KAPTUR is the ability to apply the tool to successive system developments in the same domain and have KAPTUR semiautomatically support the detection of significant differences between these systems. These differences are referred to in KAPTUR terminology as *distinctive features.* The distinctive features consist of the following:

- New functions
- New subsystems
- New placements of existing subsystems

As new systems are input into KAPTUR, the user must identify and name new capabilities or use the same name for a feature that is identical to one present in a previous system. Given this information, KAPTUR can automatically build a set of knowledge-based relationships that connect the different systems sharing common features.

The KAPTUR approach highlights the roles played by domain developers (supply side) and by system developers (demand side) in defining a reuse-based life cycle, as shown in Fig. 11.4. The develop-for-reuse expert establishes the scope of the domain knowledge that is commonly used across the systems in the domain. The domain developer organizes this knowledge in the domain library in a consumable form. The developer-by-reuse expert uses the domain library to find the resources available for development and provides them to the system developers, who apply these resources to implement systems. The system developers feed back new reuse requirements to domain developers to improve the domain library.

The domain model is stored as a hypertext network to represent system structure. The network includes system features such as subsystems, functions, resources (documents and people), external entities,

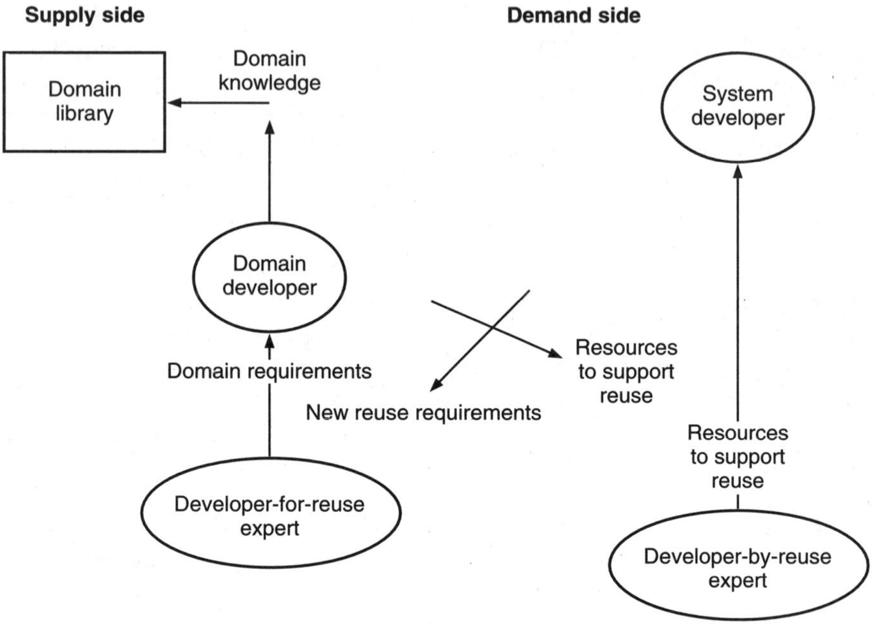

Figure 11.4 Key players in the reuse-based development process.

and parameters. In addition, the links carry relational information, such as composition and decomposition, inputs and outputs, and interactions. Because the model is intended to capture the domain knowledge of system developers, the network also includes design decision information. This includes justifications that represent design issues, positions, and arguments, as well as explanations to help users understand the system. The method also advocates the use of entity relationship and data flow diagrams as conventional specification methods. One of the salient features of the KAPTUR tool is its ability to store and trace the decision process that leads to a specific architecture. (KAPTUR is a product of Computer Technology Associates [CTA] as a domain analysis method.)

The Genesis System

The Genesis System has developed a *database compiler* to synthesize customized database management systems (DBMSs) from prewritten components. The developer, Don Batory, of the University of Texas, reports, "Enormous increases in software productivity are achieved by exploiting reusable and plug compatible modules."

The system has been under development for more than 10 years and can now generate centralized relational DBMSs with various configurations. Current efforts include extending the prototype to support object-oriented and distributed databases. The developers used domain analysis techniques to formulate a building-block technology for file management systems. According to Batory, their approach uses "existing systems, published algorithms, and structures to discern generic architectures for large classes of systems." The Genesis method also defines the generic architecture as the primary product of the domain analysis. While the method recognizes the need to gain a full understanding of a domain in order to construct the architecture, Genesis does not give specific techniques for obtaining or representing this understanding.

The Genesis generic architecture is a template for constructing systems. Building-block modules with standardized interfaces can be plugged into this template by the Genesis tool at the direction of the user. The Genesis approach recommends studying domain information, including systems, algorithms, and data structures, to produce architecture and interfaces that cover the class of systems. The product forms a blueprint for constructing software systems from building blocks. The Genesis approach describes two steps to the analysis process, as follows:

1. *Defining a generic architecture:* A software architecture is defined in terms of a hierarchy of independently definable objects (IDOs)—objects whose implementations have no impact on other objects. For each IDO, there are operations, standard interfaces, and a collection of algorithms that implement the operations. The method does not produce a domain model, a domain terminology dictionary, or a method of mapping the DBMS problem domain to the IDO.
2. *Defining standardized interfaces to objects:* In addition to the architecture information, the Genesis method also produces information about the interrelationships between the building blocks, that is, the IDOs, operations, and algorithms. When the tool is executed, these constraint rules eliminate all building blocks that are incompatible with others already selected by the user. Genesis offers some guidelines for software architecture, but in general the method relies on the knowledge, experience, and creativity of domain experts to create the architecture. A developer using the Genesis tool must be an expert in the domain and should know what to select and the implications of the selection. To improve its utility, the tool should provide users with an interactive design aid that explains the effects of each design decision. The Genesis developers have recognized the following issues:
   a. Establishment of the proper decomposition of the domain is essential. If the subdomains are too restricted, the analysis may lead to interfaces that are unstable, requiring changes each time new algorithms or structures are introduced. If the decomposition

is too broad, the grouping of algorithms and structures will link objects that really should be separate.

b. Development of the architecture does not mean simply listing algorithms and structures and allowing a developer to select what appears to support the requirements. The domain analysis must provide architecture for building a system from these orthogonal units (IDOs).

c. The technology embodied in Genesis is intended to support the exploration of solutions to problems in the domain. The architecture provides a platform on which to implement a class of previously identified solutions.

The developers of Genesis have validated a reuse approach based on domain analysis. Their method is built upon identifying the underlying IDO of a domain, fashioning a generic architecture for structuring the IDO, constructing the building blocks to implement these structures, and implementing the tools to perform system synthesis. (The Genesis System was developed by Don Batory of the University of Texas.)

Design Recovery

The Design Recovery (DESIRE) method gathers design information from source code, organizes the information, and abstracts a design. The DESIRE tool performs these steps and allows domain experts to display and restructure the design, incorporating their knowledge. The recovery results have been positive, and there are active users of the tool that can process C and C++ programs of moderate size (5 to 100,000 lines of code).

The main product of this method is a generic design that is called a *domain model.* Various aspects of this model, such as the calling structure and module structure, can be captured and displayed using the tool. However, there is no way to abstract the design model into an architecture model (e.g., a layered architecture that shows packaging of routines) or to access design decision information. The design recovery method also does not provide any model of the problem space.

DESIRE is used primarily as a tool for maintaining or reengineering existing code. To truly support domain analysis and reuse, the design recovery method and tool must provide knowledge to support an analysis of the features of the problem domain. A developer could then use the tool to explore the extent to which existing systems exhibit these features and extract their implementation. The information extracted from the code could be structured to represent the implementation in a format, such as a design template, that could be reused in other developments.

The domain analysis method is primarily embodied in the Reuse of Software Elements (ROSE) system. The tool attempts to capture domain knowledge to support an early reuse decision and is aimed at meeting the following goals:

1. *Featured-based selection:* Identifying domain objects and associated components from their known features
2. *Constraint-based analysis:* Analyzing a set of user requirements based on known domain dependencies and relationships
3. *Domain-driven completion:* Performing completeness checks to ensure there are no missing requirements in a system specification
4. *Domain-driven refinement:* Collecting and applying design issues as the criteria for support of design decisions

Integrated Computer-Aided Manufacturing (ICAM) Definition (IDEF) Process Model

IDEFo [U.S.DOD] is a top-down diagramming technique that starts with a general process and decomposes it into subprocesses. IDEFo starts with a single context diagram that represents the entire process. This is decomposed into successively more detailed diagrams, collectively called an *IDEFo model.* An *actigram* is the decomposition level as represented by an activity diagram. Each box in the model represents a process consisting of a group of activities to accomplish the process. The information or data necessary to carry out the activities of the process and the information or products generated by the process are represented in an IDEFo diagram by arrows. Figure 11.5 illustrates an IDEFo process model.

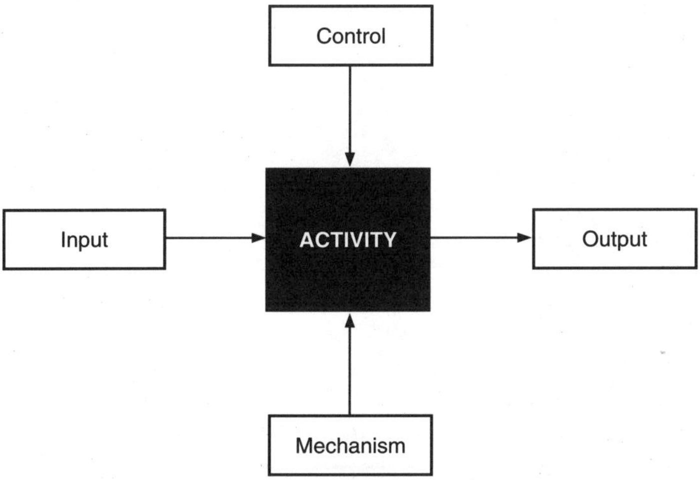

Figure 11.5 A sample IDEFo process model.

An IDEFo diagram consists of boxes and arrows. The box represents activities, or functions. Arrows denote objects, or data. The placement of the arrows in relation to the boxes has specific meaning. Arrows on the left going into the box are the inputs, which initiate the activity and are transformed. Arrows coming out of the box on the right are the outputs, the results produced by the activity. Arrows going into the box from the top are the controls that regulate or guide the activity. Arrows going into the box from the bottom are the mechanisms that are used to perform the activity. The IDEFo process model is a technique that enables professionals to understand systems and communicate with others in a simple way. The IDEFo process model is a series of diagrams that represent the understanding thus gained. The diagrams are organized in a hierarchical method, decomposing the main box into more detailed boxes as its components in a top-down fashion. Each part shown on a detail diagram is again partitioned, and so forth, until the desired level of detail is reached. The higher-level diagram is called the *parent* of the lower-level *detail* diagram. The inputs, outputs, controls, and mechanisms of a lower-level diagram balance with those of its parent diagram. The lowest level of IDEFo models leads to the identification of *objects*.

Figure 11.6 shows an example of IDEFo's main box for an object-oriented system development. Figure 11.7 shows the lower-level diagram. If the end of an arrow has small brackets, there is no match on the detail diagram for that arrow and it will not be shown in the lower level. If an arrow head has small brackets, there is no match on the parent diagram for the arrow, but it will be shown in the lower level. If an arrow splits, it means that the same data is going in two differ-

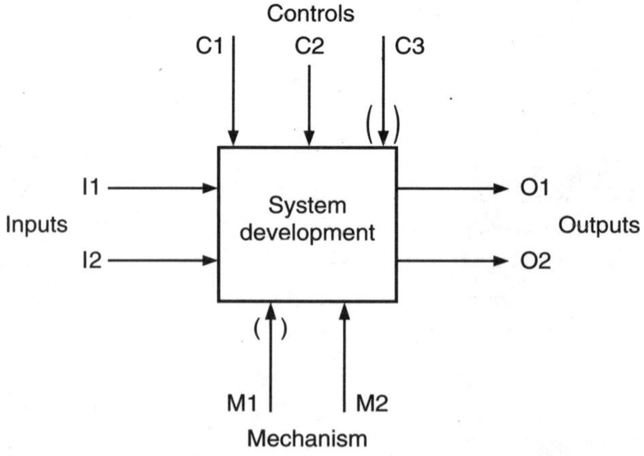

Figure 11.6 Object-oriented system development sample.

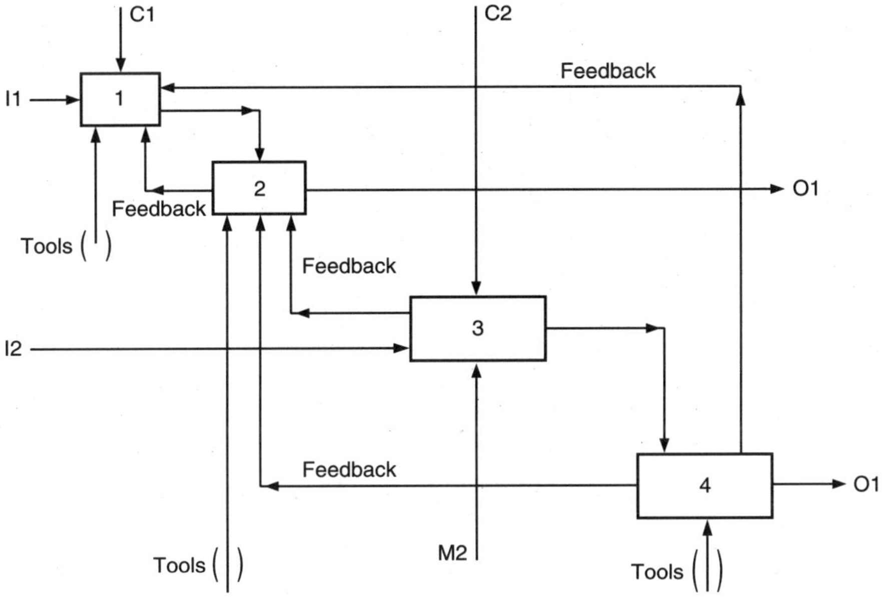

Figure 11.7 Detail diagram, level 1.

ent directions. If two different pieces of data merge into one arrow, it means that one piece of data is combined with the other piece. A node number begins with the letter *A* (for "activity"), followed by a digit for every node traversed. Each decomposition level has the node number of its parent with the specific box number appended. The top is desig-

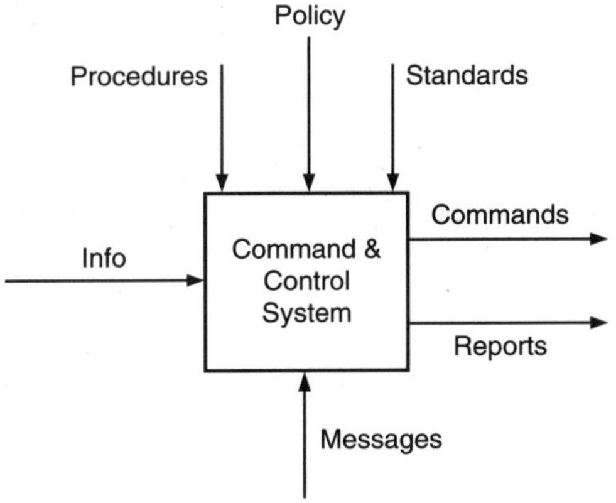

Figure 11.8 Level 0 IDEFo model.

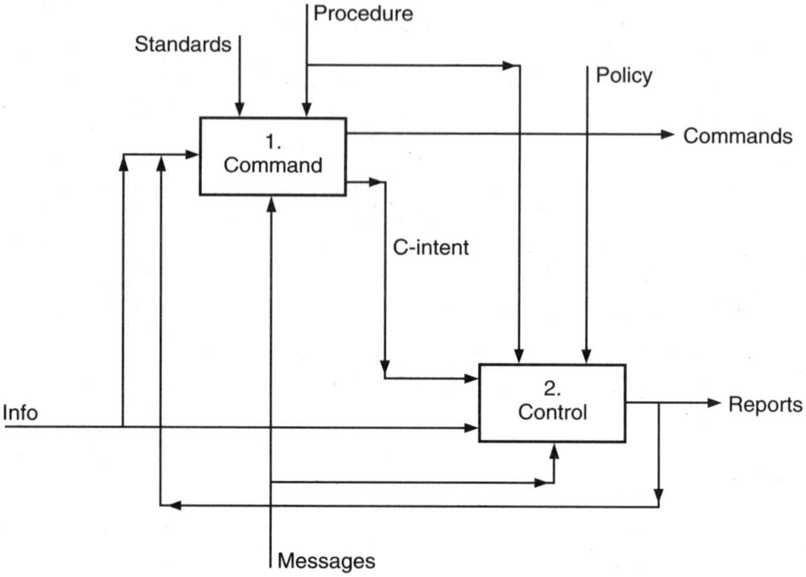

Figure 11.9 Level 1 IDEFo model.

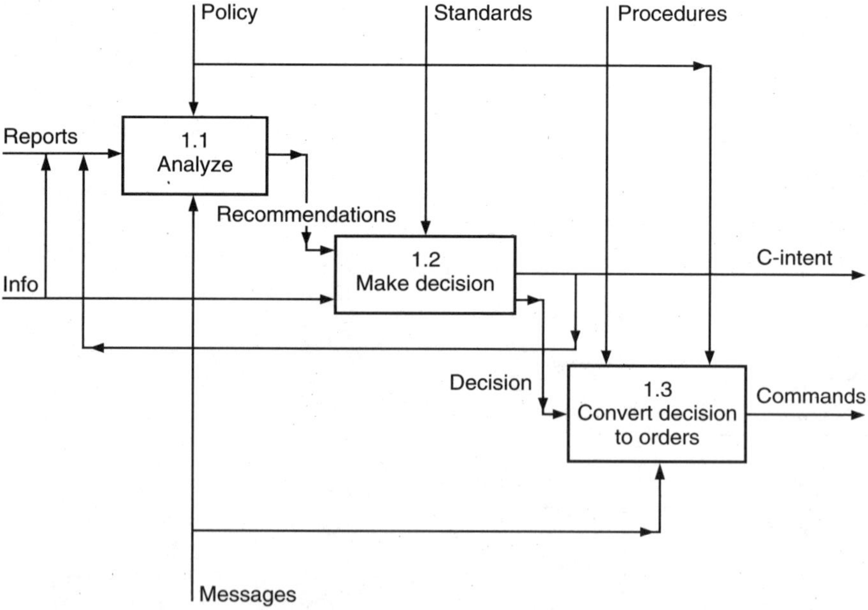

Figure 11.10 Level 2 IDEFo model.

nated A0. A single box diagram summing up the A0 diagram and stating the purpose and viewpoint is designated A – 0 (A minus 0) and is the usual starting point for a model. The context diagrams showing the environment of the model can have negative numbers.

Case Study 11.1

A commander of the Command & Control System acquires information, evaluates it, makes appropriate decisions, issues further instructions, and monitors results. The commander is authorized to use available resources to accomplish certain missions in accordance with the established policy, procedures, and standards.

The input is “info” and the outputs are “commands” and “reports.” There is a mechanism for sending and receiving messages.

Discussion. Figure 11.8 illustrates the context diagram. Figures 11.9 and 11.10 show sample IDEFo models.

Chapter

12

Feature-Oriented Domain Analysis

The feature-oriented domain analysis (FODA) method focuses on identification of prominent or distinctive features of software systems in a domain. These features are user-visible aspects or characteristics of the domain. They lead to the creation of a set of products that define the domain and also give the method its name.

The Feature-Oriented Domain Analysis Method

The feature-oriented domain analysis method supports reuse at the functional and architectural levels. Domain products, representing the common functionality and architecture of applications in a domain, are produced from domain analysis. Specific applications in the domain are developed as refinements of the domain products. The FODA method is a product of the Software Engineering Institute (SEI), at Carnegie Mellon University in Pittsburgh, Pennsylvania.

FODA Concepts

The FODA concept is to develop domain products that are generic and widely applicable within that domain. These generic products are achieved by abstracting away factors that make one application different from other applications. However, to develop applications from the generic products, those factors that have been abstracted away must be made specific and reintroduced during refinement. Not only the generic factors but also those factors that make each application unique are an important part of the domain knowledge and should be captured in the domain products. With this method, domain products are not ends in themselves, but evolve through applications.

The FODA Modeling Technique

Software development, like other engineering fields, can benefit from the development and reuse of *product frameworks* in an application domain. Product frameworks, in the context of software, are abstractions of the functionality and designs (i.e., architecture) of the applications in an application domain. To support the development and reuse of abstractions, the FODA method is founded on the following set of models:

- Aggregation/decomposition
- Generalization/specialization
- Parameterization

Aggregation

Abstracting a collection of units into a new unit is called *aggregation.* For example, school is an aggregation of students, teachers, and so on. Refining an aggregation into its constituent units is called *decomposition.* The model primitive allows composition of components into a new aggregated component or decomposition of an abstract component into its parts.

Generalization

Abstracting the commonality among a collection of units into a new conceptual unit that suppresses detailed differences is called *generalization.* Refining a generalized unit into a unit that incorporates details is called *specialization.* For example, the conceptual entity *employee* is an abstraction of secretaries, managers, technical staff, and so on. The model primitive allows the development of generic components that can be refined in many different ways.

Parameterization

Parameterization is a component development technique in which components are adapted in many different ways by substituting the values of parameters that are embedded in the component. It allows codification of the way adaptation is made within a component. The Ada generic is one example of parameterization.

The FODA method applies the aggregation and generalization primitive to capture the commonality of the applications in the domain in terms of abstractions. Differences between applications are captured in the refinements. An abstraction can usually be refined in many different ways, depending on the contexts in which refinements are made. Parameters are defined to uniquely specify the context for each specific refinement. The result of this approach is a domain product consisting of a collection of abstractions and a series of refinements of each abstraction with parameterization. Whenever a new refinement is made, the context in which the refinement is made must be defined in terms of parameters before it is incorporated into the domain product. Therefore, in the FODA method, a domain product is not the end product; it expands and evolves through application. The FODA method focuses on identifying factors that cause differences among applications in a domain, both at the functional and at the architectural level, and uses those to parameterize domain products.

Product Parameterization

The purpose of parameterization is to develop generic components that are adapted in many ways by supplying values to parameters. This concept has been put into practice through the reuse of subroutines, generics, macros, and preprocessors. The FODA method applies this concept to software engineering other than code. Identifying and understanding *factors* that result in different applications or different implementations of similar applications in a domain are the basis for parameterization. The factors considered in this method for parameterization are largely classified into commonality and differences as follows:

- Capabilities of applications in a domain from the end user's perspective
- Environment in which applications are used and operated
- Application domain technology based on which requirements decisions are made
- Implementation techniques

Although they provide a large set of common capabilities, applications in a domain also provide different sets of capabilities, which distinguish each application from the others. These capabilities, from the perspective of end users, are modeled as features. Applications may run in different operating environments. They may run on different hardware or operating systems, or interface with different types of devices. Understanding the commonality and differences among the external components with which the applications interface is essential to abstracting the functionality of those external components and defining common interfaces to them. There are many ways to provide the features desired by end users. Different people involved in the development can make different decisions, all of which affect the way the features are implemented.

Levels of Abstraction

To maximize reusability, the FODA method advocates that applications in the domain be abstracted to the level at which differences between the applications are not revealed. This abstraction is accomplished by using the model primitives. The factors that make each application unique are subsequently incorporated into the refinements of the abstractions, but incorporation should be delayed as long as possible. Generic components that capture only the common characteristics of applications in a domain are free of those factors that have a high degree of reusability because of generality. However, the productivity increase from the reuse of a generic component may not be as high as that from the reuse of a component that is less generic but addresses specific features of the intended application. The FODA method offers the benefits of both approaches by providing generic components and also refinements of those components at various levels. As generic components are refined, the factors that make applications unique are incorporated into the refinements. Components can be reused at the level that is most appropriate for an application.

Information Sources

Domain products embody a wide range of domain knowledge. During the domain analysis, the knowledge is collected from various sources and then organized and represented as domain products. Table 12.1 provides an overview of information sources to use while gathering information for the domain analysis.

Regarding the use of existing applications, it should be pointed out that systems should be selected that are as divergent in functionality as possible, while still being in the domain. This helps to minimize the number of systems that must be examined. As a guideline, at the very least three systems should be used as inputs to the domain analysis.

Activities and Products

Domain products are produced through a number of activities. The domain analysis process consists of a number of activities, and many models are produced from the process. Table 12.2 groups the activities into phases, with the inputs to and outputs from each activity, and shows how the outputs from one activity are used in other activities.

TABLE 12.1 Advantages and Disadvantages of Information Sources

Source	Advantages	Disadvantages
Textbooks	Good source of domain knowledge, theories, methods, techniques, models	Reflects only author's views May use idealized or biased models
Standards	Represents standard reference model for domain	Model may not be current with new technology
Existing applications	Most important source of domain knowledge Can be directly used to determine user-visible features Requirements documents available for domain model Detailed design and source code show architectures	Cost of analyzing many systems is high
Domain	Can provide context/rationale information unavailable elsewhere Can be consultant during domain analysis and validation of products afterward	Experts have different areas of expertise; several experts may be needed

The models produced from a domain analysis are used to develop applications in the domain, as shown in Fig. 12.1. The context model can be used by the requirements analyst to determine if the application required by the user is within the domain for which a set of domain products is available. With the help of the feature model, the requirements analyst negotiates the capabilities of the application in a domain with the users. The feature model identifies common, alternative, and optional features. If the terms relevant to the features are new or unclear, the domain terminology dictionary contains descriptions of their meanings. Typically, a data flow model contains definitions of internal functions and does not contain the information that the user needs most, which is a description of the external, or user-visible, aspects of the system. The feature model is a better communication medium because it provides this external view that the user can understand.

The entity relationship model can be used by a requirements analyst to acquire knowledge about the entities in the domain and their interrelationships. An understanding of the domain will help the analyst to deal with the user's problems. The analysis can determine if the functional model, consisting of the data flow model and the finite state model of the domain products, can be applied to the user's problems to define the requirement of the application. If all the user's problems are reflected in the feature model, then the requirements may be easily derived from the models by tracing the features embedded in the models as parameters. Otherwise, new refinements of the abstract components may have to be made. The architecture model is used by the designer as

TABLE 12.2 FODA Method Summary

Phase	Inputs	Process	Product	Description
Context analysis	Operating environments Standards	Context analysis	Context model	Environment in which the applications will be used and operated
Domain modeling	1. Features context model	1. Features analysis	1. Features model	1. End user's perspective of the capabilities of the applications in a domain
	2. Application domain knowledge	2. Entity relationship modeling	2. Entity relationship model	2. Developer's understanding of the domain entities (objects) and their relationships
	3. Domain technology Context model Features model Entity relationship model	3. Functional analysis	3. Data flow model Finite state machine model	3. Requirements analyst's perspective of the functionality of the applications
Architectural modeling	Requirements Implementation technology, context model, model, entity design information	Architectural modeling	Process interaction model Module structure charts	Designer's perspective of the high-level structure (architecture) of the applications

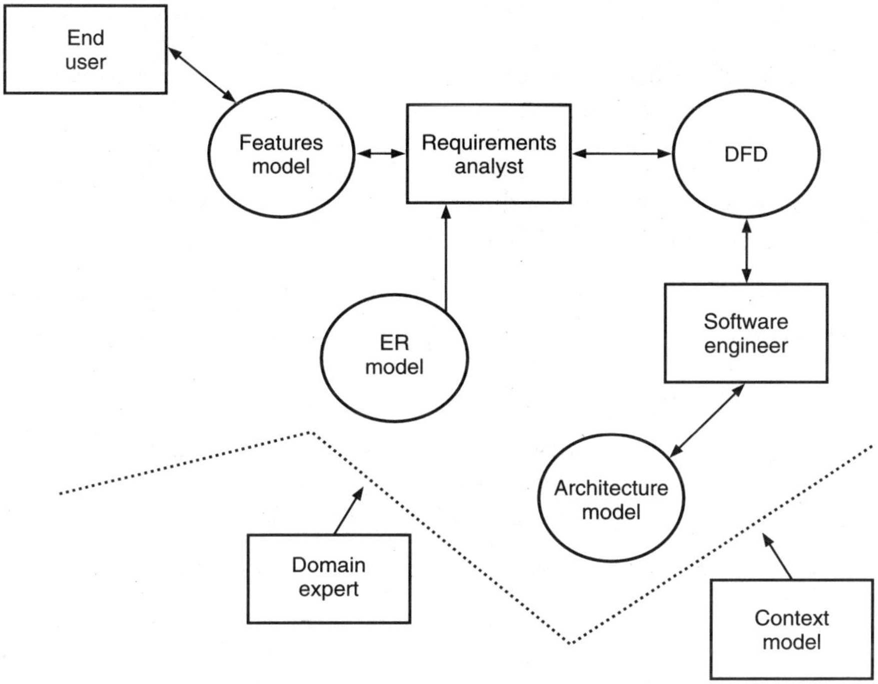

Figure 12.1 Use of FODA products in software development.

a high-level design for the application. Again, if the user's problems are reflected in the feature model, a design may be easily derived from the architecture model. If the problems are not represented, then the architecture model should be further refined from other domain products.

FODA Context Analysis

The FODA context analysis defines the scope of a domain that is likely to yield exploitable domain products. In the context analysis phase, the relationships between the candidate domain and the elements external to the domain are analyzed, variability of the relationships is evaluated, and the external conditions are also evaluated. The results of the context analysis, along with other factors such as availability of domain expertise, domain data, and project constraints, are used to scope the domain. The final results of the context analysis are documented in a context model. This context model defines the boundary of the domain—that is, the scope of the domain modeling that follows the context analysis.

A context model consists of one or more structure diagrams and data flow diagrams. A structure diagram is an informal graphical block. The target domain is placed in the structure diagram relative to higher, lower, and peer-level domains. Any other domains that interface with the target domain must also be in the diagram. A data flow diagram shows data flow between the target domain and all other domains, and entities with which the target domain communicates standards or other domain analysis results that apply to the external entities should be identified in the diagram. For each entity in the context model, the following information is included in the document:

- Name of the entity (an object in the diagram)
- Description of the function for a functional entity or description of the contents for a data entity
- Applicable standards and/or reusable components
- Description of variability, including the range, frequency, and binding time—compile time, activation time, and runtime
- Other items describing the attributes of the entity
- Source for the information or for additional information

One of the necessary conditions for building software is an understanding of different contexts in which the reusable software is to be incorporated or operated. The context model defines the scope of a domain analysis. Other subsequent analysis activities, such as feature modeling, functional modeling, entity relationship modeling, and architecture modeling, are performed within the scope defined in the context diagram.

Checklist for the context model

To yield domain products that can be exploited in other applications, the scope of a domain should be decided considering the following factors:

- Commonality of the domain in existing systems
- Availability of information on the domain and domain expertise
- Expected usage of the domain products
- Project resources and constraints

Keeping these factors in mind, the following activities for context analysis and domain scope are identified:

1. Make an initial cut of the target domain and the domain boundary. Identify the existing applications in the domain or applications using the domain. Identify information sources and any previous works on the domain, including domain analysis products, standards, and books and technical papers.

2. For each application identified for the analysis, describe the context of the candidate domain in terms of structure diagrams and data flow diagrams. Verify that the domain has a clear physical boundary within the application. If there are any previous domain analysis results or standards, determine if they address each application adequately; record problems, if any.
3. Understand the usage of the target domain, any recent technical developments that will affect the domain, and any future plans or requirements.
4. Analyze the variability of the usage and the contexts of each use as follows:
   a. Based on the features of applications in the domain, begin the definition of a feature model.
   b. Identify the environmental differences.
   c. Identify any assumptions on which the target domain is based.
   d. Construct a common model by classifying specifics of the contexts into general categories so that each context is defined as an instantiation of the common model.
5. Evaluate the model against the applications used in the analysis and incorporate the variability information into the context model.
6. Evaluate the commonality of the applications, feasibility of constructing domain products, and potential uses and benefits of the domain products.
7. Estimate the resources for the subsequent activities considering the availability of domain experts, previous work, and the maturity of the domain.
8. Document the context model; define the terms used in the model in the domain terminology dictionary.
9. Validate the model against at least one application that is not included in the analysis. Also, have the model reviewed by domain experts. Record the validation results in the context model documentation.

FODA Domain Modeling

For the domain that is scoped in the context analysis, the commonality and differences of the problems that are addressed by the applications in the domain are analyzed in the domain modeling phase and a number of models representing different aspects of the problems are produced. The FODA domain modeling phase consists of feature analysis, entity relationship modeling, and functional analysis.

Feature analysis

The feature analysis captures in a model the end user's understanding of the general capabilities of applications in a domain—typically, data flow diagrams that have been used by software developers as a medium to communicate requirements with customers and designers. Customers need to know the essential capabilities of applications that will satisfy their needs. These capabilities include features such as:

- Services provided by the application
- Performance of the application
- Hardware platform required by the application
- Cost

Features are the attributes of a system that directly affect end users. The end users have to make decisions regarding the availability of features in the system, and they have to understand the meaning of the features in order to use the system. Figure 12.2 shows an example of features involved when a person buys a car.

A feature model represents the standard features of a family of systems in the domain and the relationships between them. The structural relationship consists of a logical grouping of features. Alternative or optional features of each grouping must be indicated in the feature model. Each feature must be named distinctively and the definition should be included in the domain terminology dictionary.

The feature model serves as a communication medium between users and developers. To the users, the feature model shows the standard features, other features they can choose, and when they can choose them. To the developers, the feature model indicates what needs to be parameterized in the other models and the software architecture, and how the parameterization should be done. Other domain models and the software architecture should be defined around the standard features. Alternative and optional features must be incorporated into the models and architecture, but should always be parameterized with the corresponding features so that instantiation of the models and architecture can be done easily. The feature analysis process consists of the following:

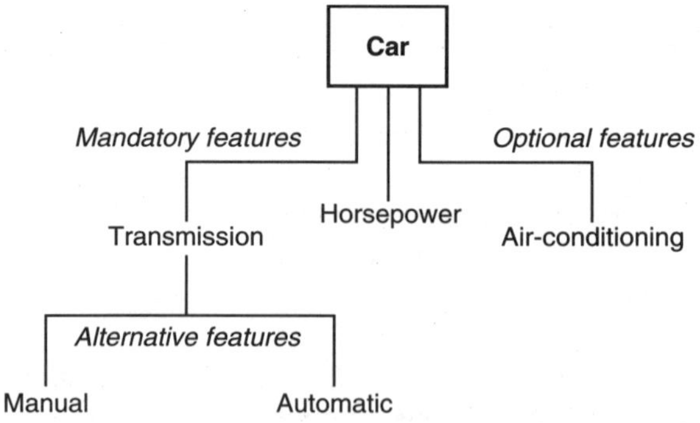

Figure 12.2 Example of car features.

- Collecting source documents
- Identifying features
- Abstracting and classifying the identified features as a model
- Defining the features
- Validating the model

Entity relationship model

The entity relationship model captures and defines the domain knowledge that is essential for implementing applications in the domain. Those who maintain or reuse software have to reacquire this knowledge in order to understand the problems that the application addresses. Therefore, the purpose of entity relationship modeling is to represent the domain knowledge explicitly in terms of domain entities and their relationships, and to make them available for the derivation of objects and data definitions during the functional analysis and architecture modeling.

The basic building blocks of the model are entity classes and "consists-of" and "is-a" relationships. Entity classes represent abstractions of objects in the application domain, and the relationship types "is-a" and "consists-of" represent generalization and aggregation relationships, respectively. Aggregation relationships specify composition structures between entities, while generalization relationships specify commonality and differences among entities. An example of the entity relationship diagram notation is shown in Fig. 12.3.

The primary use of an entity relationship model is to support analysis and understanding of the domain problems and to derive and structure the domain objects used in the applications development. Entities are units of domain information that have to be processed and maintained by the systems. They, with their definitions of attributes, are used to identify domain objects. The domain objects are then used to define data flows, data stores in the functional model, and object-oriented development.

Functional analysis

The functional analysis identifies functional commonality and differences among the applications in a domain. It abstracts and structures the common functions in a model from which application-specific functional models are instantiated with appropriate adaptation. The feature model and entity relationship model are used as guidelines in developing the functional model. The mandatory features and the entities are the basis for defining an abstract functional model. Specifications of a functional model are classified as specifications of functions

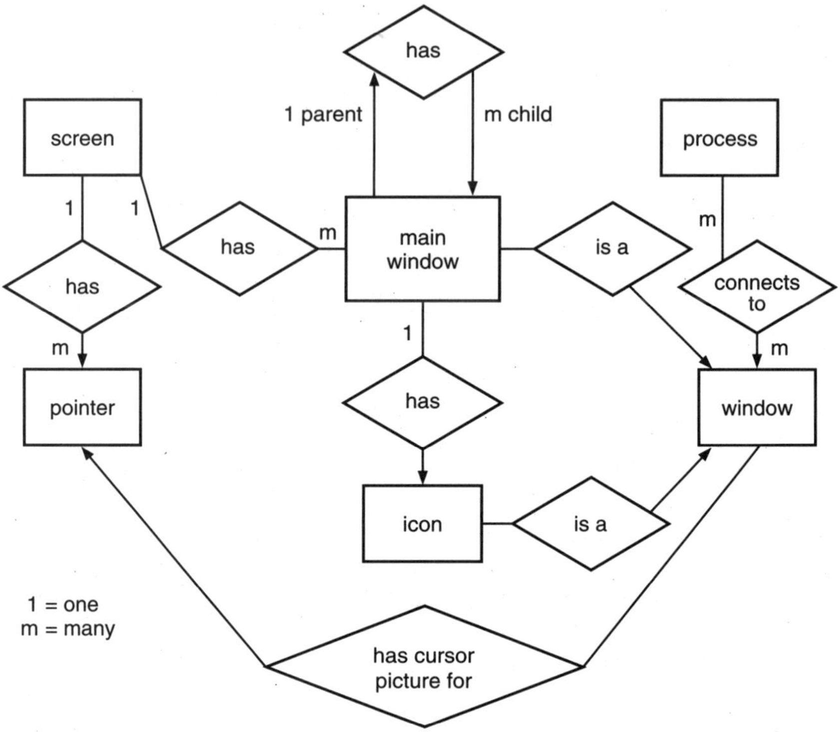

Figure 12.3 Window manager entity relationship diagram.

and specifications of behavior. The specification of functions describes the structural aspect of an application in terms of inputs, outputs, activities, internal data, logical structures of these, and data flow relationships between them. The specification of behaviors describes how an application behaves in terms of events, inputs, states, conditions, and state transitions. The primary uses of the functional model are in understanding the domain problems and reusing models in the requirement analysis.

FODA Architecture Modeling

The FODA architecture modeling provides a software solution to the problems that have been defined in the domain modeling phase. An architecture model is developed in this phase, and from it, detailed design and component construction is done. A primary goal of the FODA method is to make domain products reusable. In the development of an architecture model, architecture layering is done so that reuse can occur at the layer appropriate for a given application and the impact of technical and requirements changes to the model can be localized. A FODA architecture is a high-level design of the applications in a domain. Therefore, the FODA method focuses on identifying concurrent processes and domain-oriented common modules, and on allocating the features, functions, and data objects that have been defined in the domain model to the processes and modules. An architecture model addresses the problems defined in the domain in such a way that the model can be adapted to future changes in the problems and technology. A layered architecture is shown in Fig. 12.4.

The domain architecture layer is represented as a model showing the concurrent domain processes and the interconnections between them. This is also called a *process interaction model.* The domain utilities layer shows the packaging of functions and data objects into modules and the interconnections between them. This is also called a *module structure chart.* Domain-oriented modules that are common across the applications in the domain are also identified. The common utilities layer contains modules that are used across different domains. Modules for interprocess communication and synchronization and for data management belong in this layer. Any utilities provided by the operating systems and programming languages, such as semaphores and the Ada runtime environment, belong in the systems layer.

An architecture model is used for the following:

- To make a detailed design and identify opportunities for reusable components
- To provide a reference model for future systems development and for the evolution of existing systems
- To ascertain the reusability of candidate components
- To provide a model for managing (classifying, storing, and retrieving) software components in a domain

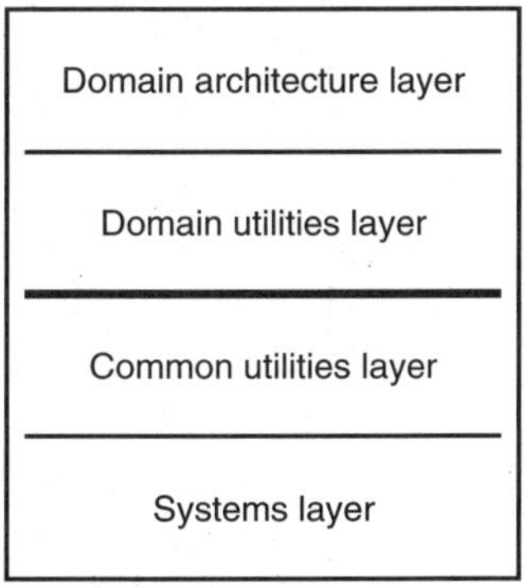

Figure 12.4 Architecture-layer sample.

A process for developing an architecture model is outlined as follows:

1. Identify the major concurrent processes from data flow diagrams and finite state machine diagrams.
2. Identify other concurrent processes.
3. Allocate the functions and data to each process and check that all the functions and data in the data flow diagrams are properly allocated to the processes.
4. Define process interactions.
5. Design each process.
6. Parameterize modules for the compile-time features so that they may be instantiated for different selections of compile-time features.
7. Specify the components identified. Specification of each module should include operations and parameters, a high-level internal logic, and allocation of features and functions.

Case Study 12.1

A window management system is a type of interactive user interface that enables users to work with multiple separate applications at the

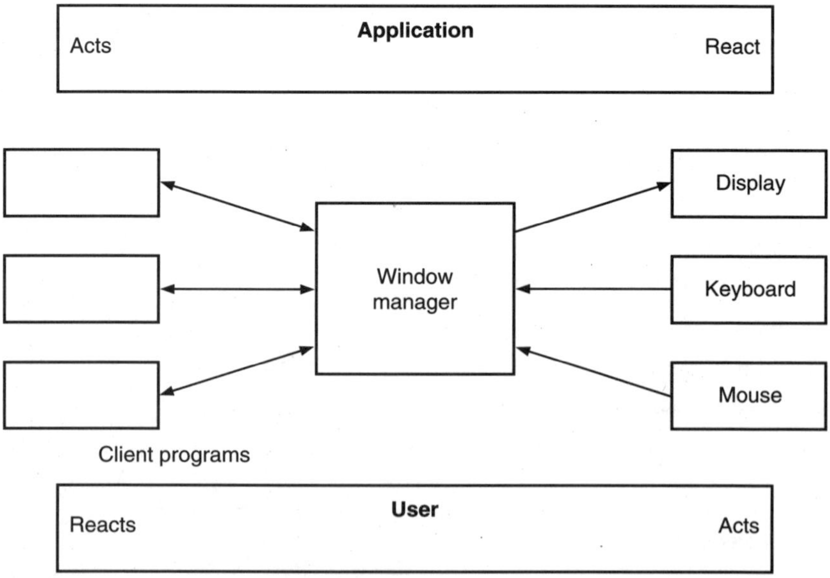

Figure 12.5 Function of a window manager.

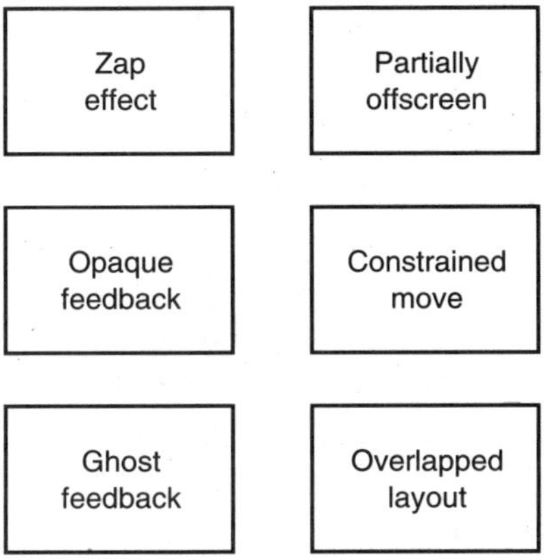

Figure 12.6 Sample user features found in a window manager.

same time. This is achieved through the use of a desktop metaphor, in which each process is associated with a graphical window, which is visually analogous to a paper or a document on a physical desktop. Users may switch back and forth between different applications, much as a person at a desk might choose between different documents on a desktop in the course of a day. A window management system provides the functionality to create and manipulate this display of multiple processes. Partial graphic representation of such a system is shown in Figs. 12.5 through 12.9.

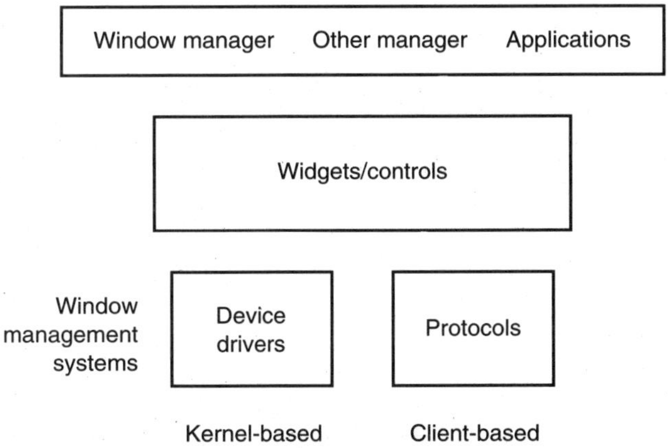

Figure 12.7 Structure diagram: relationship of window managers to window management systems.

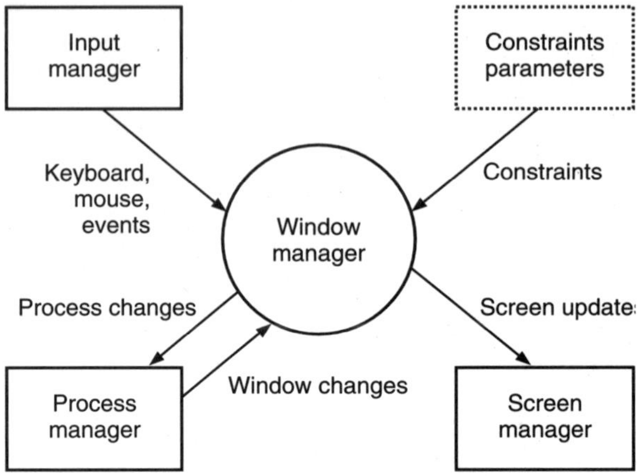

Figure 12.8 Context diagram: major data flows of window management systems.

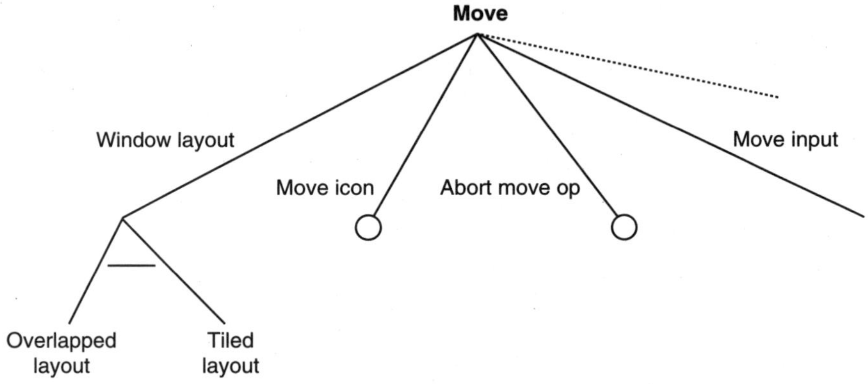

Figure 12.9 Features for the window manager move operation.

Chapter

13

The Joint Object-Oriented Domain Analysis Method

The Joint Integrated Avionics Working Group (JIAWG) Reuse Subcommittee has initiatives in several areas to demonstrate that reuse can effectively support the JIAWG programs and that the creation of reusable assets is an essential element of the reuse process. Domain analysis is the process that identifies what is reusable, how it can be structured, and how it can be used. Software objects are more understandable, more adaptable, and less likely to change than functions. This chapter covers some of the major characteristics of the JIAWG joint object-oriented domain analysis (JODA) method.

JODA

JODA defines a domain model that can be used to produce reusable software objects (RSOs), especially reusable requirements. The information in the domain model is collected using modified Coad/Yourdon Object-Oriented Analysis (CYOOA) techniques. Domain analysis is part of the domain engineering process that uses the domain model to define reusable software architecture, to design reusable code, and to define the structure of the domain. The domain structure is the organization of the parts as dominated by the general character of the whole. The domain structure is defined by the CYOOA diagrams that define the composition of the domain through whole-part diagrams and the variation in objects using generalization-specialization (gen-spec) diagrams. Objects are defined by their services and attributes. The domain structure is defined through whole-part concepts, variation in objects, services, attributes, and concepts, and the relationships between these objects and concepts.

JODA Context for Domain Analysis

The JODA context for domain analysis consists of business planning, methodology planning, domain engineering, and application engineering, as shown in Fig. 13.1. Business planning and methodology planning are necessary parts of both application engineering and domain engineering, while domain engineering is not a necessary part of application engineering. Feedback from application engineering is shown in Fig. 13.1 in order to highlight its importance. Each application that is reuse-based acquires new information that needs to be entered into the domain model. The new information may require the creation, modification, or deletion of RSOs. Without this feedback, the maximum return on the reuse investment cannot be achieved, and the domain model and RSO will not be current or viable.

Business planning identifies and selects high-level domains that will be considered for domain analysis. The criteria for identifying a domain are as follows:

- Is the domain well understood?
- Is the technology predictable?
- Is domain expertise available to support domain engineering?

Methodology planning defines a set of methods for domain engineering that are compatible with the methods for applications engineering. If the methods are not compatible, then the domain knowledge and

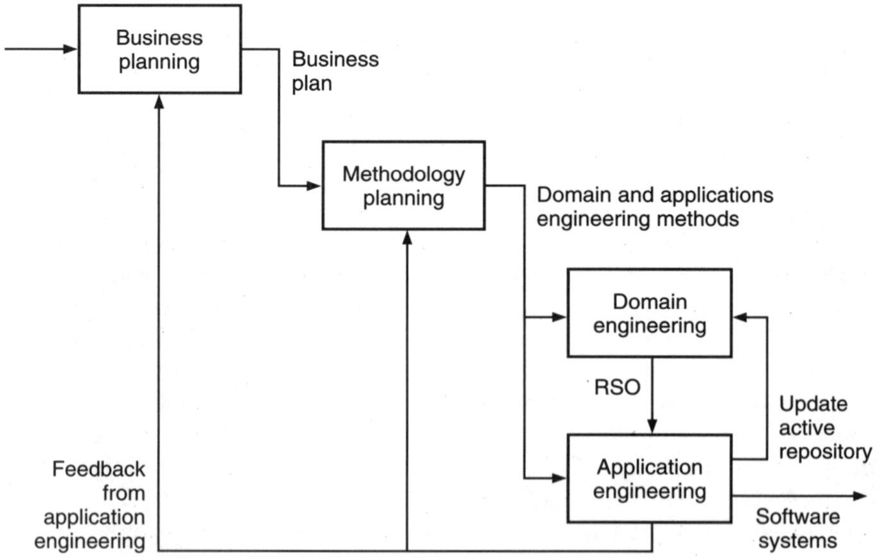

Figure 13.1 Reuse-based software development in JODA context.

software objects may not be reusable. Figure 13.2 shows more detailed information about the domain engineering activity, including the flow of specific data within domain engineering and the data that are input to applications (software) engineering. Domain engineering acquires information and creates RSOs that are reused during applications engineering. The goal of domain engineering is to capture, organize, and represent the domain from which RSOs are produced to support the implementation of any member of the domain (a family of systems). The activities in domain engineering are similar to those in software engineering, but there are two significant differences. First, domain engineering attempts to define a software solution (a family of systems) for a large problem space, while software engineering constructs only one solution (a single system) that is usually a subset of the large problem space. This difference between domain engineering and software engineering is analogous to the difference in providing a solution to the quadratic equation, $2Ax + Bx + C = 0$, as opposed to finding the solution to one specific equation such as $2x^2 - 113x - 1235$. Variation in the problem space makes one solution more general than another solution. The second difference is that software engineering does not attempt to represent and deliver the domain knowledge that has been acquired.

The goal of domain analysis is to define the domain structure and requirements and capture them in a domain model. Domain experts are interviewed to define high-level domain abstractions and to verify the information obtained from the analysis of existing systems. The domain model should not contain requirements that are obsolete, one-of-a-kind, or arbitrarily allocated. Abstract requirements that capture the essence of several requirements are preferred over more detailed requirements. If the domain analysis team determines that a require-

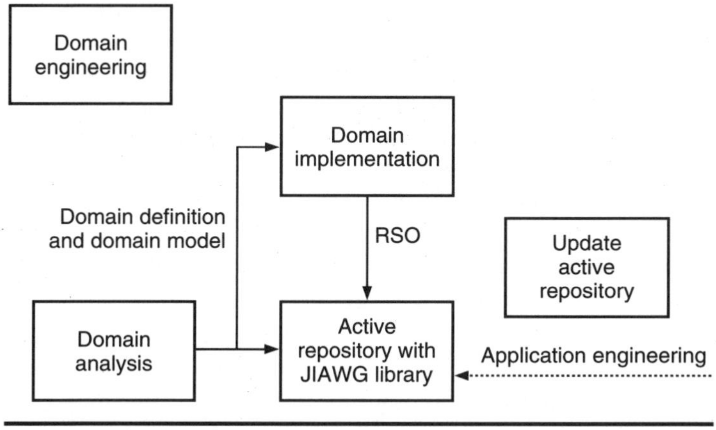

Figure 13.2 Applications engineering based on domain engineering.

ment is unique or obsolete, or that it should not be included, and the domain experts concur, then that requirement will be excluded.

The domain implementation produces RSOs. At the minimum, domain implementation should produce reusable software architecture, reusable code designs, reusable code, and reusable tests. The reusable software architectures are a set of high-level designs that can be used to implement any member of the domain family. The design information that is obtained and represented includes tasking, data allocation, the user interface, and the packaging of the requirements from the domain analysis. The roles identified in domain analysis support the definition of the user interface, and the triggers, events, and parallelism support tasking definitions. The software architectures and the rationale for selecting one over another are also recorded in the active repository. Traceability from the domain model to software architecture is added to the active repository when the architecture is added.

The active repository makes RSOs available during application engineering. During domain analysis, a domain definition and model are produced and stored in the active repository, but the model is not reused directly. The tools and techniques to support the storage, retrieval, and maintenance of the domain model and other RSOs in the organization standard form part of the active repository. The traceability is added during domain implementation because the software architectures and code do not exist during domain analysis. Furthermore, multiple implementations are possible from a single domain model, and the different implementations need to be traceable from the model.

JODA Applications Engineering

For each system that is constructed using reuse techniques, the goals for that application need to be defined. These goals depend on the coverage of the domain, the maturity of the RSO, and the experience of the development team. To determine if the reuse goals have been met, data must be collected during application engineering. Without data to measure the reuse goals, the benefits and problems cannot be identified and the reasons for success or failure may not be determined. Another reason for collecting data is to permit comparison of subsystems that are developed from reusable assets and against the subsystems that are developed without reuse. This data can be used to develop more accurate economic and planning models for reuse-based systems.

The JODA Process

The JODA process consists of three phases: prepare domain, define domain, and model domain. The prepare domain phase is a complex, time-consuming, and detailed task that requires the development of high-quality abstractions of existing and proposed systems, as shown in Fig. 13.3. This phase requires access to information from domain experts, artifacts from the development of previous systems, domain reference materials, and knowledge of emerging technology and future trends in the domain. The domain definition is delivered and maintained in the active repository. This top-level view of the domain uses the same notation as the domain analysis. The definition bounds the domain and is used by the analysis to clarify what is and what is not available for reuse. Potential users can quickly determine whether their needs can be met by the results of the domain analysis. The domain definition includes the following diagrams:

- Top-level subject diagram
- Top-level whole-part diagrams
- Top-level generalization-specialization diagram
- Domain services
- Domain dependencies
- Domain glossary
- Textual description

The domain definition identifies top-level objects and defines visible services in the domain. Therefore, the JODA domain definition would describe all the objects as real number objects.

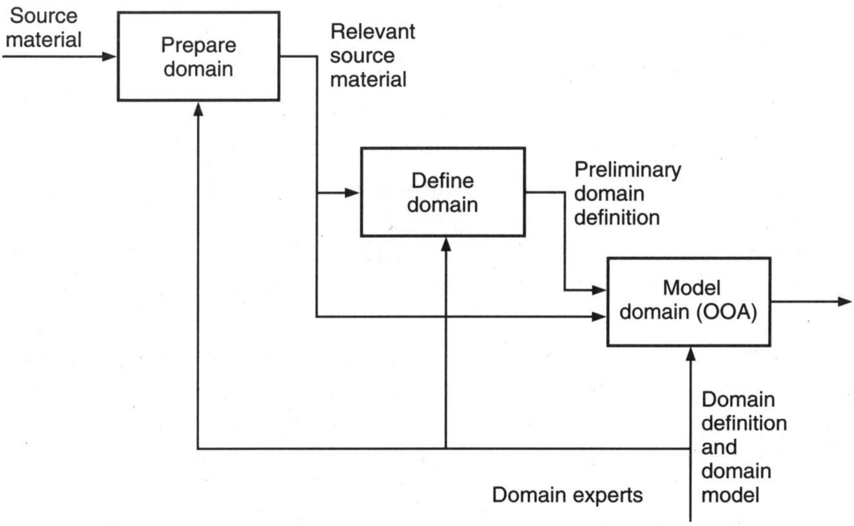

Figure 13.3 Domain analysis process.

The model domain phase contains three activities: examine object life histories and state-event response, identify and walk through scenarios, and abstract and group objects. These activities are iterated because all relevant information cannot be identified in one pass. These activities are neither discrete nor do they occur sequentially. The domain analysis team moves freely between activities, but the scenario and abstraction activities are more effective when a basic model has been identified.

JODA Products

The JODA products consist of the domain model and the domain definition. The domain model is a complete view; it contains the codified knowledge that is extracted from domain experts, the existing systems, and the future trends, and it represents the analyst's understanding of the domain. The domain definition is a top-level view of the domain; it defines the attributes and services of visible objects, the highest-level whole-part structure, a high-level gen-spec structure, and a top-level subject diagram.

Case Study 13.1

An office building elevator system specification is described as follows.

1. There are one or more elevators serving two or more floors.
2. On board each elevator is a set of destination push buttons, one for each floor, which backlight when depressed and remain lit until arrival at the selected floor.
3. On board each elevator are two directional signal lights, one for going up and the other for going down.
4. On board each elevator is a set of lights, one for each floor. One of these lights is always lit, indicating that the elevator is at that floor.
5. On each floor there are two summons push buttons, one for summoning the elevator to go up and the other to go down. These backlight when pushed and remain lit until an elevator arrives that will go in the selected direction. The top and bottom floors each have only a single summons push button.
6. On each floor beside each elevator are two floor directional lights. When an elevator arrives at the floor, the appropriate light shows the direction the elevator will take when leaving the floor. The top and bottom have only a single directional light each.
7. Each elevator has doors that are either closed or not closed. Opening, closing, or emergency stops are not considered. On each floor,

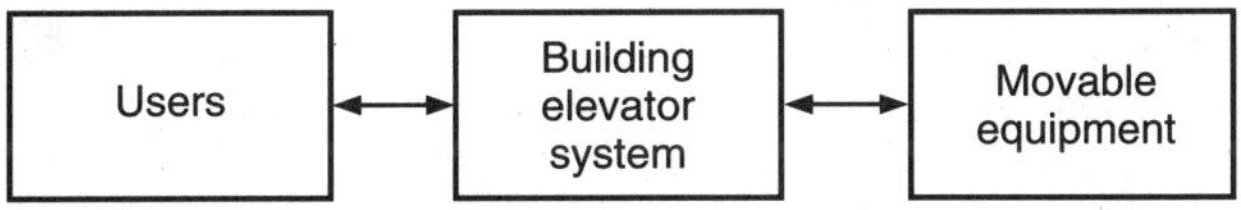

Figure 13.4 Top-level subject diagram for the office building elevator system.

there are doors for each elevator. Both the elevator doors and the floor doors have to be open for people to enter or leave the elevator at a floor.

8. The specification is not concerned with what happens under failure conditions.

A partial graphic representation of the system is shown in Figs. 13.4, 13.5, and 13.6.

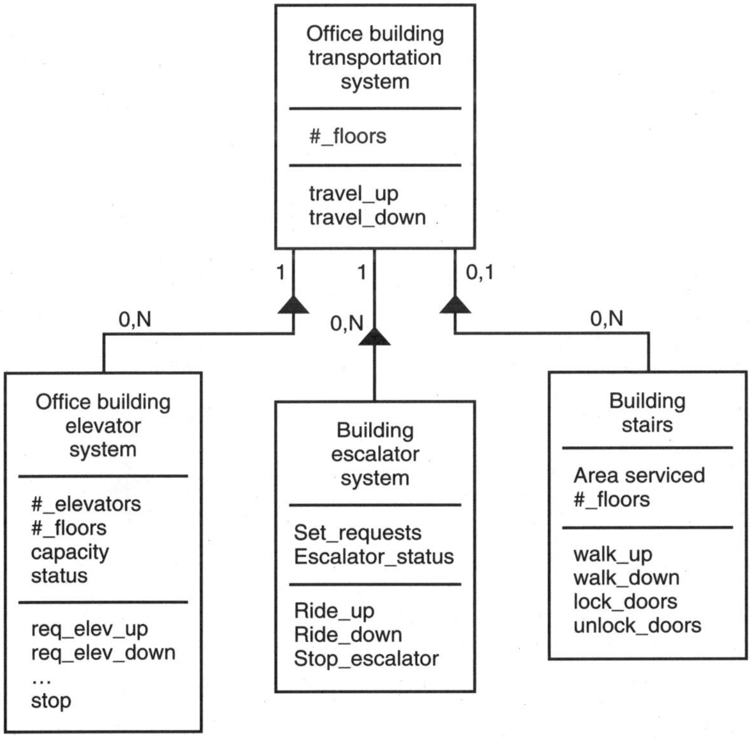

Figure 13.5 Assembly structure where the office building elevator system is a part, solid triangles indicate that this is a whole-part diagram, and the triangle points from the part to the whole.

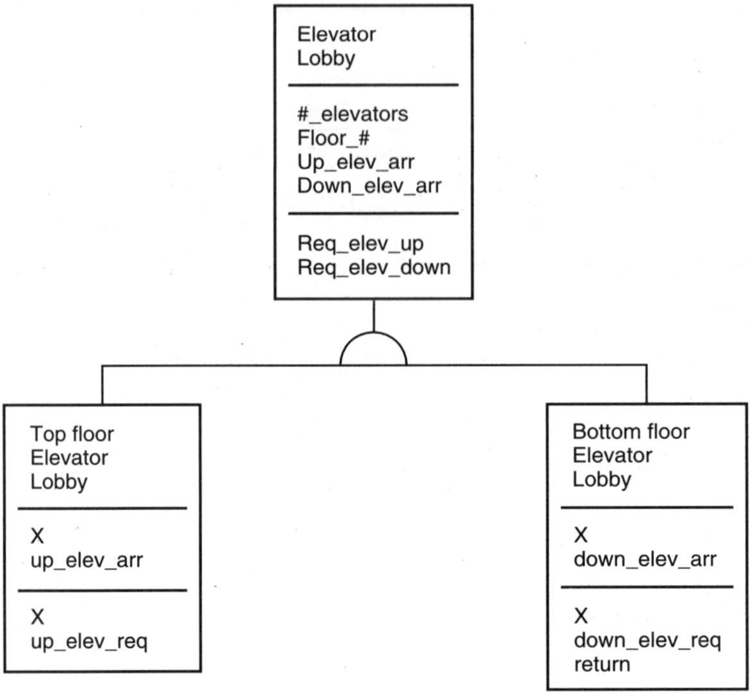

Figure 13.6 Gen-spec diagram. X means that this class does not possess that attribute or service. Notation in order: class, attributes, service.

Chapter

14

The Domain Analysis and Design Process Method

The domain analysis and design process (DADP) method focuses on software and systems reuse processes. Software and systems reuse means that reusable assets can be employed in more than one application system. This chapter covers some of the major features of the DADP method.

The DADP Concept

The DADP concept depends on specific domain analysis and domain design. Systems engineering describes a problem space and constraints. This representation is stored in a life-cycle support environment, where iterations with software, hardware, and human-factor engineers are used to evolve a solution space. Within any application domain, a progression of engineering is applied. Domain engineering is used first to define the problem space, its constraints, and its vocabulary. For a desired product line, generic solution architecture (GSA) is then defined that includes its constraints and interfaces, as shown in Fig. 14.1. This GSA becomes the basis for reuse-in-the-large for this product line in this domain.

The *domain* is defined as the problem space for an applications family with similar requirements. The *life cycle* is the concept that culminates in retirement of the software system. *Domain engineering* is defined as the analysis, design, implementation, and maintenance and evolution of domain models and domain-specific software architecture (DSSA).

Domain-specific software architecture is the structure and relationships among the software segments of generic solution architecture for a product line within a domain. Such DSSA is the basis for reuse-in-

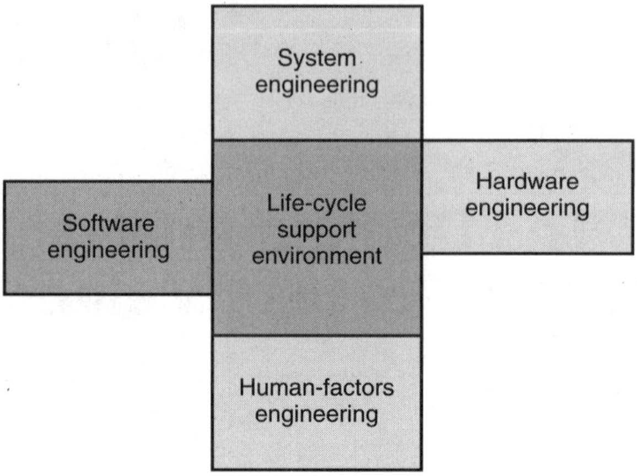

Figure 14.1 Domains, product lines, and engineering relationships.

the-large for future applications of the product line within the domain. The *product line* is defined as a solution to some portion of an application problem space. A *life-cycle process* describes how an organization does its work in evolving and sustaining products in a product line within a domain.

Application engineering consists of analysis, design, implementation, and maintenance and evolution of instances of products and product lines within a domain. This process defines the way an organization performs and manages its work. A process can be the logical organization of people, machines, tools, methods, and procedures into work activities designed to produce a specified end result. The DADP follows an object-oriented approach because many experts agree that object-oriented techniques are more disciplined than conventional structured techniques. An object-oriented approach leads to reusable classes and is more stable over time than other representations. The DADP uses a combination of top-down and bottom-up approaches to identify maximum reuse potential.

The DADP promotes understanding of an application area, or a class of applications, by identifying characteristics that are common (horizontal reuse) and domain-specific (vertical reuse). The process of identifying common application properties can lead to increased levels of software reuse across the domain.

The Domain Analysis Process

The domain analysis process is to collect, organize, analyze, and present information to identify reuse opportunities within a family of systems known as the domain. Domain analysis identifies and models problems for a group of related systems in a domain and develops generic requirements to address recurring problems in the domain to ensure that domain capabilities will remain viable over changes in technology, time, needs, people, and budget. The domain analysis process establishes a relationship among domain design, application engineering, the domain repository, and domain implementation, as shown in Fig. 14.2.

The Domain Design Process

The domain design process constructs a design that reflects the requirements of a product line within the domain. The domain design process constructs generic, domain-specific solutions and architecture that facilitate development of new applications in the domain. The domain design evolves generic solution architectures for domain-specific product lines. A generic architecture facilitates user validation of solutions to the existing problems and serves as an adaptable framework for similar application software evolutions, as shown in Fig. 14.3.

DADP Method Procedure

The DADP method procedure is to identify, derive, organize, abstract, and represent commonality and differences in a particular domain in order to facilitate the reusability of life-cycle work products within an organized body of domain knowledge. The objectives are as follows:

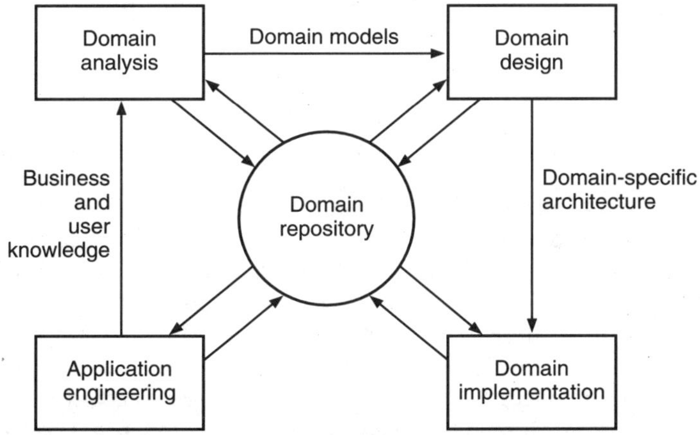

Figure 14.2 Relationship among domain analysis, domain design, application engineering, the domain repository, and domain implementation.

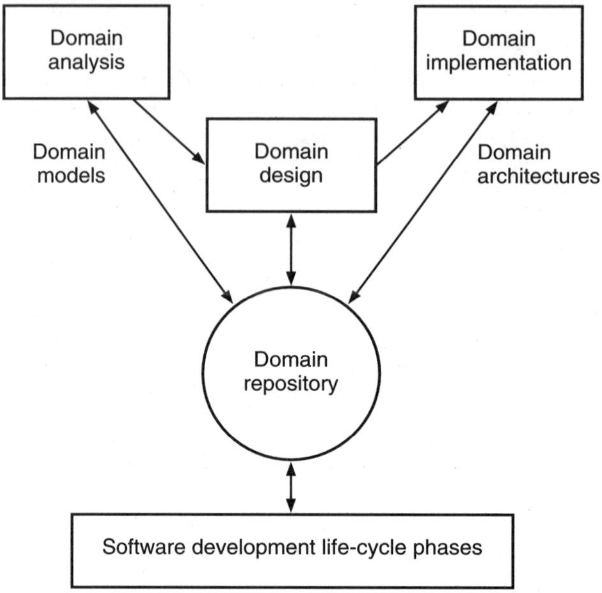

Figure 14.3 A reuse-based software engineering environment.

- To define and adopt a domain analysis methodology
- To conduct the DADP in accordance with the selected methodology
- To express the analysis and design in a transferable and usable format
- To drive the population and maintenance of the domain knowledge base
- To supply the results of the domain analysis and design to application developers
- To support integration of DADP products in application engineering

IDEFo is a top-down diagramming technique that starts with a general process and decomposes it into subprocesses. A single context diagram represents the entire process (see Fig. 14.4). This is decomposed into successively more detailed diagrams. An IDEFo model is a graphical representation of a hierarchical structure of the DADP decomposed with a specific purpose in mind. Each box in the model represents a process consisting of a group of activities to accomplish the process. The information or data necessary to carry out the activities of the process and the information or products generated by the process are represented in an IDEFo diagram by arrows. (IDEFo was discussed in Chapter 11.)

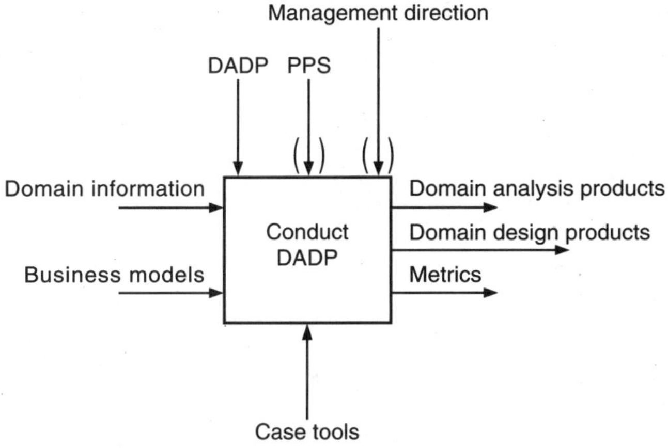

Figure 14.4 DADP IDEFo level 0.

The input in Fig. 14.4 is the domain-relevant information that can be used to determine how to implement software solutions to domain problems. This information can be acquired from the following sources:

- Previous or ongoing domain engineering efforts
- Concept planning documents
- Existing systems documentation and source code
- Technical literature including textbooks and trade journals, system surveys and user questionnaires, technology newsletters, conferences, and seminars
- Applicable domain expertise in engineering disciplines such as systems analysis and design
- Configuration management profiles
- Business models

The outputs are domain models and generic architecture (GA). The control includes management guidelines and PPS. The mechanisms are CASE tools.

The DADP method procedure consists of identifying the domain, scoping the domain, analyzing the domain, and designing the domain, as shown in Fig. 14.5. Each logical process is described in terms of its objectives, inputs, products (outputs), and activities. Each logical process can be partitioned to describe its associated responsibilities and activities. The DADP is presented in IDEFo notation.

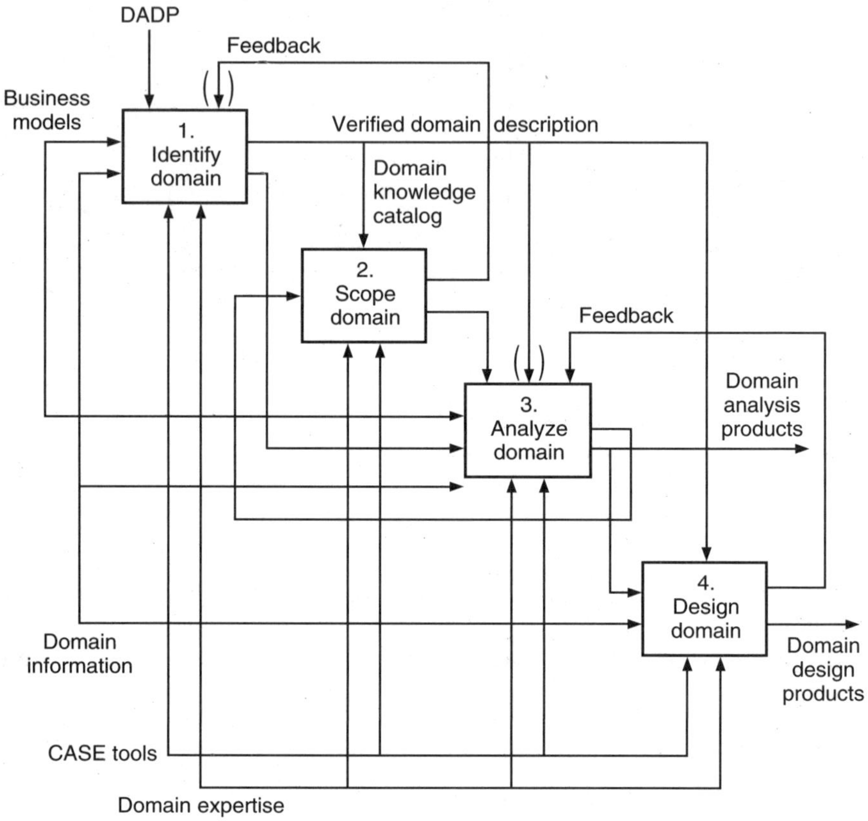

Figure 14.5 IDEFo Level 1.

Identifying the domain

Identifying the domain provides organization and direction to the remaining processes. The major phases of identifying the domain are identifying information services, gathering initial domain information, describing the domain, and verifying the domain description. Identifying the information services provides necessary information for reliable domain expertise and documentation resources that will be helpful in gaining an understanding of the domain. The domain resources will be used for soliciting, collecting, and extracting relevant domain information. The domain resources will be further used for developing and verifying domain models and other domain analysis products.

The next phase, gathering initial domain information, involves collecting domain information and developing an initial understanding by preparing a description of the domain. System questionnaires and interview worksheets are used to extract an initial set of pertinent domain data as follows:

- Business models
- Brief system descriptions
- System capabilities
- Available domain models and GA
- Identifiable common system patterns
- Operational environments
- External interfaces
- Systems with similar capabilities
- Known reuse opportunities
- Available system documentation

The purpose of this phase is to develop a domain knowledge catalog to record sources and the types of the documents, and to install this catalog in the organization repository. The third phase, describing the domain, develops a general description of the domain. In this phase, a domain is characterized in terms of its subdomains and established relationships to other domains. This phase provides a basis for understanding before proceeding with the analysis and is used to predict and assess the level of effort that will be required to conduct the analysis. The description of the partition of the domain's systems into groups is based on the system commonality, common functionality, and capabilities. The characterization of the type of systems and associated subsystems in the domain is based on common system attributes. Following are some of the major activities in this phase:

1. Define the domain's context.
   a. Initially scope the domain to determine its objects.
   b. Determine the responsibilities of the domain.
   c. Determine the services provided by the domain.
   d. Identify the dependencies and relationships the domain has with external domains.
   e. Determine the high-level functions of the domain and their interactions.
2. Construct a context diagram illustrating the interfaces between the domain and the external domains. Use existing systems context diagrams as a foundation for developing the domain context diagram. Show data and control flows in the context diagram.

3. Use the information provided by the system questionnaire, survey responses, and other possible sources to develop a general description.
4. Use the domain knowledge catalog as an index for referencing key documentation in constructing the context diagram and extracting information for a domain description.
5. Identify obvious boundaries and interfaces between different groups of systems and subsystems identified.
6. Determine the general categories or types of systems based on system similarities, and group systems accordingly.
7. Determine the general relationships between the different types or families of systems and subsystems identified.
8. Develop a general description for the initial set of systems and related subsystems under consideration and describe the system relationships.
9. Continuously refine and update the description to reflect the scope of the domain.

The purpose of the next phase, verifying the domain description, is to confirm that the description output from the previous process matches the actual domain. Domain experts independently verify the correctness of the context diagram and the domain description. This phase elaborates the problem domain as understood by domain analysts. It includes the available business process model (IDEFo) and data model (IDEFx). This phase also utilizes requirement specification documents as a framework for authenticating the domain description.

Scoping the domain

It is necessary to scope a domain when it is large and complex. The primary objective is to identify a portion of the domain on which to focus subsequent domain analysis efforts. Scoping also allows multiple or concurrent domain analysis efforts to be initiated. The process of scoping a domain establishes criteria for the scope, defines domain boundaries, and verifies the domain scope.

Scope criteria are a way to screen out domains that have little chance of being successfully analyzed. Analysis and design consist of establishing technical conditions to balance the domain's scope against available resources. Assessing the reuse potential of the domain defines the purpose and goals of the analysis. The conditions that drive the domain analysis effort need to be identified. These conditions are usually economic considerations. It is useful to examine a sample set of applications that are truly representative of the domain and identify factors that will be used to determine the depth of the analysis and the breadth of the domain. Examples of scope criteria include the availability of domain expertise, a consistent domain development methodology, and the quantity and quality of available documentation. The following are some of the activities involved in establishing scope criteria:

1. Derive scopes from a reasonably successfully DADP method. Keep in mind that if a domain has less than three systems, the potential for commonality across the domain diminishes.
   a. Projected new systems and redesigned systems that can benefit from a reuse analysis of the selected domain
   b. Vertical reuse—potential for sharing assets of a given application in similar applications within the scope of the same domain
   c. Horizontal reuse—potential for sharing assets within or across multiple domains
   d. Reuse and domain knowledge and team experience
   e. Availability of domain models, business process, systems documents
2. Define domain and subdomain boundaries. Focus domain analysis on the subdomain that offers the best opportunity to identify commonality and provides enough information to produce domain-specific software architecture. After scoping the domain and subdomain, select two families of systems, as a start for domain analysis, that have potential for showing both horizontal and vertical reuse.

Verifying the domain scope ensures the correctness and completeness of the domain and subdomain identified in the define boundary. Domain experts check this process to determine that the decision on where to focus domain analysis efforts is objective rather than subjective. They further confirm that domain boundaries are clearly defined to expedite the domain analysis effort and to maximize the identification of commonality and differences. Management direction concentrates on the feasibility of the domain analysis effort by assessing the depth and breadth of the domain.

Analyzing the domain

Analyzing the domain involves organizing and synthesizing problem space information, identifying commonality, determining common object adaptation requirements, and verifying the domain model. The objective of organizing and synthesizing problem space information is to merge and categorize existing systems analysis information, and to identify and gather reliable, detailed domain information and evaluate it for future use. To achieve the objectives of this phase, reverse engineering of existing source code is sometimes necessary.

The diagrams for analyzing the domain are object-oriented (class), process (IDEFo, DFD), relationship (ERD), and behavioral (STD). Identifying commonality relates to identifying objects and their relationships, determining behaviors, identifying constraints, developing common object models, and verifying the domain common object model. An object-oriented modeling technique helps to tackle more challenging problem domains and to increase the internal consistency of analysis results. All attributes and services should be described, seeking three types of operations for each object:

- *Constructor* A service that alters the state of the object
- *Selector* A service that evaluates the current state of the object
- *Iterators* Services that permit all parts of the object to be traversed

Common objects or operations should be identified with meaningful identifiers and clear, concise definitions. Object attributes can be identified and described in a general manner. Classes of objects and attributes should be identified. Services that are common to a class should be identified and the processing performed on or by it should be defined.

Each class is considered as a generalization. Inheritance is inherent in class structures and it enhances understanding and decreases complexity and redundancies. For aggregation assembly structures, consider the assembly as parts, the container as contents, and the collection as members.

The necessary connections and interfaces between objects should be determined. Reusable domain models should be constructed. Message connections between objects are identified by combining the event response and data flow attributes. Concentrate on messages being sent from one object to another. Existing entity relationship diagrams should be used to compile message connection data. The processing dependencies of an object should be identified, indicating its services. Identify object behaviors to understand and determine the way each object interacts, functions, responds, or performs. The behavioral model yields the following three basic components:

- States that an object exhibits
- Its transition conditions from one state to another
- Actions performed by, or on, an object

The development of a domain creates common object models and integrates the object relationship model, the object behavioral model, and object constraint diagrams. The required concurrency aspects for each class and object should be defined, as well as the logic/algorithms for every class and object service. External interfaces should be specified with the associated external class or object names.

Designing the domain

Designing the domain means constructing a design that reflects the solutions to the problems of the domain model within the domain constraints. The domain design identifies and evaluates alternative generic architectures. A model of requirements and constraints should be formed; several generic architectures are possible as solutions. However, to minimize risk in future applications, to leverage probable improvements in future technology, and to maximize life-cycle reuse, some generic architectures are better solutions than others.

The domain covers are designed to identify domain constraints, solution space information is collected and organized, domain-specific parts are surveyed, DSSA and guidelines are developed, and DSSA is validated.

The domain implementers and designers utilize the domain design catalog and identify potential design components. They compare the components to the requirements in the domain model and determine the level of requirement satisfaction by identifying compliance requirements of design and code. They remove unqualified components from the domain design catalog.

Metrics are used to assess the effectiveness of reuse and as future guidelines. A comparison of the gathered metrics with the reuse criteria will determine whether to accept the component as a potential candidate, reject the component, or decompose the component to allow a more complete assessment. Following are some of the activities involved in the development of domain design.

- Follow standard design practices as defined in the PPS, with an emphasis on abstraction of implementing dependencies.
- Consider these elements in determining the structure of the DSSA:

  The architectural components' flexibility, efficiency, reusability, ease of use, and protection against misuse

  The nature of language bindings to communication packages

  Hardware assignment of objects after examination of system design and assessment of timing and sizing estimates
- Research the solution space of existing system design and extract every potentially viable solution architecture.
- Establish traceability between the DSSA and the identified design components.

- Identify design strategies to enable the effective implementation of adaptation requirements.

Case Study 14.1

A retail supply business requires that enough inventory be maintained to meet daily sales. Customers can request items, and cancel or modify their orders. The business maintains a catalog for promotion. The problem is to design a system to effectively regulate and maintain the retail inventory.

If stock is available, then the inventory is decremented and an issue receipt is provided. Then the stock is issued. The objects are Transaction, Inventory, and Catalog. The attributes are transaction, inventory, and catalog. The operations on Transaction are to accept incoming request and to cancel/modify outgoing request. The operations on Inventory are to receive stock, issue stock, perform inventory, and maintain stock level. The operations on Catalog are to query catalog, update catalog, and disseminate catalog. A partial solution is shown in Figs. 14.6 through 14.9.

Benefits of the DADP

The DADP can provide a significant return on investment if done properly; however, if executed with errors of commission or omission, the errors in the domain models will lead to errors in the generic archi-

Retail supply

- Transactions
- Inventory
- Catalog

- Accept incoming request
- Cancel/modify incoming request
- Prepare outgoing request
- Cancel/modify outgoing request
- Receive stock
- Issue stock
- Perform inventory
- Maintain stock level
- Query catalog
- Update catalog
- Disseminate catalog

Figure 14.6 Retail supply domain model of common objects.

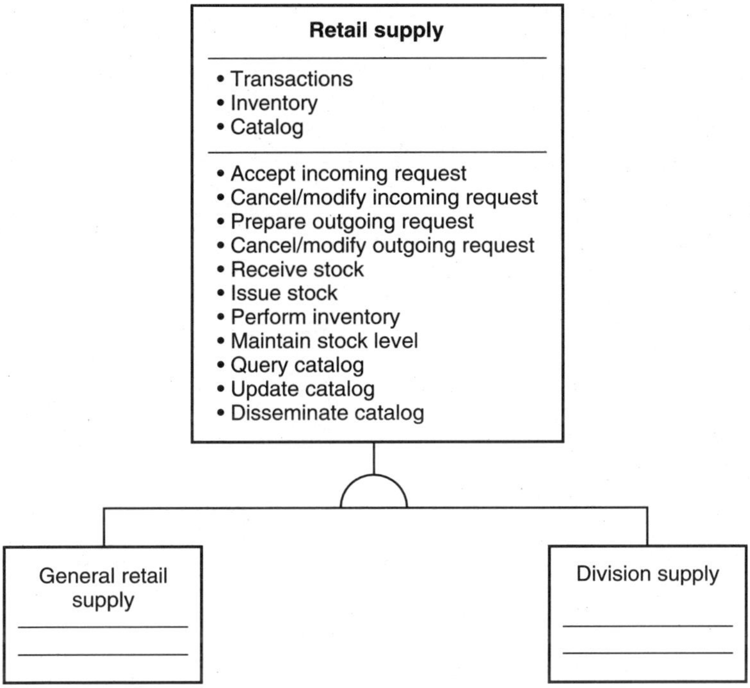

Figure 14.7 Retail supply adaptation model.

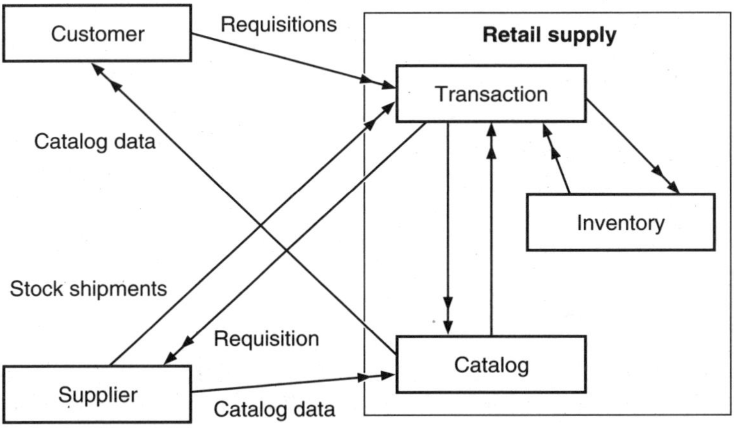

Figure 14.8 High-level retail supply DSSA.

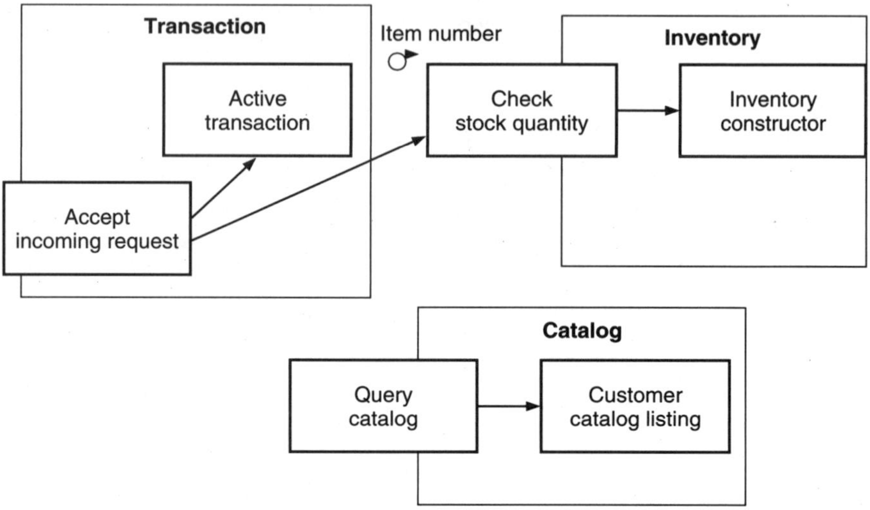

Figure 14.9 Retail supply DSSA showing an execution thread for an issue transaction.

tectures. In turn, these will lead to errors in the implementation of the assets that meet the requirements of the generic architectures, which will lead to errors in the deployed and operated application systems that employ these implementation assets. Good domain engineering can pay dividends; sloppy domain engineering will cost. Some of the benefits of DADP are as follows:

- It minimizes redundant software development efforts.
- It improves process productivity.
- It improves product quality in system/software development and maintenance life cycles.
- It reduces costs and schedules.
- It increases user suitability.
- It reduces risk.
- It increases opportunities for competition by lowering domain knowledge base barriers.
- It facilitates technology insertion.

Among the organizations that have benefited from using the domain-specific reuse approach is Fujitsu Software Development for Electronic Switching Systems (SDESS). Before implementing the DADP, 20 percent of the company's product was delivered on schedule;

afterward, 70 percent was delivered on schedule. Nippon Electronics Corporation (NEC) Software Engineering Laboratory reports that it has integrated a reuse library into the process and products of life-cycle support environments, resulting in a 6.7-fold productivity improvement and a 2.8-fold quality improvement. Many other organizations have been practicing such software reuse, including IBM and Hewlett-Packard. (The DADP was produced for DISA by Charles Mckay.)

Part

5

The Domain Design Process

Method will teach you to win time.

GOETHE

Chapter

15

Domain Design Methods

Domain design methods are object-oriented. This chapter covers some of the object-oriented methods available in the industry.

Domain Design

The purpose of domain design is to construct generic, domain-specific solution architectures that facilitate the development of new applications in the domain. Domain design evolves generic solution architectures for domain-specific lines and facilitates user validation of solutions to existing problems. Domain design serves as an adaptable or configurable framework for similar application software evolution.

The primary objective of domain design is to construct a design that reflects the requirements of a product line within the domain and to provide generic solution architecture. The domain analysts and designers capture and structure domain-relevant information for reusability and use-process guidelines. The necessary information is gathered from existing system documentation, domain experts, and other reuse analyses or studies.

Criteria for Selecting a Correct Object

Determining the criteria for selecting a correct object is important. There are four major tests that are useful because they do not accept false objects:

- The *uniformity test* is based on the definition of an object, and each instance of the object must have the same set of characteristics and be subject to the same rule.

- The *more-than-a-name test* is applicable to those objects that cannot be described by attributes. This object has no characteristics other than its name. Probably it is an attribute of another object. It is already defined that every object has attributes.
- The *or test* is conducted on the object description. If the inclusion criteria in the object description uses the word *or* in a significant manner, then it is probably a set of diverse things rather than an object.
- The *more-than-a-list test* is conducted on the object description. If the inclusion criterion is in the object description, then it is simply a list of all specific instances of the object, and it is most likely not a true object.

Object-Oriented Domain Design Methods

The industry offers a number of object-oriented methods for domain design: Rumbaugh, Shlaer/Mellor, Booch, Coad/Yourdon, and Martin/Odell. Which to choose is an important decision. There is no one standard object-oriented method, and each one of these methods has pluses and minuses. Selection of the one that is best suited to your domain requirements and environment is not easy. Each one of these methods will be addressed and its respective strengths and weaknesses will be explored. We will examine these methods in the context of object-oriented semantics, such as inheritance, aggregation, and association. Explicitly, we mean here by inheritance "is a kind of," by aggregation "is a part of," and by association "is related to." The object-oriented method that is selected should cover both analysis and design phases and support other phases of the object-oriented software development life cycle. The selected method should be easily understood and followed, and it should be sufficiently matured and well tested in various object-oriented software development environments. The method should also support a CASE tool. Proper education and training should be available for the selected method.

The Rumbaugh object modeling technique

The Rumbaugh method is known as the *object modeling technique* (OMT) and is one of the easiest techniques for object-oriented analysis and design. The OMT consists of the object model, the dynamic model, and the functional model. The *object model* is like an entity relationship diagram. It shows classes and their attributes that include operations and relationships among classes. The relationships include inheritance, aggregation, and association. The object model provides the data view. The *dynamic model* contains a state transition diagram (STD) for each class in the object model. The *functional model* is the data flow diagram (DFD), which provides the link to objects by partitioning so that the lowest level of the DFD bubble is operations on classes.

This method has been tested in various applications. The symbol notations for these models are easily followed. This method is well documented in *Object-Oriented Modeling and Design* [Rumb91]. The method supports many CASE tools, and several training courses are available for it. The OMT was originally developed in the General Electric Research and Development Center, in New York. The strength of this method is that it is easily followed and consists of familiar notations. Its weakness is that it is still evolving.

The Shlaer/Mellor object-oriented method

The Shlaer/Mellor object-oriented method is a recursive system development process. This system process consists of domain partitioning, domain analysis, the application domain, service domains, the software architecture domain, and the implementation domain. Object-oriented analysis (OOA) is a derivation of the domain analysis. It provides three viewpoints: the information model, state models, and the processes model. Classes are modeled in the data view, which provides association and subtyping. Each class is then given a state transition diagram. Here, actions are described by a DFD. Classes are connected by messages and this initiates the architectural view. Different notations are used that describe the design for classes and their interactions, which is actually a weakness for this method in transitioning from analysis to design. This method is documented in *Object-Oriented Methods for Software Development* [Sodh96], and there are many CASE tools available for it.

Many training courses are available for this method. The strength of the method is that the recursive design will facilitate transition of the design model into a working system. Its weakness is that there is no smooth transition from analysis to design.

The Grady Booch object-oriented method

Grady Booch's object-oriented method is well known in the industry. Booch describes entity relationship diagram (ERD) features in the data view as a "class diagram." Dynamics are illustrated with an STD within a class. Booch shows interactions between objects by timing diagrams and object diagrams. This method shows the logical architecture with object diagrams and class categories that use object partitioning. It also shows the physical design with module and process diagrams. This method covers object diagrams, which provide object partitioning, and also the relationship with object behavior.

This method is well documented in *Object-Oriented Analysis and Design with Applications* [Booc94]. There is a CASE tool available for this method, and many training courses are also available. The strength of this method is that it has matured more than any other object-oriented methods. Its weaknesses are that the notations are not familiar and are not easily put into practice.

The Coad/Yourdon method

The Coad/Yourdon method relates to the data view with the ERD. It shows aggregation, association, and subtyping. This method shows behavior by naming operations on the classes and defining them within the class by service charts. The service charts consist of state transition charts and flowcharts. The method shows the behavior among the objects by the placement of message connections on the ERD. The classes are grouped into subjects in the architecture.

There are many training courses available for this method. CASE tools are available for this method. The strength of this method is that the whole system can be described in a single diagram, which is considered to have many layers. This diagram lends itself to the user viewing different layers of the system. The weakness is that for a large system, the various-layers view may not work well.

The Martin/Odell method

The Martin/Odell method describes the data view as a binary rather than an entity relationship. The method explains that the objects change class during their lifetimes. This method supports subtypes, class expression, and dynamic classification. It states behavior in the ERD. The events are linked with the data view. A CASE tool compiles an event diagram into executable code. This method defines the architecture with the help of an object flow diagram that uses a functional partitioning schema.

CASE tools are available for it. The strength of this method is the analysis phase, which involves an event-driven approach that identifies events first, after which these events define objects. The weakness of this method is that it is not easily followed.

The unified modeling language

The unified modeling language (UML) is a methodology for modeling object-oriented systems. The UML is a mixture of three object-oriented methodologies: Grady Booch's, James Rumbaugh's object modeling technique, and Ivar Jacobson's use-case driven object-oriented software engineering model.

The UML is a recognized methodology for specifying, visualizing, and documenting the assets of an object-oriented system. The components of the UML are a metamodel and a system notation that can be used to express relationships between entities in a business system or between the objects that represent those entities in a component-based application. The metamodel is a graphical representation of how a model should look. The UML includes the following diagrams:

- Use-case diagrams that illustrate the software from the user's point of view
- Class diagrams that show the static structure of the classes within a system
- Object diagrams that show the objects within a system
- State diagrams that show different states that an object can have at any time and how an object transitions from one state to another
- Sequence diagrams that illustrate how several objects work together and how they communicate over time
- Collaboration diagrams that show the operating context of the objects
- Activity diagrams that illustrate control flow
- Component diagrams that represent the physical structure of the system in terms of actual components
- Deployment diagrams that show how a project is deployed

The UML represents an iterative model of software development, the importance of software architecture, and component reuse. The choice of an object-oriented method depends on the environment and the nature of the domain requirements.

The Object-Oriented Method

The object-oriented method (OOM) captures in detail the particular domain-specific knowledge of the application in a form that lends itself to careful, point-by-point verification by domain experts. Through formal models of the problem domain, the OOM provides a detailed and well-documented foundation from which requirement decisions can be made. The methodology transfers the domain knowledge accurately to the software engineers and communicates the requirement analysis in a form that is easily understood and mapped into an object-oriented design.

The concepts behind the OOM are to facilitate an understanding of the customer's requirements, to graphically show the logic to the customer, and to enable understanding of the stated requirement. Then objects are determined, relationships between objects are established, instantiation criteria for objects and their relationships are determined, and functional processes are developed. An object is a mental abstraction of a set of real-world things. This method uses concepts from object-oriented and structured approaches that include abstract data types, inheritance, and module coupling and cohesion. It uses graphical models with proper documentation that transfers the requirements from one phase to another for implementations. The OOM couples its analysis into object-oriented design and is implemented in any suitable object-oriented programming language that includes Ada. This concept maintains the traceability of the requirements for embedded systems. The OOM method provides the project controls and communication tools for management, quality assurance, and documentation formats. Such systems can be developed cost effectively and efficiently, and they can be effectively maintained for a longer time. The following basic models constitute the OOM:

- Object analysis model (OAM)
- Object information model (OIM)
- Object behavior model (OBM)
- Object process model (OPM)
- Requirements definition model (RDM)
- Object-oriented design (OOD)

The object analysis model

The object analysis model (OAM) consists of all the analysis that is needed to understand the customer's requirements. This model also contains information with regard to all the identified external interfaces. This step is especially important for the embedded systems. These interfaces are linked with external systems, as illustrated in Fig. 15.1. The purpose of this graphic is to show the customer's requirements in an unambiguous method so that the customer understands the stated requirements. (Requirement analysis has been thoroughly discussed in previous chapters.) Identifying processes, data storage, and data flows can extend the model.

The goal is for the requirements to be mutually understood and recorded in the proper document before proceeding to any further analysis or design activity. The notations that are used in the graphic should be clearly defined and properly recorded in the document for understandability. The object data dictionary can be initiated at this level by the recording of this essential information.

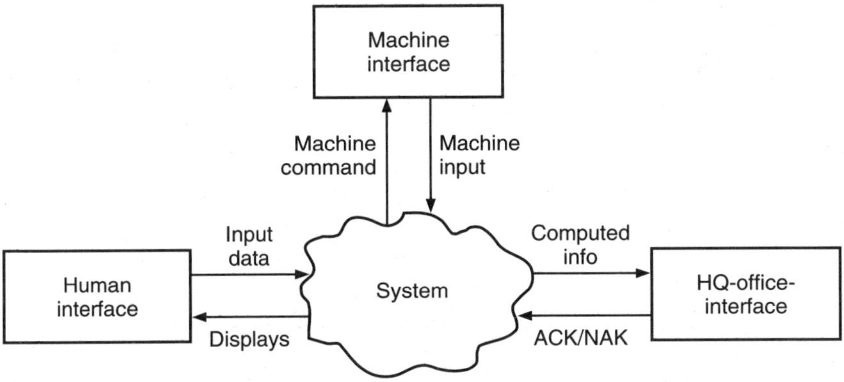

Figure 15.1 OAM diagram.

The object information model

The object information model (OIM) identifies the conceptual entities of the problem and formalizes them as objects and attributes. A complete and unambiguous understanding of the problem is the goal. The OIM is the beginning of the analysis phase. It identifies things about the problem and the relationship of these things to the problem; things and associations are modeled here. The model is simple enough to be easily read and understood. Significant emphasis is placed on formalization of the relationships between objects. A model is developed and depicted graphically, as shown in Fig. 15.2. The textual descriptions are used in the definition of the model's semantics.

In Fig. 15.2, abstraction of like things is grouped together into sets. Things are alike if they behave in the same way and can be described by the same characteristics. Naming an object is a first draft for this. The characteristics, which all elements of the set have in common, are called *attributes* of the object. An attribute is the abstraction of a single characteristic, which is possessed by all entities and was abstracted as an object. The set of attributes must be complete, fully factored, and mutually independent. Attributes use a dot notation, for example:

```
Object.Attribute
```

There are three types of attributes: descriptive, naming, and referential. The descriptive attributes provide facts that are intrinsic to each instance of the object. The naming attribute provides a fact about the arbitrary name carried by each instance of the object. The referential attribute links an instance of one object to an instance of another object.

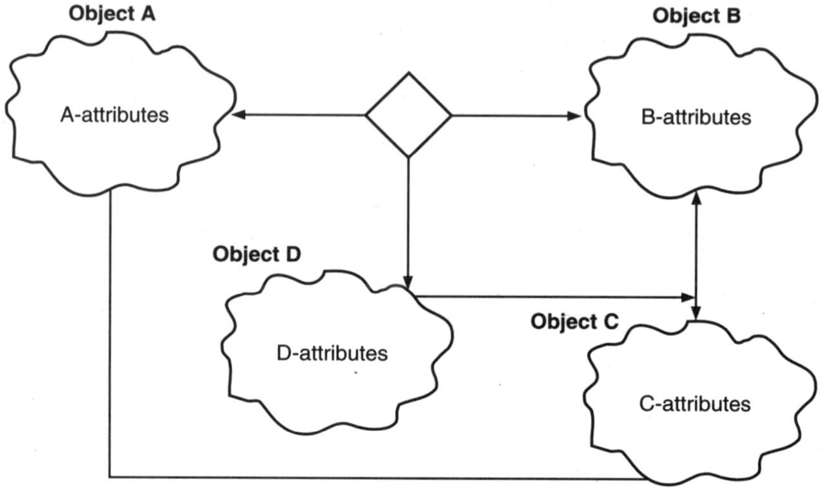

Figure 15.2 OIM diagram.

Tables are used for defining the types of questions, which can be answered by inspection of the objects. The table name is the name of the object. Each column of the table is an attribute of the object, and each row is an instance of the object. The instance is the specific element of the set and is denoted by that object name. As illustrated in Fig. 15.3, every box in a table contains exactly one value. Attributes of an object should not contain internal structure. Tables are the basic formal structure of the OIM because they are simple and adequate. The object representation by the table assists in the identification of the objects and attributes. The table also helps in the representation of instances of objects.

Associations exist between things in the real world. These associations must be formalized in this model. They can be recognized by verb phrases in the descriptions. For example:

Object A

Attribute A1	Attribute A2	Attribute A3
Instance A1	Instance A2	Instance A3
Instance A11	Instance A22	Instance A33
Instance A111	Instance A222	Instance A333

Figure 15.3 OIM table and object relationship.

The car has tires.

Thus, a relationship is named by a verb phrase. It can be phrased in both directions of the relation. For example:

A class is composed of students.

and

Students compose a class.

The same two objects may have more than one relationship between them. This depends on the type of their relationship. An object may be related to itself. There can also be a relationship between multiple objects. For example:

The floppy disk was formatted on the disk drive.

The floppy disk is owned by a student.

The floppy disk contains disk files.

This type of relationship that involves two objects can be classified into three fundamental forms and called *multiplicity* (see Table 10.1).

A graphical notation is necessary for the replacement of a table for complex objects, as shown in Fig. 15.4. The graphical notation eases the handling of complex systems. This graphical notation represents spatial compression of the model. Thus, OIM notation representations are illustrated in Fig. 15.5. Supertype and subtype constructs are shown in Fig. 15.6. The correlation relationship symbol is illustrated in Fig. 15.7.

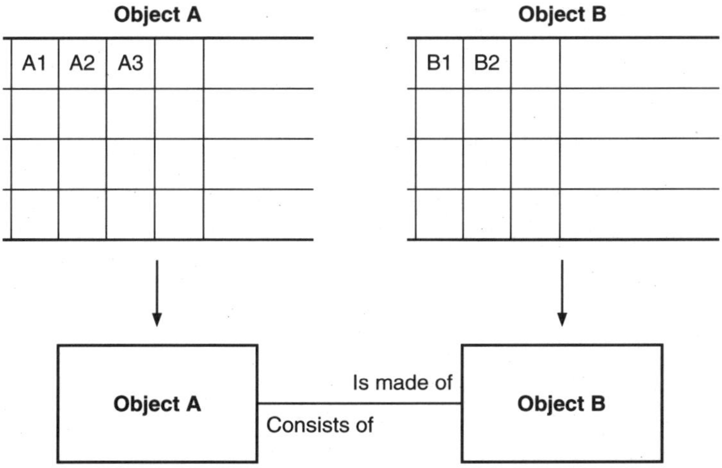

Figure 15.4 OIM table and object relationship.

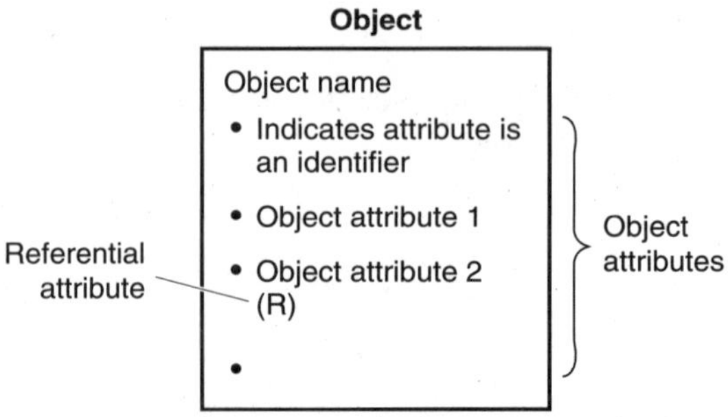

Figure 15.5 OIM notations.

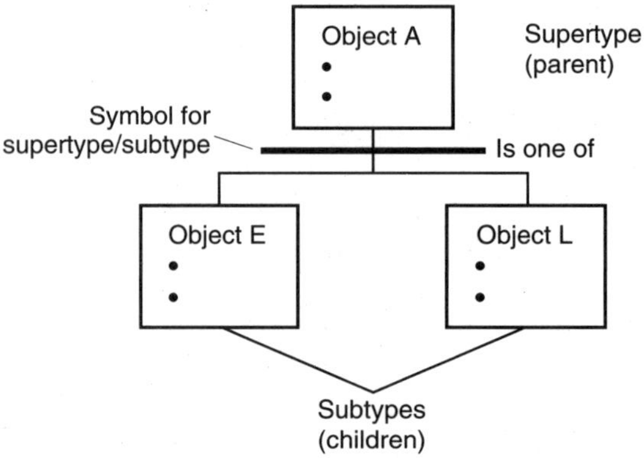

Figure 15.6 Supertype/subtype constructs.

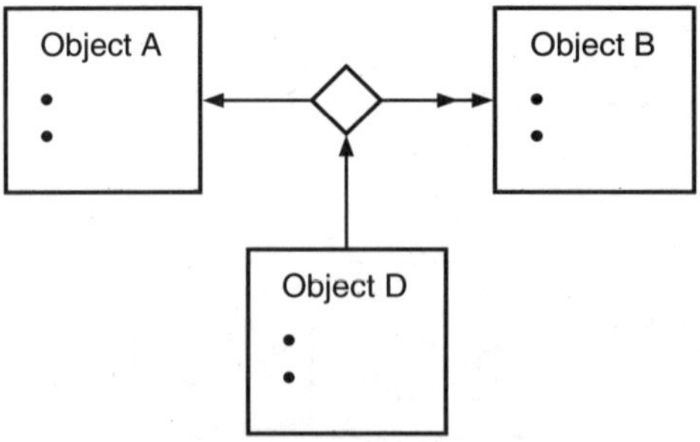

Figure 15.7 Correlation symbol.

Object data dictionary. The object, attributes, and their relationships are documented in an object data dictionary (ODD). This document consists of a written description of the objects and it formalizes the identification of the objects, forms part of the formal system specification, and separates descriptions that are written for each object. This is a live document and should start at the beginning of the software engineering and be enhanced throughout the software development and maintenance phases.

The object behavior model

The object behavior model (OBM) formalizes the life or event histories of objects and relationships, as identified in the OIM. Things go through various states during their lifetimes in the real world. The life cycle of an object is therefore the behavior of an object during its lifetime. An example of the object lifetime diagram is presented in Fig. 15.8.

An object may be in only *one* state at a time. The states are mutually exclusive. These states are discrete, and transitions can occur instantaneously. Transitions from any state to any other state are not always allowed. Incidents cause transitions of things between states. Some incidents cause a progression only when the thing is in certain states of its life cycle. Similar characteristics of real-world things have a common life cycle. Thus, the OBM is a formalization of the life cycle of an object in regard to the following parts:

- States
- Events
- Transitions
- Actions

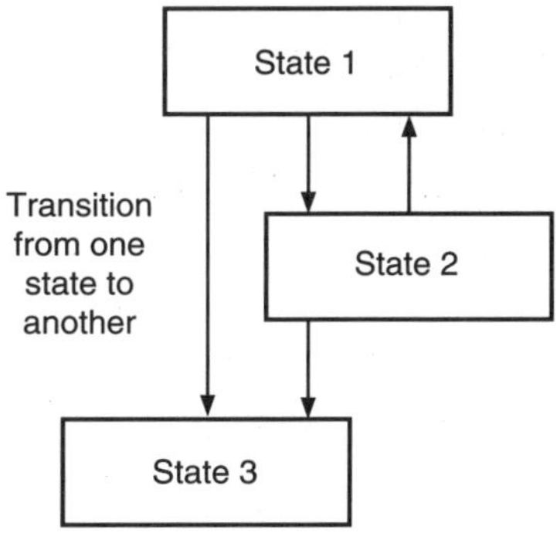

Figure 15.8 Object lifetime diagram.

The *state* of the OBM corresponds to the state of an object's life cycle. An *event* is an incident or action that causes a progression to another state or to the same state. The *transition* is the new state of an object if a particular event occurs while the object is in a particular state. The *action* is the function that is performed immediately when entering a new state. Each state can have only one action, but that action might consist of many processes.

A sample OBM is shown in Fig. 15.9. The boxes represent the states, and the lines represent the events. The event causes the transition to the new state.

Figure 15.10 represents an alternative version of a state transition diagram (STD), which is a kind of OBM. An alternate form of state model representation is the state transition table (STT), as shown in Fig. 15.11. In the STT the rows represent states, the columns represent events, and the cells represent the effect of each event in each state. When a particular event cannot happen for a particular state of the object, then the cell entry cannot happen. The event may be prevented from happening for many reasons such as a physical impossibility, definition of the object, or any constraints. If a particular event can happen for a specific state of the object but the object does not respond to the event, then an "event ignored" entry is made in that cell. If the event is ignored, then the object stays in the same state. The advantages of the STT are that it can be extended by adding an additional column for action and is associated with entering each state. The information contained in the STT or STD is the same, but the development of the STT from the STD will catch one of the most common errors in developing the OBM. This is illustrated in Fig. 15.11.

The OBM is built for each dynamic object in the OIM. The following are suggested guidelines for constructing an OBM:

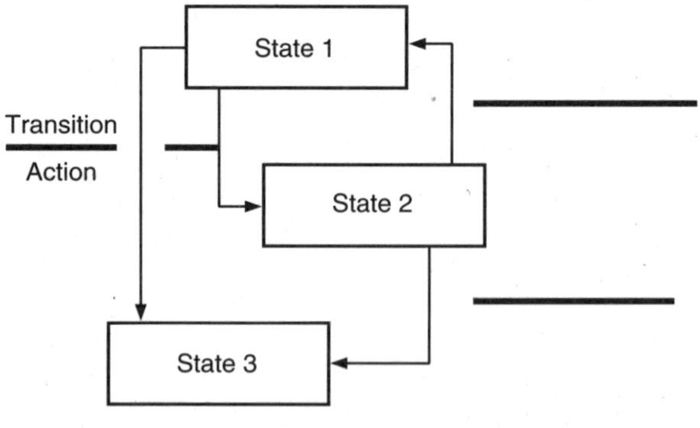

Figure 15.9 OBM sample.

	Event 1	Event 2	Event 3		
State 1	Effects of Event 1 in State 1				
State 2		Effects of Event 2 in State 2			
State 3	Effects of Event 1 in State 3				

Figure 15.10 STD table sample.

- Take one instance of the model and analyze and record the life cycle of that instance.
- Record the various states for that instance.
- Find the states that consider all relationships of the object.

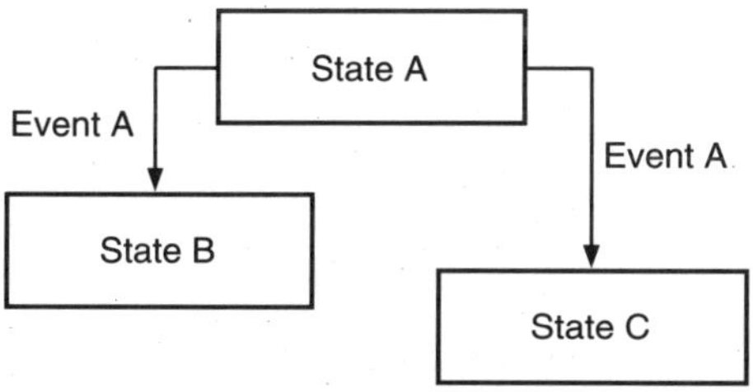

Error

	Event A	Event B	Event C		
State A	State B or State C				
State B					
State C					

Figure 15.11 STT check.

- Build an STT.
- Check the table for new or additional states.
- Define the action that will be executed upon entry into a state.
- Identify nonfinal states.
- Identify events that the object must generate so it can exit nonfinal states.
- Expand actions that generate these events.
- Add the new events to the STT.
- Complete the STT.
- Complete the STD.

The object process model

The object process model (OPM) makes use of data flow diagrams and develops the required processes that drive the objects through their event chains. The principle of data flow diagrams has been discussed in the book, *Software Engineering Methods, Management, and CASE Tools* [Sodh91]. Only a few of the concerns about objects will be discussed here.

The following is a list of suggested processes for the development of a data flow diagram of a single object:

- Develop an OBM that formalizes the behavior of an object over time.
- Analyze the action that is performed when the state is entered.
- Break the action down into a sequence of processes.
- Depict each process as a data flow diagram.
- Place each action data flow diagram on a separate page.

The data of an object are represented as a data store in the data flow diagram. The data store will be recorded in the object data dictionary (ODD). The data store for the object contains all the attributes of the object. The instances of the object are created and stored in the data store. The data store holds all data and all attributes of all instances of the object. The data store is shared by all action data flow diagrams. The data flow diagram involves data stores, which are made up of attributes of those data. These processes are discrete.

The requirements definition model

The requirements definition model determines the information and processes that will be used within the automated system as opposed to those that will be carried out by operators or other external agents. It describes the boundary statements and clarifies the system specification.

OOM MIL-STD-498/IEEE 1498

The OOM fits under MIL-STD-498 requirements for software development. A set of formal reviews and audits is necessary at different phases of the software development and testing. The standard should be tailored and produce necessary documentation. Some OOM notations should be identified with respect to the standard. The object and its life cycle should be considered as a capability. Each capability should be correlated with the matching requirement in the system specification. Its purpose should be stated clearly and its performance should be described in measurable terms. The data item description specifically refers to an established relationship of the capability to the state and modes of the system.

The external interfaces are established and OOM models further identify the internal interfaces. The data elements of the standard can be recognized by the organization of objects and attributes. A computer software configuration item corresponds to the system/problem domain of the OIM. The computer software components correspond to the identified objects, and the computer software units relate to the processes.

IEEE working groups are producing standards for software reuse. Many organizations are developing their own standards for reuse to be followed by the practitioners in the organization.

OOM benefits

The OOM is stable under changing requirements. It does not require system boundary. The notations used are simple and understandable. This method aids in minimizing code.

OOM weaknesses

The OOM is evolving and has not yet matured. There is a lack of standardization. External stimulus and responses are not apparent.

The object-oriented methodology represents the emergence of an object-oriented approach, a data structure approach with entity relationship modeling, and a functional process approach. The OOM is an open-ended, teachable, and easily transferable methodology. The choice of an object-oriented method depends on the environment and the nature of your domain requirements.

Chapter 16

Domain Implementation

Domain implementation implies to collect, classify, catalog, browse, and search assets. This chapter presents the domain implementation, repository mechanism, maintenance, certification, and validation processes.

The Object-Oriented Software Life-Cycle Model

The object-oriented software life-cycle model encompasses many concepts throughout the various stages of software development, from project management through system design and software coding to maintenance. Software requirements may change over time. There might be a bug that is identified in due time. With the advent of modern technology, software has to be reengineered. Thus, the life cycle provides a way of looking at the various phases of object-oriented software development for a system. These phases assist the process of interpreting the various aspects of software development into a common language, which may be graphic, so that the effects of changes to the development process can be recognized.

A software life-cycle model is either a prescriptive or a descriptive characterization of software evolution. *Prescriptive* means the level of detail that is supplied by the method insofar as providing direction on how to accomplish the various activities. A prescriptive life-cycle model is easier to develop. Many software development details can be ignored, glossed over, or generalized. This, of course, should raise concern for the relative validity and robustness of such life-cycle models when developing different kinds of application systems in different kinds of settings. In contrast, a *descriptive* life-cycle model characterizes how software systems are actually developed. They are less common and more difficult to articulate for one obvious reason: observation and data collection must be performed throughout the development of a software system. This development period is an elapsed time usually measured in years. Also, descriptive models are specific to the systems observed and are only generalized through systematic analysis.

A graphical notation is necessary for the replacement of a table for complex objects. The graphical notation eases the handling of complex systems. This graphical notation represents the spatial compression of a model.

Object-Oriented Software Life-Cycle Issues

Object-oriented software evolution represents the cycle of activities that are involved in the development, use, and maintenance of software systems. Systems software comes and goes through a series of passages that accounts for its inception, initial development, productive operation, upkeep, and retirement from one generation (version) to another. In turn, models of software evolution date back to the earliest projects in which large systems software was developed. The apparent purpose of these object-oriented software life-cycle models was to provide an abstract scheme that accounted for the "natural" or engineered development of systems software. Such a scheme could therefore serve as a basis for planning, organizing, staffing, coordinating, budgeting, and directing software development activities. The specific set of activities is as follows:

- *Activity 1:* System initiation/adoption identifies the origination of systems. Many new systems replace or supplement the existing processing mechanisms.
- *Activity 2:* System requirements engineering involves segregating hardware and software requirements. The specified software requirements are allocated to computer software configuration items. The object-oriented database management system is identified for object-oriented software.
- *Activity 3:* Domain engineering addresses domain analysis and architecture engineering as well as the creation and evolution of particular assets or components for reuse in object-oriented software development.
- *Activity 4:* Object-oriented software requirement analysis and specification identifies the problems that should be solved. The software architecture process determines what will be produced. This involves requirement identification, analysis, representation, communication, and development of acceptance criteria and procedures.

A suitable object-oriented method is selected for software development.

- *Activity 5:* Functional specification/prototyping/simulation identifies and potentially formalizes such subactivities as the objects of computation, their attributes and relationships, the operations that transform these objects, and the constraints that restrict system behavior.
- *Activity 6:* Partition and selection for the given requirement. The functional specification divides the system into manageable pieces that denote logical subsystems. Then it is determined whether new, existing, or reusable software systems correspond to the needed pieces.
- *Activity 7:* The architectural configuration specification activity defines the interconnection and resource interfaces between system modules in ways that are suitable for their detailed object-oriented design and overall configuration management.
- *Activity 8:* A detailed component object-oriented design specification defines the object-oriented/procedural methods through which each module's data resources are transformed from required inputs to provided outputs.
- *Activity 9:* Component implementation and debugging codify the preceding specifications into operational source code implementations and validate their basic operation.
- *Activity 10:* Software integration and testing affirm and sustain the overall integrity of the software system architectural configuration through verification of the consistency and completeness of implemented modules, verification of the resource interfaces and interconnections against their specifications, and validation of the performance of the system and subsystems against their requirements.
- *Activity 11:* The documentation revision and system delivery package rationalizes the recorded system development description into systematic documents and user guides. All this is in a form that is suitable for dissemination and system support.
- *Activity 12:* Training and practice provide system users with instructional aids and guidance in understanding the system capabilities and limits that need to be understood for effective system use.
- *Activity 13:* Object-oriented software maintenance sustains the useful operation of a system in its host/target environment that provides requested functional enhancements, repairs, performance

improvements, and conversions. Maintenance represents ongoing incremental iterations throughout the life-cycle activities that precede it.

- *Activity 14:* Software retirement is not very common. Most retired system software is considered useless and, hence, not in existence. These retired systems were once created for some special purpose, with a special language and for a special computer. Use of these components, which are well tested and efficient, is better than the creation of new ones. Understanding and identifying the reusability and viability of existing software components for the new systems is important. The model of a new system can be compared with the existing model of the retired system so that identification of suitable software components for reuse can be made. The reuse of these pretested software components will definitely save time and expense and improve the quality of the new software products.

The model concept, taken at a high level of abstraction and applied to software development, is called the *software life cycle.* This life-cycle notion exists beyond the design and programming stage of development. The life-cycle concept implies that software exists even in the conceptual stages of problem definition, that it needs to be maintained after formal development has been completed, and that it functions until retirement.

The Object-Oriented Life-Cycle Model and MIL-STD-498/IEEE 1498

The object-oriented life-cycle model can represent a combination or a single model. The main features of an object-oriented model are that objects should be identified in the problem space during the requirement analysis activity. The same objects are mapped in the solution space during the design activity, and are implemented with the help of the object-oriented programming language during the implementation activity.

MIL-STD-498 identifies three examples of life-cycle models. The *grand design* model is essentially a once-through model. Simplistically, it calls for determining user needs, defining requirements, designing the system, and integrating the system, followed by testing, fixing, and delivery. In this model all the requirements are defined first.

The *incremental* model determines user needs and defines the system requirements, then performs the rest of the development in a sequence of builds. The first build incorporates part of the planned capabilities, the next build adds more capabilities, and so on, until the system is complete. Multiple developments are permissible in this model. All the requirements can also be defined first. Field interim products may be possible in this model.

The *evolutionary* model also develops a system in builds, but differs from the incremental model in acknowledging that the user need is not fully understood and all requirements cannot be defined up front. In this model, user needs and system requirements are partially defined up front, then they are defined in each succeeding build. In this model, multiple development cycles are permissible. Field interim products are also possible in this model.

IEEE has recently released a new international standard, "Standard for Information Technology Software Life Cycle Processes Software Development Acquirer-Supplier Agreement," which will replace IEEE 1498.

Asset Collection

Asset collection is a process to identify and collect the potential reusable candidates. The identification of potential components is determined by the result of domain analysis. The domain analysis provides formal software problem descriptions that can be used as a general reference throughout the asset identification phase. These assets are evaluated to provide the information necessary to determine its initial certification level. The assets are collected from domain analysis, requirement analysis, design, models, code, software testing, specifications, training, and system documentation.

Selection Criteria for Reuse Assets

The selection criteria for reuse assets imply that the potential reuse asset is a candidate. These criteria do not confirm that the selected asset will be placed in the repository. Further analysis is necessary for inclusion in the repository. The process determines that the selected candidate is suitable to the domain and has potential for future inclusion in the repository.

The selected asset encompasses a single common function or capability within the domain. The candidate asset follows the organization PPS, analysis, documentation, design, coding, or reuse standard applicable to the product. The requirement that the selected asset satisfies has the potential for future use within the domain. The code is a highly cohesive set of interfaces that do not have any undesirable side effects. The included algorithms are stable, efficient, and accepted within the domain. The software testing products provide complete test coverage. The specification and documentation are written in an unambiguous language. The system training is documented properly.

Asset Submitting Schema

The submitting schema requires that the asset meet the specified selection criteria. The information should include the submitter's name, organization, department, section, address, and phone number. The location includes the full pathname and filename of all files associated with the submitted asset. The following must also be provided: a complete identification of the reuse asset and originating system; a text abstract file that provides a full description of the asset, including constraints, required assets, special conditions, and other pertinent information; identification of supporting documentation; and a list of keywords the submitter believes a user may need in searching the repository to identify the asset.

Asset Accepting Schema

The selected asset is refined and prepared for repository population. The repository should be populated with the assets that are compatible with the organization domain. These assets should be complete, with all the supporting documents. They should be robust, mature, reliable, stable, and well tested. The domain engineers perform the necessary analysis to accept the assets. The domain repository manager prepares assets for inclusion into the repository system.

Asset Certification

Asset certification is a process to facilitate the reuse of software components. This process is accomplished by cataloging the reusable components and making them available for populating the repository. The repository contains the reusable assets from all phases and activities of the object-oriented software life cycle. Software developers then use the repository to find and evaluate reusable components that are suitable to their needs.

Asset certification criteria

The certification process uses applicability criteria and domain engineering, software engineering, and quality criteria. The certification process produces a certification level for a potentially reusable software component. After evaluation, some components require reengineering to initially prepare them as candidates for populating the repository. The reusable components are in response to user requests for a particular component in a high-demand category that requires some modification. Analysis determines the reengineering investment that is required to increase the level of certification. If the reengineering cost is too high, the component is discarded in favor of an alternative with similar characteristics that already meets minimum reusability criteria. Once any reengineering and associated testing are completed, the component is recertified at a higher level and is populated in the repository.

Levels of certification

Levels of certification relate to the completeness and the quality of reusable assets. They are determined by the degree of testing that has been performed on these reusable assets. Four levels of certification have been identified:

- *Level-1 certification* identifies the components as approved for repository population on the basis of customer demand only. These components have not received any measurement, testing, or documentation beyond that originally provided by the donor. The completeness of the components is not known. A level-1 component is provided to users quickly, but offers the lowest level of confidence in quality and completeness.
- *Level-2 certification* identifies the components as released to users and verified for completeness. Components with source code must compile for this level. While level-2 components offer a greater degree of confidence than level-1 components, these components are not tested and thus do not have user manuals.
- *Level-3 certification* identifies the components that have met the requirements of level 2 and also have complied with reusability criteria and functional validation and verification. The components are tested and the test data and test results are available. When a user extracts the components, the test data are transmitted along with the component. Level-3 components are the best compromise between cost and timely population of the repository.
- *Level-4 certification* adds a user's manual to the level-3 requirements. When a user extracts a level-4 component, the user's manual is transmitted with the component. Level 4 offers the highest level of quality assurance, completeness, and reusability. The efforts associated with certifying a component at level 4 are important and are comparable to developing a new component of similar size and functionality.

Repository Mechanism

The repository mechanism is a process to properly classify and catalog the collected potentially reusable assets before inclusion in the repository. After the candidate components are accepted for populating in the repository, all their related documents and the reusable assets themselves are brought under configuration control. Configuration management approves that the reusable assets are complete and possess all the necessary documents. It allocates numbers to the reusable assets and their documents for identification and for the record, and verifies that all assets are present according to the organization's established PPS. Once controlled, the reusable assets under CM control are not available for any change. Configuration management maintains its own database. Any problems that arise in this process are resolved with the data review board.

The repository mechanism assists the process of browsing, searching, and retrieving the necessary information conveniently. Repository maintenance is an important operation. The information in the repository should be accessible and easily extracted by the users. The repository should be operational all the time and should maintain a hot line on the Internet, as well as a telephone number, where users can easily request information in case of any problem. Many organizations also maintain a help desk, which users can call to receive assistance.

Accessing the Repository for an Asset

Accessing the repository for an asset is a process. The user receives an access account and a password to connect with the repository. The password provides the user with access to log in on his or her computer with the repository. The user then browses the repository to identify assets that might meet the need and to extract the asset of interest. The user requests that the domain administrator provide the asset of interest identified from the repository catalog as hard copy or magnetic medium. The user can also extract assets of interest from the repository using file copy, file transfer protocol (FTP), or any other extracting media.

The repository should be linked with other repositories via the Internet for easy access. Sometimes a firewall is used for security reasons and protection of an organization's data.

The Reuse Asset Anomaly Process

This process identifies discrepancies between the observed performance of reuse assets and the expected performance based on previously established requirements. The anomalies are submitted formally and analyzed. Anomalies are resolved with the data review board.

Collection of Metrics

Collection of metrics is a process whereby the collected data for each reuse asset are recorded and graphically presented. The metrics reflect the number of users accessing the repository, the number of times a specific reuse asset has been extracted, the number of reuse assets extracted, and the number of user accounts that have been issued every month.

Return-on-investment data are collected to verify estimated against actual data: how beneficial the reuse applications have been in the organization in terms of saving time and money and increasing the quality of products. To achieve the best result, accurate data should be collected for these metrics. The metrics process should be stable and predictable. This process should be continually improved.

Chapter

17

Application Development with Reuse

Application development with reuse software is a reality. The benefits of reusable software components are achieved if the reusable software can successfully be used in another application development within the domain or in any other domain. This chapter covers the important issues of application development with reuse software, understanding customer requirements, and future trends.

Building a System with Reuse Assets

Building a system with reuse assets requires a good architectural design of the domain. A system requires identification of hardware for which the software will be developed. Identification of hardware depends on the customer. The customer provides the necessary tools and instruments that will be used by the software developers. This process assists the software developers in ensuring that the software is tested in accordance with the requirements. Any further discussion of hardware is beyond the scope of this book.

Reusability is one of the promises of the object-oriented approach. But reuse is not free—you have to work smart and hard to achieve the benefits of reuse. There are many different versions of reuse in the industry: code, inheritance, template, component, framework, pattern, artifact, asset. The bottom line is that you cannot call something reusable if it is not used more than once. Identification of software depends on whether it is a new development, a reuse of available existing software, a reengineering of the software, or a reverse-engineering process. A substantial amount of COTS software is available that suits the requirements of reuse. The domain knowledge and experience of the system analyst/engineer play a major role in this decision of selection. Thus, this selection entails developing the right software for the right requirements.

New development

In new development, it is customary that various software development phases are met. The major phases are domain analysis, requirement analysis, design, and implementation. Commonalities and differences are identified in domain analysis. These can be further divided into subphases. Most of these phases are iterative. This is an example of a typical waterfall model. The models must be shared among the group of developers who seek to integrate software. The model must be well designed, consistent, and based on the proper object-oriented design method. The model may be constantly evolving with new requirements or modifications.

New development normally follows a set of prescribed standards and methods, and uses prescribed CASE tools. Traditionally, the process moves from high-level abstractions and logical, implementation-independent designs to the physical implementation of a system. It follows a sequence that goes from requirements through the design of the implementation and leads toward a new development of software throughout the life-cycle phases. The initial phase is analysis of the new requirements and proceeds through the development of all phases of analysis until the project is completed.

Reusable software is developed in response to the requirements for one application and can be used in whole or in part for the satisfaction of requirements of another application. The domain analyst must find a way that the existing software, which is pretested and cost and time efficient, can be reused. The basic approach involves configuration and specialization of preexisting software components into viable application systems. Initial use of reusable software during the architectural design specification is a way in which implementation can be speeded.

Reverse engineering

Reverse engineering extracts design artifacts and builds or synthesizes abstractions that are less implementation dependent. This process implements changes that are made in later development phases of the existing software and automatically brings back the early phases. The process starts from any level of abstraction or any stage of the life cycle. It covers a broad range that starts from the existing implementation, then recaptures or recreates the design, and, finally, deciphers the requirements that are actually implemented by the system.

Reengineering

Reengineering is the renovation, reclamation, examination, and alteration of the existing system software for changing requirements. This process reconstitutes the existing system software into a new form and the subsequent implementation of the new form. The reengineering process dominates during the software maintenance life cycle. This helps to identify and separate those systems that are worth maintaining from those that should be replaced.

System Environment

A system environment includes everything that is not in the system itself. The environment is the circumstances under which a system will be employed. The software developer models the customer/user's environment. The model can be graphical and describe the system capabilities and functionality in the environment. The environment identifies at a high level the reuse component candidates that can be imported from other related domains. These components need further domain analysis for software reuse.

System Boundary

A system boundary separates the system from the environment. The software developer models the boundary of a system. The models can be graphical representations of the system within the boundary. The boundary describes the operational and functional capabilities of the system. The software developer interviews the customer/user in order to understand the system requirements and create the boundary for the system. This process is enhanced when the software developer conducts domain analysis and prototyping of the system. The software developer also conducts trade-off studies and activities and explores system requirement feasibility, cost effectiveness, and risk reduction analysis.

Understanding the Software Requirement

Understanding the software requirement is essential for reusing assets in building a system. Software requirements must be stated clearly, unambiguously, and completely. The requirements must be testable and measurable. Prototype models should be used to generate test cases and use cases. The requirements should be modeled to enhance understanding of test cases.

Multiple models are available for this process. The models should reflect as many aspects of the software requirements as possible. The goal of the models is twofold: to satisfy the customer and ensure he or she understands the implementation of the requirements, and to assist the software developers so the software design can continue. The commonalities among these models are the types of products they eventually produce. The model will differ depending on the software development process used. The abstract life-cycle model assumes the following types of products:

- Requirements model
- User view/operational model
- Information flow model
- Implementation model

Specifications describe all subsets of the aspects of a software process. They also describe a product at some level of abstraction and from a point of view that uses some degree of formalism. The purpose and context of the particular process or product type determine the desirable aspect, the desirable level of abstraction, the proper perspective, and the desirable degree of formalism within the software life cycle.

The *requirements model* provides a view at various levels of the software refinement process for the entire system, subsystem, or modules. This details the "what" requirements that are essential for the software development—the needs that the proposed software system should fulfill.

The *user view / operational model* provides the requirements that concern the software problems—the functions, from the customer's point of view, that the system must perform so that these needs are met. The model's main function is to communicate between the customer and the software developer. The goal is to correct any omission in the early stages, improve productivity, and increase the quality of the produced software. The model provides assistance and guidance to the customer and the software developer. It provides a more detailed understanding of the requirements and how they will be implemented in the software development.

The *information flow model* provides the necessary detailed requirements information for software development. This supplements the flow of information and what is essential for the customer's point of view. The type of information should be specified and based on the purpose and context of the specification product.

At this time the information is a matter of looking for commonality and differences. The commonality search captures common states and transitions in the state charts. It also captures the common activities and data flows for input and output in activity charts. The difference parameters are captured by conditions in control flow in the state charts. The difference parameters are also captured by the optional data flow in activity charts.

The behavioral aspect shows the way the system responds to specific inputs—the states it will adopt, the outputs it will produce, and whether it will meet the boundary conditions on the validity of inputs and states. This includes a description of the environment that produces the inputs and consumes the outputs. It also includes constraints on performance that are imposed by the environment and function of the system. The information model includes finite state and data/object models.

The *implementation model* products actually lead and build the system in accordance with the customer's requirements. This provides the details about how a system will be built and how it behaves, as it has been described in the software requirement analysis and specification. The code is written and tested so it actually can be implemented on the computer while a particular object-oriented method is used. Any change requests will be entertained and executed in the process. An existing system should be changed to correct some inherent incorrectness, to better fulfill changed requirements, or to adapt to a changed environment of both hardware and software. Depending on the severity of the change, change requests can trigger the creation of new product versions at various levels in accordance with the changed requirements.

In the maintenance phase, the intended changes to the system must be specified. In addition, new updated versions of various levels of existing products should be developed. Specifications of processes and products permit the incorporation of changes in a formal way.

Case Study 17.1

This case study revisits Case Study 9.2, "A-Bank Information System" (see Chapter 9).

Discussion. This discussion presents the difference between distributed object technology and other approaches on the reusability of the business object services. Since no such services exist before the first application is built, little tangible value is perceived in this area until a second application can be developed. Provided that the first application is good architecture, the cost to develop other applications should be reduced by reusing the components that were built as part of the earlier applications. The investment of time and energy in developing an object model, as shown in Fig. 17.1, that truly represents the business process will easily be justified by the resulting reuse benefits as additional client applications are developed.

Figure 17.1 shows how a bank's products relate to one another in a simplified way. Products consist of accounts that can be owned by a customer, and services, such as bill payment, that can be used by a customer. For each object type, the set of possible functions or operations that can be performed on the object are defined. Each of these opera-

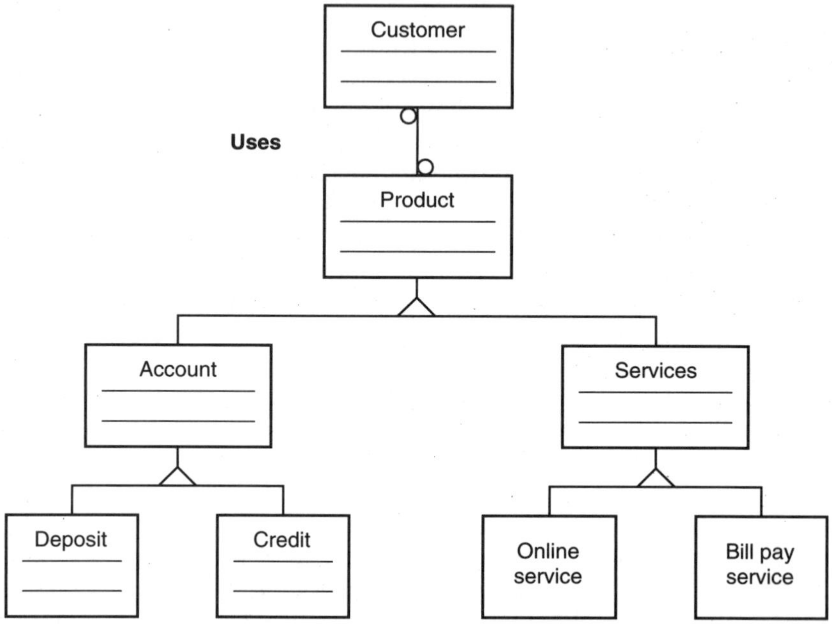

Figure 17.1 Object model for banking business.

tion definitions includes a set of input and output arguments that must be specified by the client of the object. The model also defines the attributes, or data values, stored to describe an object. For instance, a Checking Account object type might include attributes such as Ledger Balance and Overdraft Limit. The model further describes relationships between object types, as suggested by the relationship between the Customer and Product object types depicted in Fig. 17.1.

The Trend for the Future

The trend for the future in the industry is to follow the successful footsteps of other engineering faculties: "reuse, reuse, reuse" to save time and money, as has been achieved in other branches of engineering. The lesson to learn from the computer hardware industry is that by practicing reuse they have been able to reduce prices for architecture and components. When building a house or factory, the contractor does not invent new products but reuses whatever is already available in the market. There is a lot of knowledge available on the Internet—extract as much knowledge as possible from the Internet and reuse it. More research is being conducted to make the Internet efficient in handling visual information.

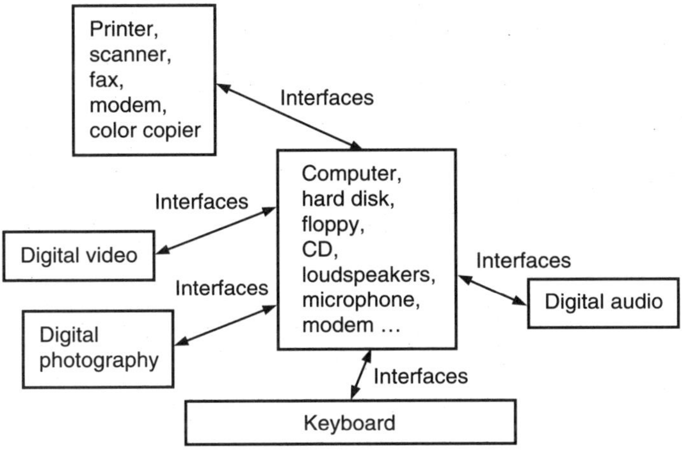

Figure 17.2 A PC workstation system with reusable components.

It is also valuable to capture the knowledge gained through human experience when such a person retires. Much of this valuable knowledge is currently being wasted by retiring with the person who possesses these valuable years of experience. New electronic chips need to be invented, along with knowledge-based systems software, and continuous feedback for improvement is also important. Perhaps a software mechanism could be invented that would capture the valuable knowledge based on experience so it could be reused by others who will perform the same type of duties in the future. Thus, instead of starting from the beginning, the new person can have access to the knowledge based on experience and can thereby avoid going through the same ritual training. This process can save a lot of expense and time, while adding to the experience of the new person on the job and sharing valuable contributions in a short time. The data from such knowledge can be populated into a personal, domain-specific repository to be reused in the future. This system can be employed at various levels and in various fields of endeavor in both industry and life in general.

There is a common saying in the industry that a computer is as good as the engineer who designed it, and this is proven by reusing well-tested hardware components. Furthermore, the computer software is as good as the system/software engineer who designed it, and this, too, is borne out by reusing well-tested software components as provided by the domain engineer. These engineers have worked the smart way (and not the hard way) to save money and time and generate a quality product. A typical example of a PC workstation incorporating reusable components is shown in Fig. 17.2.

Part

6

Samples

Fits like a glove

A WESTERN SAYING

Chapter

18

Repositories and Assets

Domain repositories consist of assets for reuse. Most of this information is available and easily accessible on the Internet. This chapter examines samples of assets in repositories: Asset Source for Software Engineering Technology (ASSET), the Digital Concepts and Analysis Center (DCAC), the Guide to Available Mathematical Software (GAMS), the IIUG Software Repository Index, the Laboratory for Advanced Software Engineering Research (LASER), and the Public Ada Library (PAL).

The Asset Abstract

The asset abstract contains a brief description of an asset in a repository. The allocated unique number and name identify the reuse assets. For example, a reuse asset has the identification number 0010 and the name "Hash Table Bounded." Following is a brief description from the abstract in the catalog:

> This generic bounded hash table package provides hash table manipulation operations necessary for most applications where a hash table data structure is needed. In building this package, we always strive for the following: the operation provided in this package must be primitive, complete, and sufficient.
>
> A primitive operation is an operation that cannot be implemented effectively without knowing the underlying representation of a particular object (in this case our object is HASH TABLE). By complete we mean that a user will find that the following operations will be the only operations needed to manipulate a bounded hash table in almost any application. Whenever necessary, a user will be able to build other operations based only on the operations provided in this package.

A bounded hash table is a stack whose maximum number of buckets must be specified when a hash table object is declared. A fixed amount of storage will then be allocated for that particular hash table object.

In another example, the asset name is "Unbounded Multiset Operation" and the identification number is 0039. The abstract is as follows:

The generic unbounded multiset package will allow the user to work with elements from a universe of elements and multisets of those elements by allowing

- the user to see if an element is a member of a multiset
- to clear a multiset, to delete an element from a multiset
- to add an element to a multiset
- to determine the cardinality of a multiset
- to see one multisubset of another multiset
- to copy one multiset to another multiset
- to check whether a multiset is empty
- to see if a multiset is a proper multiset of another multiset
- to find the number of occurrences of an element in a multiset

In addition, the generic unbounded multiset package will allow the user to unite a multiset with another multiset, to intersect a multiset with another multiset, to take the difference of a multiset and another multiset, and to take the additive union of a multiset with another multiset.

This generic unbounded multiset package provides the objects and operations necessary to capture the abstraction of an unbounded multiset. Any additional operations needed can be built out of the operations provided in this package.

The term unbounded means that a multiset may, conceptually, have an unlimited number of elements in it.

Asset Source for Software Engineering Technology (ASSET)

The ASSET repository is managed by Science Applications International Corp. (SAIC) and includes assets developed by both SAIC and the Software Engineering Institute (SEI). From the home page of ASSET, you can examine domains of the repository and the list of assets in the repository. The SAIC/ASSET World Software Reuse Discovery (WSRD) library contains over 1000 products cataloged by subject area and application in over 35 domains. The index of domains is as follows:*

*This list is copyright 1997 by SAIC.

- Ada programming
- Ada standard and bindings
- Artificial intelligence
- C++ programming
- C3I
- Clean-room software engineering
- Computer graphics
- Computer security
- C programming
- Database management
- Data structure utilities
- Distributed processing
- Domain analysis and engineering
- Image engineering
- Information storage and retrieval
- Math utilities
- Network communication
- Object-oriented software development
- Operating systems
- Planning and scheduling systems
- Process engineering
- Process models and definitions
- Project management
- Reuse library
- Runtime support
- Simulation
- Software development—specification
- Software development process
- Software development tools
- Software engineering education
- Software engineering environment
- Software quality and measurement
- Software reuse

- Software reuse—domain-specific
- System utilities
- Text processing
- User interface
- U.S. government standards

A list of unrestricted assets is available that can be downloaded from the SAIC Web page. Most of the samples of these assets include software reuse and documentation concerning reuse strategy models, reuse training, reusability guidelines, descriptions of the reuse process, reuse economics, reuse lessons learned, and a framework for the reuse process. Unrestricted WSRD library holdings (distribution A) may be downloaded to your host by selecting the Download Button displayed on the abstract page. There are 94 assets in SOFTWARE REUSE, including:

- ASSET-B-1844 Tutorial: Software Reuse: Emerging Technology
- ASSET-B-1843 Software Reuse: Guidelines and Methods (Software Science and Engineering)
- ASSET-B-1836 Integrated Software Reuse: Management and Techniques (Unicom Applied Information Technology)
- ASSET-B-1835 Software Reuse with ADA (IEEE Computing Series 16)
- ASSET-B-1834 Software Reuse and Reverse Engineering in Practice (Unicom Applied Information Technology, No. 12)
- ASSET-B-1833 Third International Conference on Software Reuse: Advances in Software Reusability November 1–4, 1994, Rio De Janeiro, Brazil: Proceedings (proceedings)
- ASSET-B-1832 Software Reuse: Methods, Models, and Costs (Software Development)
- ASSET-B-1831 Measuring Software Reuse: Principles, Practices, and Economic Models
- ASSET-B-1830 Software Reuse: A Holistic Approach (Wiley Series on Software-Based Systems)
- ASSET-B-1829 Confessions of a Used Program Salesman: Institutionalizing Software Reuse
- ASSET-B-1828 Framing Software Reuse: Lessons from the Real World
- ASSET-A-1826 Report of the Reuse and Product Lines Working Group of WISR8 (CMU/SEI-97-SR-010)

- ASSET-A-1699 Business Analysis of Software Assets for Product Lines (CMU/SEI-96-TR-010)
- ASSET-A-1554 A Reuse-Based Software Development Methodology (CMU/SEI-92-SR-4)
- ASSET-A-1423 Perspective on Software Reuse (CMU/SEI-88-TR-22)
- ASSET-A-1335 Planning for Reuse Tutorial
- ASSET-A-1325 Bibliography of Software Reuse Publications
- ASSET-A-1290 Exploring Contemporary Topics in Systematic Software Reuse
- ASSET-R-1276 Making the Case for Inter-operating Reuse Libraries (Reference)
- ASSET-A-1232 Adding Goals for Reuse Practice to Project Plans
- ASSET-R-1175 Domain Analysis and Reuse Environment—Commercial Off The Shelf (Reference)
- ASSET-A-1142 Acquisition Reform Task Promoting the Practice of Software Reuse
- ASSET-T-1113 Developing Reusable Ada Software
- ASSET-A-1101 Software Process Reuse in an Industrial Setting
- ASSET-A-1100 Software Reuse and Reusability Metrics and Models
- ASSET-A-1099 Faster Reuse and Maintenance Using Software Reconnaissance
- ASSET-A-1098 Learning and Inquiry Based Reuse Adoption (LIBRA)
- ASSET-A-1093 Software Reuse (14-Week Overview)
- ASSET-A-1089 Reuse 95—Fourth Annual Workshop on Software Reuse Education and Training
- ASSET-A-1076 WISR 7: Seventh Annual Workshop in Software Reuse
- ASSET-C-1074 Reuse-Oriented Software Evolution (ROSE) Process Model—Draft
- ASSET-T-963 Introduction to Reuse
- ASSET-B-929 Software Reuse Survey Report
- ASSET-B-928 Annotated Bibliography on Software Reuse, Metrics, and Measurements
- ASSET-A-856 Reuse 94—Third Annual Workshop on Software Reuse Education and Training

- ASSET-R-778 Reuse-Driven Software Processes Guidebook Online (Reference)
- ASSET-R-763 Reuse Process Manager (RPM) (Reference)
- ASSET-A-705 Reuse Adoption Guidebook
- ASSET-A-702 Reuse-Driven Software Processes Guidebook
- ASSET-R-695 C/C++ Data Object Library (Reference)
- ASSET-A-683 CARDS Component Providers and Tool Developers Handbook
- ASSET-R-660 SPS Software Reuse Training and Consulting (Reference)
- ASSET-R-656 Introduction to Software Reuse and Domain Analysis (Reference)
- ASSET-R-620 Software Reuse in Ada (Reference)
- ASSET-R-616 Reuse Driven Software Development (Reference)
- ASSET-A-598 CARDS Command Center Supported Components Report
- ASSET-A-596 CARDS Acquisition Handbook
- ASSET-A-593 WISR 6—Sixth Annual Workshop on Software Reuse (1993) Proceedings
- ASSET-A-592 WISR 5—Fifth Annual Workshop on Software Reuse (1992) Proceedings
- ASSET-A-591 WISR 4—Fourth Annual Workshop on Software Reuse (1991) Proceedings
- ASSET-A-590 Sources of Reusable Software Components
- ASSET-A-542 CARDS Software Architecture Seminar Report
- ASSET-A-541 Reuse Education Workshop Proceedings—October 1993
- ASSET-A-530 NATO Standard for Software Reuse Procedures
- ASSET-A-527 Reuse Documentation Database (RDDB)
- ASSET-A-507 Software Reuse Case Study (TRILLIUM)
- ASSET-A-496 Reuse Economics Spreadsheet Model (RESSM) [MS-DOS Version]
- ASSET-A-490 Reuse Economics Spreadsheet Model (RESSM) Users Guide
- ASSET-A-439 Synthesis Reuse Process Guide
- ASSET-A-413 Reuse Economics Spreadsheet Model (RESSM) [Macintosh Version]

- ASSET-A-382 Reuse-Oriented Software Evolution (ROSE) Process Model
- ASSET-A-355 Reusable Software Components
- ASSET-A-336 Reuse Education Workshop Proceedings—September 1992
- ASSET-A-312 Federal Acquisition Regulation and Budget/Finance Impacts on Software Reuse
- ASSET-C-305 Consolidated Reuse Lessons Learned
- ASSET-A-252 Evaluating Reusable Software Assets: Criteria and Procedures
- ASSET-A-220 Rapid Storage/Retrieval of Reusable Components (RSR)
- ASSET-A-209 Reusability Guidelines—Ada Coding Guide
- ASSET-A-180 Reusability Guidelines

The Internet address of ASSET is www.asset.com.

The Digital Concepts and Analysis Center (DCAC) Repository

The DCAC consists of the World Wide Geographic Digital Database and Digital Terrain Elevation Data (DTED). The DTED consists of the following assets:

- Display software
- Raster software
- Vector graphic software
- Reusable map conversion
- Geodetic software

Display software

Display software consists of digital terrain elevation data for PCs. The objective of the PC-DTED program is to display DTED data accurately and efficiently in a DOS environment. This software optionally displays the following:

- An elevation map of an area on which elevations are color-coded by range
- A matrix of actual elevation values for smaller areas
- A gray-scale shaded aspect image

The language used is C and the platform is DOS.

Raster software

Raster software is for the PC and called PC-ARC Digitized Raster Graphics (ADRG) Software. PC-ADRG is a C-language software component that reads, extracts, and displays ADRG directly from the CD-ROM. PC-ADRG is an interactive program that supports the following options:

- *Pan left,* which shifts the view four tiles to the left
- *Pan right,* which shifts the view four tiles to the right
- *Pan up,* which shifts the view four tiles to the top
- *Pan down,* which shifts the view three tiles to the bottom
- *Zoom 2X,* which zooms two times bigger than the current mouse location
- *Zoom 4X,* which zooms four times bigger than the current mouse location
- *Save screen,* which saves the current screen
- *Overview,* which returns to the overview image
- *Zoom to full scale,* which zooms from wide angle to full scale
- *Wide angle,* which zooms two times larger than the current view
- *Latitudes,* which automatically update the latitude values in DDMMSS (degrees, minutes, seconds) format
- *Longitudes,* which automatically update the longitude values in DDMMSS format

PC-ADRG was developed and tested on an IBM-compatible 486 PC with CD-ROM. The language used is Borland C. The platform is DOS.

Raster product format (RPF) software

U-RPF (the Sun/Solaris version) and W-RPF (the DOS/Windows version) evaluate the controlled image base (CIB). The RPF software comes in two parts: an applications program with GUI called *Raster Map,* and a library of reusable filter functions in ANSI C executed from a command-line interface. Raster Map reads RPF data from a CD-ROM, displays it on the screen, and writes the data to disk. The library functions are reusable software modules. Raster Map browses an RPF volume; reads a frame file of RPF data from a CD-ROM; reads an area from CD-ROM by coordinates; extracts, decompresses, and downsamples RPF overview, legend, and frame file image sets. It displays RPF overview, legend, and frame file image sets on screen, pans and zooms, switches map scale, displays geographic coordinates, and enables point and drag to mark a rectangle for extraction to disk. Library functions perform the first four Raster Map functions:

1. Extracts the RPF table of contents and frame file metadata
2. Provides mono or stereo coverage of a specified area
3. Writes data in other formats
4. Associates RPF legend files with corresponding RPF frame files

Vector graphic software

The vector graphic software exploits vector-based digital topographic data. The vector product format (VPF) exploitation software is based on GUI and reusable software modules that allow users to perform a variety of tasks on VPF data sets. Users are able to execute operations directly from DOS- (Windows 3.1/95/NT) and UNIX- (Solaris 2.x) compliant GUIs or extract modules from the library for integration into other applications.

Reusable map conversion and geodetic software

Reusable map conversion and geodetic software consists of many reusable modules. *Geotrans* is a datum transformation and coordinate conversion software package that operates on DOS (Windows 3.1) and UNIX (Solaris 2.x) platforms. Geotrans supports the following conversions:

- Coordinates—geodetic and geocentric
- Datum shifts
- Grids
- Projections

Mercator. Mercator projection is a conformal projection for which the point-scale factor is 1 along the equator. The equator lies on the line $Y = 0$. This projection is not defined at the poles. Meridians and parallels provide the framework for Mercator projections. Meridians are projected as parallel straight lines that satisfy the equation $X =$ constant. Evenly spaced meridians on the ellipsoid project to evenly spaced lines on the projection. Parallels are projected as parallel straight lines perpendicular to meridians. Evenly spaced parallels on the ellipsoid project to unevenly spaced parallels on the projections. The spacing between projected parallels increases with distance from the equator.

Polar stereographic. Polar stereographic projection is a limiting case of the Lambert conformal conic projection when the one standard parallel approaches a pole. In this conformal projection, meridians are straight lines, parallels are concentric circles, and the point-scale factor is 1 at the pole.

Transverse Mercator. Transverse Mercator projection is a conformal projection for which the point-scale factor equals 1 along the central meridian. The line $Y = 0$ is the projection of the equator, and the line $X = 0$ is the projection of the central meridian. Both the central meridian and the equator are represented as straight lines. No other meridian or parallel is projected onto a straight line. Since the point-scale factor is 1 along the central meridian, this projection is most useful near the central meridian. Scale distribution increases away from this meridian.

Universal Transverse Mercator (UTM). UTM projection is a family of projections that differs from the Transverse Mercator projection as follows:

- Longitudes of the central meridians (in degrees) are $3 + 6n$, $n = 0 \ldots 59$.
- The point-scale factor along the central meridian is 0.9996.
- The Y value, called *northing,* has an origin of 0 m in the northern hemisphere at the equator.
- The Y value, called *southing,* has an origin of 10,000,000 m at the equator and decreases toward the pole in the southern hemisphere.
- The X value, called *easting,* has an origin of 500,000 m at the central meridian.

For the UTM grid system, the ellipsoid is divided into 60 longitudinal zones of 6° each. Zone number one lies between 180°E and 186°E. The zone numbers increase consecutively in the eastward direction. It is intended that a UTM projection should be used only in one of the 6° zones, plus the overlap area. In each zone, the UTM projection extends for a 40-km overlap into two adjacent zones. Moreover, UTM coordinates are used only between 80°S and 84°N plus the overlap region. The UTM projection extends to 84° 30′ N and 80° 30′ S to overlap with the universal polar stereographic (UPS) projections.

The Internet address for DCAC is http://arc_www.belvoir.army.mil/vert_libraries.htm.

Guide to Available Mathematical Software (GAMS)

The Guide to Available Mathematical Software project of the National Institute of Standards and Technology (NIST) studies techniques to provide scientists and engineers with improved access to reusable computer software that is available to them for use in mathematical modeling and statistical analysis. One of the products of this work is an online cross-index of available mathematical software. This system also operates as a virtual software repository. That is, it provides centralized access to such items as abstracts, documentation, and source code of software modules that it catalogs; however, rather than operate a physical repository of its own, this system provides transparent access to multiple repositories operated by others.

Currently four software repositories are indexed: three maintained for use by the NIST staff (but accessible to the public) and netlib, a publicly accessible software collection maintained by Oak Ridge National Laboratory and the University of Tennessee at Knoxville (netlib in Tennessee) and Bell Labs (netlib at Bell Labs). This represents some 10,000 problem-solving modules from more than 100 software packages.

The vast majority of this software contains Fortran subprograms for mathematical problems that commonly occur in computational science and engineering—for example, solving systems of linear algebraic equations, computing matrix values, solving nonlinear systems of differential equations, finding minima of nonlinear functions of several variables, evaluating the special functions of applied mathematics, and performing nonlinear regression. Among the packages cataloged are the IMSL, NAG, PORT, and SLATEC libraries; the BLAS, EISPACK, FISHPAK, FNLIB, FFTPACK, LAPACK, LINPACK, and STARPAC packages; the DATAPLOT and SAS statistical analysis systems; as well as other collections such as the Collected Algorithms of the ACM.

All cataloged problem-solving software modules are assigned one or more problem classifications from a tree-structured taxonomy of mathematical and statistical problems. Users can browse through modules in any given problem class. To find an appropriate class, you can utilize the taxonomy as a decision tree or enter keywords that are then mapped to problem classes. Search filters can be declared, which allow users to specify preferences such as computing precision or programming language. In addition, users can browse through all modules in a given package, all modules with a given name, or all modules with user-supplied keywords in their abstracts.

The principal search mechanism in GAMS is based on a tree-structured taxonomy of mathematical and statistical problems. Each node in this tree is termed a *problem class* and is designated by a *tag,* an alternating sequence of letters and numbers (e.g., D2b1). Each module in GAMS is assigned to one or more problem classes. To locate software, GAMS users find a class that describes the problem they wish to solve and then view the modules with that classification.

A *component* is a retrievable object associated with a package or module. Examples of module components are Source, Full-source (source plus dependencies), Documentation, and Example. Available components vary from module to module and package to package. Note that Source is not always available (it is never available for commercial software indexed in GAMS).

A cross-index collects references to information available from a variety of sources. GAMS is an example of a cross-index of mathematical and statistical software.

In GAMS the term *module* is used to denote a unit of software that can be used to solve a particular problem. A module can be a Fortran subprogram, a C procedure, a stand-alone program, or a command in a system. Modules are what you are searching for when you use GAMS. A *package* is a collection of modules related by authorship, maintenance, or distribution. A package can be a subprogram library, an interactive system, or a moderated collection of programs. A *repository* is an Internet site that maintains and distributes a collection of software packages. In GAMS some repositories are free public-access sites, such as netlib, while others are computer systems accessible only by NIST staff. (In the latter case GAMS has made special arrangements to redistribute selected components.)

GAMS does not maintain a software repository of its own. Instead, it is a cross-index of a variety of repositories maintained by others. Nevertheless, it does provide many facilities of a software repository, such as search and retrieval of source and documentation. Thus, GAMS can be viewed as a virtual repository.

Directories

Following is a list of sources of information on software reuse in an easily accessible format.

Arbitrary Precision Arithmetic Packages. An index of available packages for arbitrary precision arithmetic compiled by Mark Riordan of Michigan State University.

Automatic Differentiation Software. An index of available automatic differentiation software compiled by Chris Bischof and Fred Dilley of Argonne National Laboratory.

CFD Codes List. An index of resources for computational fluid dynamics maintained by Tomasz Plewa at the Max-Planck-Institut für Astrophysik.

Computer Algebra Information Network (CAIN). An index of systems and packages for computer algebra.

Control Numeric and Software. An index of information on numerical methods and software in control engineering developed by the German Aerospace Center.

Decision Tree for Optimization Software. Recommendations of Hans Mittelmann of Arizona State University and P. Spellucci of the Technical University Darmstadt.

Finite Element Mesh Generation. Information on current research and pointers to software maintained by Robert Schneiders of RWTH Aachen.

Global Optimization. Information on global optimization (and some additional information on local optimization) collected by Arnold Neumaier of the Computational Mathematics group at the University of Vienna.

Internet Software Guide for Engineers. Directory of software resources of particular interest to water resources engineers.

Interval Computations. Software for numerical computations based on interval arithmetic.

Linear Programming FAQ. Frequently asked questions about linear programming, posted monthly to the Usenet newsgroup sci.op-research.

Math Archives. A directory of software and other materials useful in the teaching of mathematics at the college level, maintained by the mathematics department at the University of Tennessee at Knoxville.

Mathematics on the Web. A directory of mathematics information servers maintained by the mathematics department at Penn State University.

Math-Net. Links to the mathematical world maintained by the Konrad-Zuse-Zentrum für Informationstechnik Berlin (ZIB).

numcomp-free-c.txt. A list of resources for numerical computing in C and C++.

Numerical Methods and Related Fields FAQ. Answers to frequently asked questions about numerical analysis and related fields maintained by Steve Sullivan of Mathcom Inc.

Numerical Methods Resource List. An index of resources for numerical computing maintained by Tomasz Plewa at the Max-Planck-Institut für Astrophysik.

Scientific Applications on Linux. A directory of scientific software known to work under Linux.

National Software Exchange. A software exchange system set up on behalf of the U.S. High Performance Computing and Communications (HPCC) program.

The Object-Oriented Numeric Page. A directory of software, projects, publications, conferences, and other material related to object-oriented numerical computing.

NEOS Guide to Optimization Software. A listing of optimization software packages maintained by the Optimization Technology Center of Argonne National Laboratory and Northwestern University.

Nonlinear Programming FAQ. Frequently asked questions about nonlinear optimization, posted monthly to the Usenet newsgroup sci.op-research.

Numerical Evaluation of Special Functions. An extensive survey of the literature and available software for the evaluation of the higher transcendental functions. Includes more than 600 references organized by topic.

Optimization Software Guide. A listing of optimization software packages [More93].

Statistical Software List. Maintained by the Institute of Statistics and Decision Sciences at Duke University.

Another Statistical Software List. Maintained by Stata Corp.

SymbolicNet. An information center for symbolic and algebraic computing.

Wavelet Information. A directory of wavelet information and software maintained by Amara Graps.

Repositories

Fortran 90 Software Repository. Repository of Fortran 90 software maintained by NAG.

Free Fortran Software. Repository of free Fortran software maintained by the Fortran Market.

The Geometry Center. Repository of information and software on computational geometry and geometrical visualization.

HREM and Surface Structure Facility at Northwestern University. A small collection of software for FFT and related transforms in Fortran and C.

MGNet Multi-Grid/Domain Decomposition Network Repository. Repository of information and software on multigrid and multidomain methods for solving partial differential equations.

Netlib (in Tennessee or at Bell Labs). A large mathematical software repository.

Statlib. A repository of statistical software, data sets, and other information.

ZIB Electronic Library. Software developed by the Konrad-Zuse-Zentrum für Informationstechnik Berlin (ZIB). Includes the Reduce Network Library, CodeLib, and mathematical programming software.

Freely available packages

Algae. A high-level, interpreted language for numerical analysis.

CLICAL. A calculator-type computer program for vectors, complex numbers, quaternions, bivectors, spinors, and multivectors in Clifford algebras.

CLIFFORD. A Maple V package for Clifford Algebra computations.

Data Curve Fitting. Java applets for linear and nonlinear data fitting.

Fermat. A computer algebra system for the Macintosh.

GAP. Groups, Algorithms and Programming, a system for computational discrete algebra with particular emphasis on computational group theory.

Intel Performance Library Suite. Includes Math Kernel Library (MKL) with optimized BLAS and FFT for the Pentium® Pro processor. Multiple processors are supported.

MathLab 95. Windows 95/NT software for plotting functions in 2D and 3D. Includes L-systems for expressing fractal-like plots in 2D and 3D.

MuPAD. A (parallel) general-purpose computer algebra system developed at the University of Paderborn.

Scilab. A high-level system with Matlab-like syntax for system control and signal processing applications. Available for UNIX systems as well as for Windows 95 and the Macintosh.

SymbMath. Computer algebra and symbolic manipulation system with learning. Available for PCs.

Visual Math for Java. A graphic calculator and equation solver usable from a Web browser.

The Internet address for GAMS is http://gams.nist.gov.

IIUG Software Repository Index

This section describes the mechanism to access the International Informix Users Group (IIUG) Software Repository and other Informix-related archives on the Net. Some software packages provided through IIUG are available via special condition or instruction. There are several ways to locate files in the repository. If you know the name or category of software in which you are interested, you may use the index that lists the files grouped into general categories. Some files may appear in more than one category. From the index, you may either download a file that you want from the IIUG FTP archive to your local system or view it directly using your browser.

Repository index

This index allows you to access the IIUG Software Repository and other Informix-related archives on the Net. The files are grouped into categories based on their general use or the environment in which they are designed to operate. Some files may appear in more than one category. Some software in this repository is available via special condition or instruction.

Informix-4GL files are as follows:

- 4gltags_awk Generates vi tags file for 4GL source (AWK) [Download] [View]
- 4gltags_c Generates vi tags for 4GL source (C) [Download] [View]
- 4gltree Produces a function map for 4GL source (AWK) [Download] [View]
- appstart Runs Informix applications setuid (C) [Download] [View]
- arrdemo Demonstrates a method of displaying 4GL arrays (4GL, C) [Download] [View]
- blackjack The well-known casino game (4GL) [Download] [View]
- blob_char Converts a TEXT type to a CHAR type (C) [Download] [View]
- browser Browses an array (4GL) [Download] [View]
- calx Pops up a calendar pick-list (4GL) [Download] [View]
- cfuncts Functions for use in 4GL, including a Soundex routine (C) [Download] [View]
- cgi_4gl Functions to help create WWW interface programs in 4GL (C) [Download] [View]
- check_prt Examples of printing checks with dollar amounts as words (4GL) [Download] [View]

- codereuse Article and discussion on writing reusable 4GL code [Download] [View]
- connect_4gl 4GL callable ESQL/C code for handling CONNECT, etc. (4GL, ESQL/C) [Download] [View]
- constr_err Traps constraint error and tells which constraint failed (4GL) [Download] [View]
- credit_card Processes point-of-sale credit card transactions (4GL, ESQL/C, C) [Download] [View]
- cursor_name6 Prints strings that cause problems in 4GL 6.x cursor names (4GL) [Download] [View]
- cvtdatetime Functions to convert local datetime and Universal time (4GL) [Download] [View]
- datelib_ak Date functions (C, YACC/BISON) [Download] [View]
- dbdiff2 Generates SQL that alters one database to be like another (4GL) [Download] [View]
- dbref Analyzes referential integrity and builds (un)load scripts (4GL) [Download] [View]
- dbxref Cross-references 4GL variables, labels, and functions (C) [Download] [View]
- easter Several methods of calculating Easter for a specified year [Download] [View]
- emacs_4gl 4GL mode file for emacs [Download] [View]
- fgl_crypt Several approaches to encrypting strings in a 4GL program (4GL, C) [Download] [View]
- fgl_run Runs commands without 4GL "run" statement (C) [Download] [View]
- fglpp A 4GL preprocessor/precompiler (AWK) [Download] [View]
- get_user Returns current login-ID to a 4GL program (C) [Download] [View]
- getopt 4GL version of getopt(3) function [Download] [View]
- hangman The well-known word guessing game (4GL) [Download] [View]
- iedit Simple text editor (4GL, C) [Download] [View]
- iid Informix-4GL code beautifier (C) [Download] [View]
- incerto Random number generator for 4GL (C) [Download] [View]
- inferr Scans .err files for error messages (AWK) [Download] [View]
- infmx_tidy Informix-4GL code beautifier (C) [Download] [View]

- intvl_round Rounds intervals (4GL) [Download] [View]
- kw Prints 4GL source file with keywords in upper case (C) [Download] [View]
- l_pop Handles pop-up windows for display and choosing (4GL) [Download] [View]
- look_date Allows date selection in a pop-up window (4GL) [Download] [View]
- lu_cust Replaces DISPLAY/INPUT ARRAY for customer lookup/choosing (4GL) [Download] [View]
- m4gl m4 macro to provide define/include for 4GL [Download] [View]
- maintlib Functions for writing interactive maintenance programs (4GL, C) [Download] [View]
- make_sccs Examples for using make and SCCS with 4GL [Download] [View]
- metaphone Several implementations of the Metaphone phonetic algorithm (C) [Download] [View]
- msg_pmpt Displays message box and lets user choose option (4GL) [Download] [View]
- need_inc_4gl Determines if a 4GL program requires an include file (JAVA) [Download] [View]
- noncaseqry Converts WHERE clause for non-case-sensitive query (4GL) [Download] [View]
- ppcc4gl Preprocesses 4GL source using cpp (SH, CPP) [Download] [View]
- progtest A test of 25 questions for 4GL programmers with answers [Download] [View]
- prt_decimal Methods of formatting decimal numbers for printing (4GL, C) [Download] [View]
- query_win Provides scrolling QBE pick-list in a pop-up window (4GL) [Download] [View]
- random_4gl Random number generator for 4GL (C) [Download] [View]
- reccmp Compares data in two identically structured RECORDs in 4GL (C) [Download] [View]
- recursion An example of recursion in 4GL (4GL, ESQL/C) [Download] [View]
- reserved List of I4GL and ISQL reserved keywords (C) [Download] [View]

- rpt_awk Functions to control AWK reports like 4GL or ACE (AWK) [Download] [View]
- rpt_blobs Prints BLOBs such as images and logos in 4GL reports (C, 4GL) [Download] [View]
- rpt_length Several approaches to having variable report lengths (4GL) [Download] [View]
- rpt_size Changes 4GL report dimensions at runtime (C) [Download] [View]
- scriba Tools for documenting and indexing 4GL source files (SH, AWK) [Download] [View]
- setenv An enhanced version of putenv(3) (C) [Download] [View]
- solitaire Solitaire game similar to the one on most Windows PCs (4GL) [Download] [View]
- soundex Utilities for generating Soundex codes (4GL, C) [Download] [View]
- soundex_ius Soundex function for use with Illustra/Universal Server (C) [Download] [View]
- space_usage Reports table space usage in an OnLine database (4GL, C) [Download] [View]
- split_string Functions for splitting/parsing 4GL strings (C) [Download] [View]
- sqrt_4gl sqrt() function for 4GL (C) [Download] [View]
- tbl_ring_mnu Table-driven ring menu utility (4GL) [Download] [View]
- tcl4gl Functions for interfacing TCL with Informix-4GL (C) [Download] [View]
- test4glcomp Source code to test 4GL compiler [Download] [View]
- timeout Allows 4GL programs to set input time-out intervals (C) [Download] [View]
- trigger_test Tests triggers and stored procedures from 4GL (4GL, SQL) [Download] [View]
- vari_functs Functions using variable values (4GL, C) [Download] [View]
- vertmenu Vertical pull-down menus for 4GL (C, 4GL) [Download] [View]
- vgrind_4gl vgrind definition file for 4GL [Download] [View]
- wordwrap Demonstrates using INPUT ARRAY and WORDWRAP (4GL) [Download] [View]

- work_days Methods for computing number of workdays (4GL) [Download] [View]
- zipbundle Prints bundling instructions for bulk mailing by zip code (4GL) [Download] [View]

Multifile collections

- *DAS* Utilities applicable to many Informix-related environments maintained by Dave Snyder
- *flat 4GL* C functions for processing flat files from within 4GL programs
- *inx util* Utilities to assist in Informix-4GL development maintained by Tim Schaefer
- *multiscreen* Program that is an example of doing multiscreen input in 4GL
- *rdslib* A P-code linker and librarian

ESQL/C

- dbnames Gets list of visible databases (ESQL/C) [Download] [View]
- dbstruct Generates C structs for database tables (SH) [Download] [View]
- esql_c++ Files for compiling ESQL/C programs with C++ (SH, ESQL/C, C) [Download] [View]
- esql_cpp Preprocesses ESQL/C programs using CPP (AWK, CPP) [Download] [View]
- esql_proto1 Header (".h") files containing ESQL/C function prototypes [Download] [View]
- esql_proto2 File describing ESQL/C function prototypes [Download] [View]
- esqlutil Generates C structs for database tables (ESQL/C) [Download] [View]
- gettype Article/code for getting data type from syscolumns (SH, ESQL/C, C) [Download] [View]
- hierarc_sql Handles hierarchical data like parts explosion (SQL, ESQL/C, ACE) [Download] [View]
- intvl_conv Functions to convert intervals (ESQL/C, SPL) [Download] [View]
- reserved List of I4GL and ISQL reserved keywords (C) [Download] [View]

- sqlda_funcs Functions for handling sqlda structures (ESQL/C) [Download] [View]
- tclsql Functions for interfacing TCL with Informix-SQL (ESQL/C, C) [Download] [View]
- updblob Generic program to update BLOB fields (ESQL/C) [Download] [View]

Informix-SQL

- loop_scr Generates multitable SPERFORM screens (AWK, SH) [Download] [View]
- orclproc Oracle function equivalents as stored procedures (SPL) [Download] [View]
- privproc Reports privileges for stored procedures (ACE) [Download] [View]
- random_spl Stored procedures for generating a random number (SPL) [Download] [View]
- reform_sql Reformats ISQL output to one wide line per row (AWK) [Download] [View]
- reserved List of I4GL and ISQL reserved keywords (C) [Download] [View]
- rpt_awk Functions to control AWK reports like 4GL or ACE (AWK) [Download] [View]
- sh_select Example of doing SQL queries from the shell (SH, AWK) [Download] [View]
- tclsql Functions for interfacing TCL with Informix-SQL (ESQL/C, C) [Download] [View]
- sysmast_sql SQL scripts to be used with the sysmaster database (SQL) [Download] [View]
- upper_spl Methods for upshifting characters in SPL (SQL, SPL) [Download] [View]
- upshift_spl Methods for upshifting characters in SPL (SQL, SPL) [Download] [View]

NewEra

- INDEX A listing of the FTP files and directories in /pub/informix/pub/newera [Download] [View]
- newera_make Replaces nmake.exe when PC NewEra compiles to only p-code (PERL) [Download] [View]

- nwera4gl.exe 4GL to NewEra migration tools (PC self-extracting archive) [Download]
- virtual_os Provides a wrapper around operating system type calls [Download] [View]
- pickdate Files to demonstrate the "pickdate" functionality in NewEra 2.0
- picklist Files to demonstrate the "picklist" functionality in NewEra 2.0

Database Administration

- analyse_idx Interactive program that gives information on indexes (4GL) [Download] [View]
- arch2disk Archives an OnLine database to disk (SH) [Download] [View]
- arch_hp_tape Archives an OnLine database to an HP shuttle tape drive (SH) [Download] [View]
- ckfls Reports files in $INFORMIXDIR with incorrect permissions (SH) [Download] [View]
- copy_spaces Converts onstat –d commands into onspaces commands (SH) [Download] [View]
- db_ontape Runs ontape (SH, PERL) [Download] [View]
- dbalter Alters one database to be like another (ISQLPERL) [Download] [View]
- dbamon Monitors OnLine engine performance (SH) [Download] [View]
- dbdiff2 Generates SQL that alters one database to be like another (4GL) [Download] [View]
- dbinfo_lk Displays INFO statement output (SQL, AWK) [Download] [View]
- dbldfmt Converts a fixed-field-length file to LOAD format (C) [Download] [View]
- dbref Analyzes referential integrity and builds (un)load scripts (4GL) [Download] [View]
- dbsh Splits dbschema output into a set of files (PERL) [Download] [View]
- defrag_table Defragments tables (PERL, SQL) [Download] [View]
- disk_struct Displays the disk structure for the current instance (4GL, SH) [Download] [View]

- dm Shows summary of output from various onstat commands (ESQL/C) [Download] [View]
- errmsgtbl Creates a database table of Informix error messages (SH, AWK) [Download] [View]
- extentsize Calculates extent sizing for a table (SH) [Download] [View]
- idbb Automatic Informix database backup utility (SH) [Download] [View]
- killidle Monitors and kills idle processes (AWK) [Download] [View]
- lockrep Reports tables locked by users (SH, AWK) [Download] [View]
- maxextents Determines total number of extents for a table (C, JAVA) [Download] [View]
- onlsize Reports sizes of OnLine databases (PERL) [Download] [View]
- orclproc Oracle function equivalents as stored procedures (SPL) [Download] [View]
- pres_ext Creates SQL script to preserve OnLine extents (SH) [Download] [View]
- privproc Reports privileges for Stored Procedures (ACE) [Download] [View]
- reorg_pl Reorganizes an entire database or single table (PERL) [Download] [View]
- save_idx Saves and re-creates indexes (SH, AWK) [Download] [View]
- schemadiff Compares two schemas, described in _Tech_Notes_v5, i3 (C) [Download] [View]
- space_usage Reports table space usage in an OnLine database (4GL, C) [Download] [View]
- su_ontape Does an su to user "informix," then runs ontape (C) [Download] [View]
- sysmast_sql SQL scripts to be used with the sysmaster database (SQL) [Download] [View]
- tab_col_frm Table/column information screen file (SPERFORM) [Download] [View]
- tbheader Prints header information from an Informix backup tape (C) [Download] [View]
- tbrpt Combines several tbstat options into one report (SH, AWK, SQL) [Download] [View]

- utils_ak Database administration scripts and programs (ESQL/C, AWK, SH) [Download] [View]
- utils_jl Database administration utility package (C, SH) [Download] [View]
- utils_sp Database administration scripts and programs (PERL, C, 4GL) [Download] [View]
- xtbload X application that displays OnLine status similar to xload (C) [Download] [View]

Miscellaneous utilities

- INDEX A listing of the FTP files and directories in /pub/informix/pub [Download] [View]
- areacode Utilities and data for North American telephone area codes [Download] [View]
- asql_yacc ANSI-compliant SQL parser (LEX, YACC, C) [Download] [View]
- comma2unl Several methods for converting comma-quote files to unload format [Download] [View]
- dbftosas Converts .dbf files for SAS loading (PERL) [Download] [View]
- dbldfmt Converts a fixed-field-length file to LOAD format (C) [Download] [View]
- errmsgtbl Creates a database table of Informix error messages (SH, AWK) [Download] [View]
- intvl_conv Functions to convert intervals (ESQL/C, SPL) [Download] [View]
- killidle Monitors and kills idle processes (AWK) [Download] [View]
- listiem Lists contents of Informix error message file (C) [Download] [View]
- lockrep Reports tables locked by users (SH, AWK) [Download] [View]
- makedic Makes a data dictionary listing file (4GL) [Download] [View]
- metaphone Several implementations of the Metaphone phonetic algorithm (C) [Download] [View]
- sccstools Collection of tools for working with SCCS (C, SH) [Download] [View]

- scriba Tools for documenting and indexing 4GL source files (SH, AWK) [Download] [View]
- sh_select Example of doing SQL queries from the shell (SH, AWK) [Download] [View]
- shar Makes shell archives ("shar's") (SH) [Download] [View]
- soundex_ius Soundex function for use in with Illustra/Universal Server (C) [Download] [View]
- sqlcmd Interprets SQL commands against an Informix database (ESQL/C, C) [Download] [View]
- sql_yacc SQL parser (LEX, YACC, C) [Download] [View]
- termcap_keys Helps determine special key values for termcap entries (C) [Download] [View]
- trigger_test Tests triggers and stored procedures from 4GL (4GL, SQL) [Download] [View]
- upper_spl Methods for upshifting characters in SPL (SQL, SPL) [Download] [View]
- upshift_spl Methods for upshifting characters in SPL (SQL, SPL) [Download] [View]
- ww Wraps long lines in text files without splitting words (SH, AWK) [Download] [View]

The Internet address for IIUG is http://www.iiug.org.

Laboratory for Advanced Software Engineering Research (LASER)

The Laboratory for Advanced Software Engineering Research (LASER) is a research lab in the computer science department of the University of Massachusetts at Amherst. LASER comprises several projects sharing the common goal of investigating tools and techniques to improve the software engineering process. The Reusable Components Library is a set of commonly used abstractions for use in Ada programs. The library has been designed to integrate smoothly with the object management tool set, both providing persistence operations for the types defined in the library and allowing the use of Pleiades defined types as actual in the parametric type constructors.

The library contains:

- Abstract data types
  Balanced binary tree generic
  Hash table generic

List generic
Queue generic
Set generic
Stack generic
Symbol table generic
Variable length strings

- Interface packages
  Command-line interpretation package
  Standardized command-line names

- General utilities
  Calendar utilities
  Graph layout generic
  Persistent stubs generic
  String and character conversion functions

Ada source code

The common components library contains the Index of /ftp/language_processing/language_independent. This directory contains IRIS, a language-independent graph representation of programs, and the IRIS Support Tools, a set of tools for the manipulation of IRIS graphs and repositories.

Index of /ftp/common_components contains

pleiades_library_2.0 . . .	23-May-96 12:42	36k
prettyada_1.1e.tar.Z	23-May-96 12:42	38k

This directory contains common components used by other software and distributed by LASER.

- components A library of reusable persistent data structures including stacks, queues, etc. Used by virtually all LASER software.
- dag_layout A library to support the automated layout of directed graphs. Developed at UCI.
- pleiades_library The core support library required for Pleiades clients. Pleiades is a database programming language developed by LASER. Used by virtually all LASER software.
- prettyada An Ada source code formatter library used by LASER tools that output Ada source.

Pleiades object management tool set

The Pleiades object management tool set is an object management system that facilitates the definition, manipulation, and maintenance of complex objects and their interrelationships. Its focus is on providing the capabilities in a way that is both easy to use and flexible enough to support a wide variety of complex applications, such as software engineering environments.

Type Evolution Support System (TESS)

TESS is a tool set to support the evolution of persistent type definitions. TESS semiautomatically constructs transformers that convert persistent instances of an old type definition into instances of a new one.

Software engineering tools and libraries from LASER

All of the software distributed by LASER is distributed as Ada source. To build the software, you must have an Ada compiler and a POSIX library for your system. The following software is available (by category):

- Object management tools
- Language processing tools
- Software analysis tools
- Reusable components

The Internet address for LASER is http://laser.cs.umass.edu.

Public Ada Library (PAL)

The PAL is a library of Ada and VHDL software, information, and courseware that contains over 2.5 billion bytes of material (mainly in compressed form). All items in the PAL have been released to the public with unlimited distribution, and, in most cases (the exceptions are shareware), the items are freeware.

Ada is an international standard computer programming language that is used in a wide variety of applications, including real-time control systems, medical systems, business data processing systems, communications systems, X/Motif applications, Microsoft Windows applications, entertainment software, and software development systems.

Ada83 is an object-based language that achieved international standardization in 1983, and Ada95 is an object-oriented language that achieved international standardization in 1995. Ada95 is upward-compatible with Ada83, and, while both languages may be called "Ada," it is more appropriate to use the term "Ada" to refer to the current version of the language, Ada95.

VHDL is an IEEE standard computer programming language that is based on Ada83. VHDL, which stands for VHSIC Hardware Description Language (VHSIC stands for "very high speed integrated circuit"), is used to design PC boards and integrated circuits.

The PAL is based on the Washington University Archive (WUArchive). WUArchive is composed of two host computers:

- wuarchive.wustl.edu, which contains the files of the PAL and supports anonymous FTP, Gopher, remote NFS mounts, and the World Wide Web
- mail.wustl.edu, whic]h handles several electronic mailing lists for the PAL

The PAL is managed from an administrative host computer at Monmouth University (this administrative host computer is not available to the public) and directly at the main PAL site, wuarchive .wustl.edu.

The PAL includes:

- Free Ada83 and Ada95 compilers
- Reference manuals in text, Postscript, and hypertext of the Ada83 and Ada95 languages, along with rationales for the design of these languages
- Over 80 sets of courseware in topics such as software engineering, object-oriented design and analysis, software reuse, domain engineering and analysis, and Ada83 and Ada95 (including computer-assisted instruction courses)
- Hundreds of reusable software components and tools written in Ada83 and Ada95
- Bindings from Ada to several horizontal domains, including X11, Motif, POSIX, and SQL, as well as standard interfaces, including ASIS, IRDS, and PCIS
- Software for Ada compiler evaluation and benchmarking, including ACES, ACVC, and PIWG

- Technical reports on Ada, comparing Ada with C++, software engineering, domain engineering, object-oriented design (OOD), object-oriented programming (OOP), software reuse, and other topics
- VHDL models, simulations, and information

The PAL contains copies of material available to the public from several other sites on the Internet (the PAL mirrors these sites) and documents this material in the PAL database. These sites include:

- The Ada Information Clearinghouse
- The GNU New York University Ada95 Translator Project
- The Software Engineering Institute
- The AdaSAGE project at the Idaho National Engineering Lab
- The VHDL Repository at the University of Cincinnati

The PAL Frequently Asked Questions (FAQ) list answers most questions posed by new (and old) users of the PAL and is updated approximately monthly. The PAL Card Catalog makes it easy to search the PAL. This card catalog is available in hypertext (available for viewing via the World Wide Web). For your convenience, there are two main World Wide Web entry points to the PAL Card Catalog:

- The Taxonomy of the PAL Card Catalog allows you to view the PAL by subject area (e.g., Ada compilers, courseware, and software components).
- The Index of the PAL Card Catalog allows you to use your World Wide Web client software (e.g., Netscape) to search for items in the PAL by keyword.

Also you may run the PAL Card Catalog from its copy at the Walnut Creek CD-ROM PAL mirror site.

- The world's largest Windows archive (mirrored from winsite.com), including Windows 3.1, Windows 95, and Windows NT.
- Linux, Linux, Linux; pick your distribution:
  RedHat (from www.redhat.com)
  Debian (from www.debian.org)
  Slackware (from Walnut Creek CDROM)
- Linux on PowerPC!
  MkLinux (from mklinux.apple.com)
  Linux-PPC (from www.linuxppc.org)

- A complete mirror of SunSite's Linux archive (from sunsite.unc.edu)
- A good collection of security and privacy software for Linux (from www.replay.com)
- Choose your BSD:
  FreeBSD
  NetBSD
- For Macintosh users:
  A complete mirror of the Info-Mac archives
  Files from the Arizona Macintosh Users Group
- Aminet, the Internet's largest Amiga software archive
- The complete archive of all 3D Realms and Apogee games and demos, exclusive to wuarchive.
- Over 2100 MIDI files of modern and not-so-modern music from filecity.com

For those who just want to browse, here's the full off-the-root-directory listing:

- */doc* Documentation and other textual information
- */edu* Educational programs and materials
- */graphics* Graphics programs
- */languages* Programming language–specific archives
- */multimedia* Multimedia: audio, video, and images
- */packages* Packages running on many different systems
- */systems* System-specific programs and data
- */usenet* Archives of selected Usenet newsgroups

PAL top-level taxonomy

The PAL top-level taxonomy consists of movement within the PAL Card Catalog as follows:

- Ada compilers
- Benchmarks
- Bindings
- Communications
- Copies and mirrors
- Courseware

- Database management tools
- Distributed processing
- Documentation development tools
- Documents
- Miscellaneous tools
- Project management tools
- Software components
- Software development tools
- Testing
- User toolkit
- VHDL

PAL Card Catalog entry

The User Support Tools are a collection of tools to support the user of PAL. The toolkit directory tree has not been certified per se. It is used extensively, and the tools are written mostly in C. The toolkit contains a variety of useful and reliable tools, and the PAL Certifier uses many of them on a regular basis.

The PAL User Toolkit is a collection of tools to support the user of PAL. This tree includes binaries for MS-DOS, MAC, and VMS, as well as source code. This collection contains tools that can help the user of the PAL manipulate the files in the PAL. These tools include various versions of TAR (the UNIX tape archive) for several platforms:

- Various versions of compress (the UNIX file compression program) for several platforms
- Various versions of GNU ZIP (the GNU file compression program) for several platforms
- Various versions of UUENCODE and UUDECODE (the UNIX binary-to-text and text-to-binary file conversion programs)
- Various versions of ZIP and UNZIP by the Info-ZIP group.

Info-ZIP provides a very good ZIP and UNZIP file/directory archive compression tool that runs on virtually every platform. For several platforms, the pager2 program is available, which concatenates and tears apart text files. There are also the t2t (text to text), u2m (UNIX to MS-DOS), and m2u (MS-DOS to UNIX) text file format conversion programs. Source code to many of these programs is included, so they may be ported to other platforms as the user desires.

The "all" directory tree contains many such items. Each tool in the PAL toolkit has either an associated abstract (*.abs) or README file. These files contain author information and some user instructions. They should be read before the user employs the tool.

With Version 1.3 of the toolkit, Mosaic has been added. The version of Mosaic in the win_31 tree includes a socket driver for stand-alone execution of Mosaic under Microsoft Windows 3.1 without a network.

The Internet address of PAL is http://wuarchive.wustl.edu.

Chapter

19

Domain Analysis and Design Examples

Example 1: Processing a Customer Order

A factory household outlet store carries only brand-name items for sale at wholesale prices. It carries items such as household furniture, kitchen utensils, fans, dining room tables, chairs, and electrical fixtures. The store provides credit to customers to increase sales and maintains adequate inventory so a customer can buy an item and carry it home. The store also accepts orders for those items that are not in stock. The management uses a computer to run the business efficiently.

The store has many employees to assist in this operation. These employees are well trained in their fields. The company offers a good benefits package to attract workers.

Figures 19.1 through 19.4 provide a sample domain analysis and design process for this example.

Data dictionary

Computer systems = {hardware + software}

Payment = [cash | check + (ID) | charge card]

Personnel = {general administration + order clerk + inventory control manager + credit manager + shipping personnel + financial manager + sales personnel}

Software = {order entry system + order approval system + financial system}

Discussion. This is a generic case study for processing a customer order. The design can be applied to situations with similar requirements.

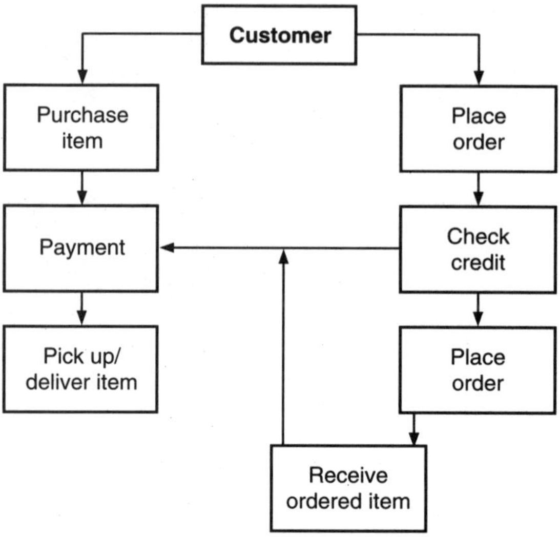

Figure 19.1 Architecture model for processing a customer order.

For example, how does this situation differ from ordering any other item in your life? The process is the same. Therefore, it saves both money and time to reuse some of the existing assets for handling such transactions. You have to look around for such assets—a good resource is the Internet.

Example 2: Postal Mail System

One of the major problems at a post office during the holiday season is a backlog of mail that must be delivered on time. A solution should reduce the waiting times associated with these backlogs.

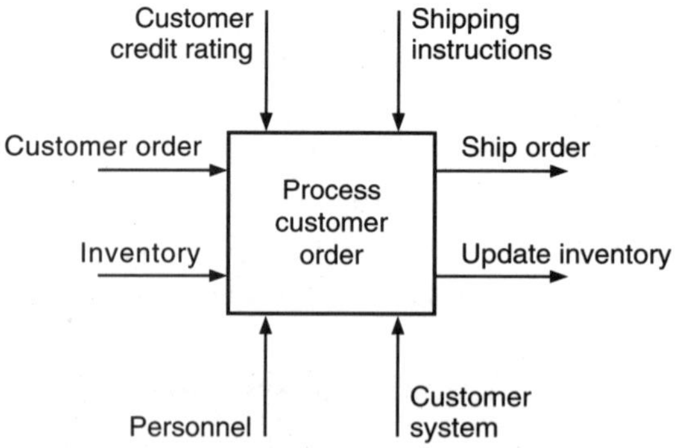

Figure 19.2 Context diagram—process customer order.

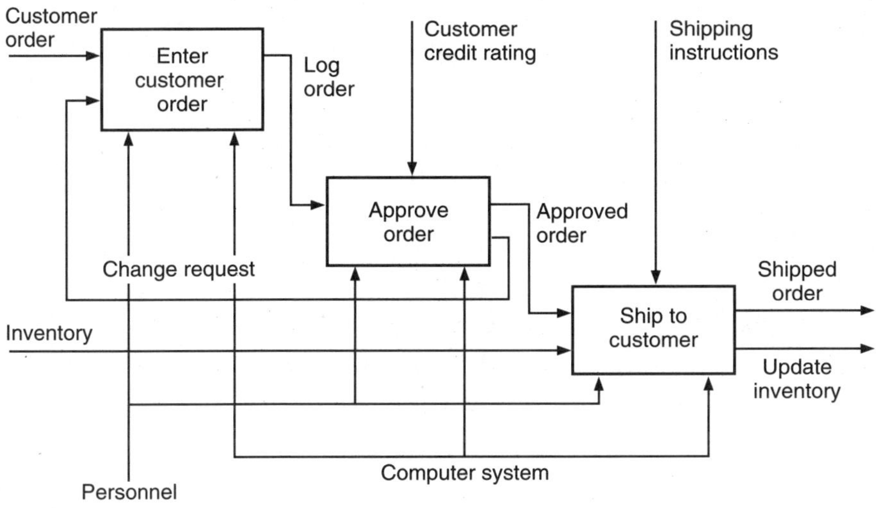

Figure 19.3 IDEFo lower-level diagram for processing a customer order.

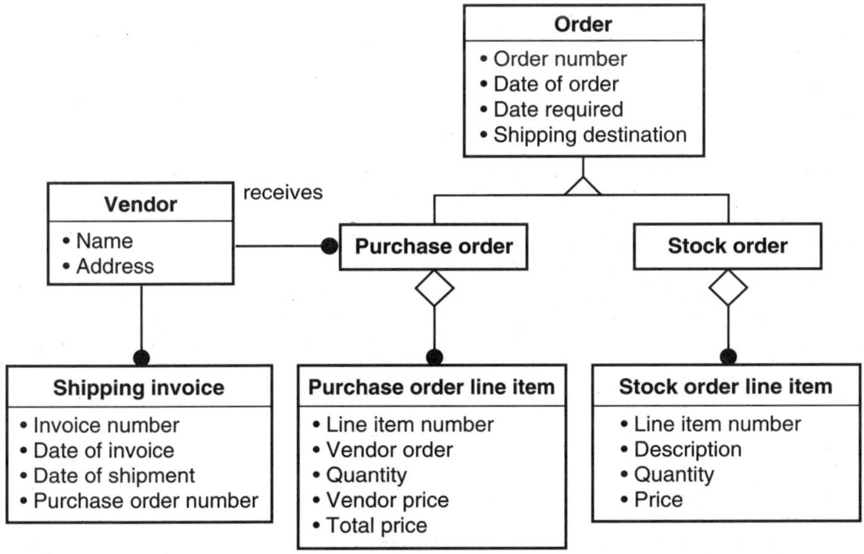

Figure 19.4 Object design diagram for processing a customer order.

There are three major types of mail that arrive at a post office: one-day delivery, Priority mail, and regular mail. A postal worker normally selects a piece of mail, giving precedence to Priority mail, reviews it for any errors, and hand-feeds it into a scanner. Once a piece of mail is scanned, it is automatically forwarded to the right destination.

Figures 19.5 through 19.8 show the sample models for this generic example.

Data dictionary

Customer mail = personal + company

Personal = letters | bulk mail | certified | package

Letters = certified (receipt due) | Priority

Priority = one day | two days | three days

. . .

Postal rules = rate | size of package | contents

Destination = known address

Validated mail = correct address + size + postal stamp

Correct object = correct legal contents + instructions

Discussion. There are many post offices in the country that perform the same types of services. Once money is spent to design it, a good sys-

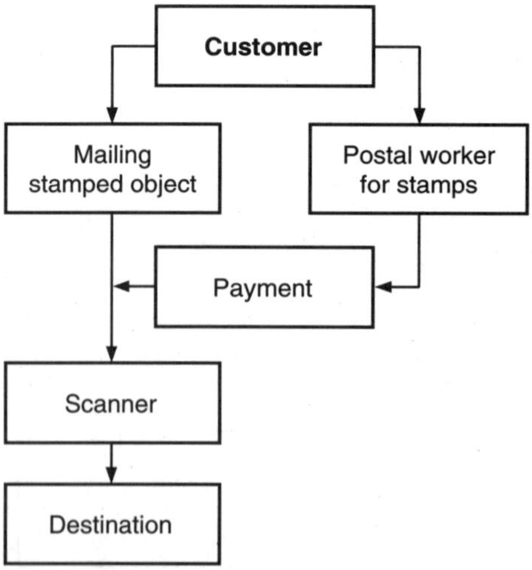

Figure 19.5 Architecture of a postal mailing service.

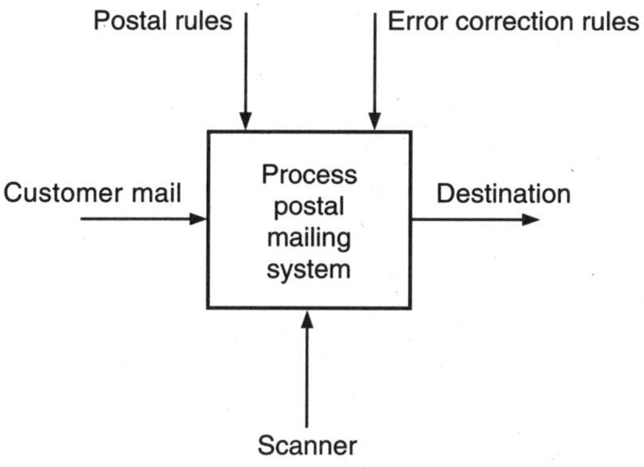

Figure 19.6 Context diagram—postal mail system.

tem can be reused again and again. Some of the requirements should be tailored to fit into existing designs.

Internationally, postal service is practically the same process. The same design can be reused with some modification and creation of interfaces. Even UPS and Federal Express services are not much different from the postal services.

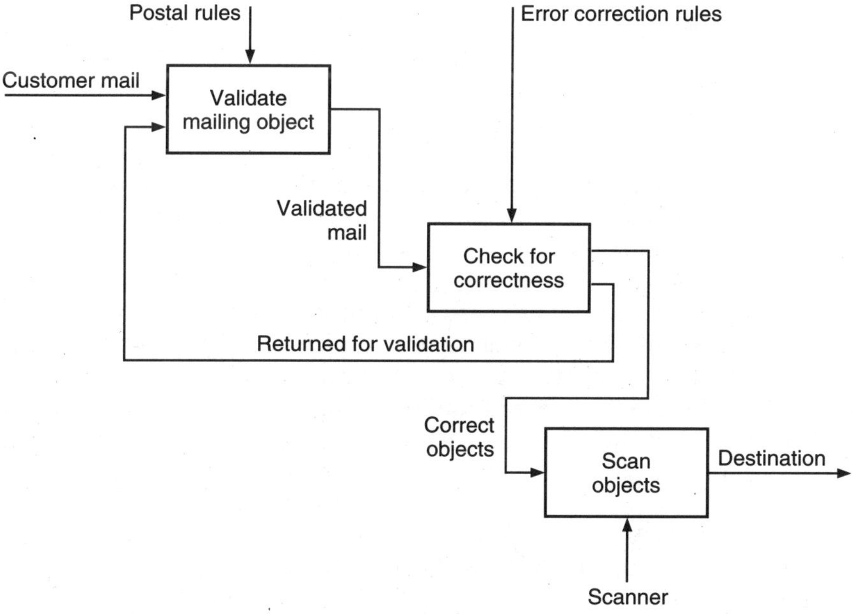

Figure 19.7 IDEFo lower level—processing in postal mail system.

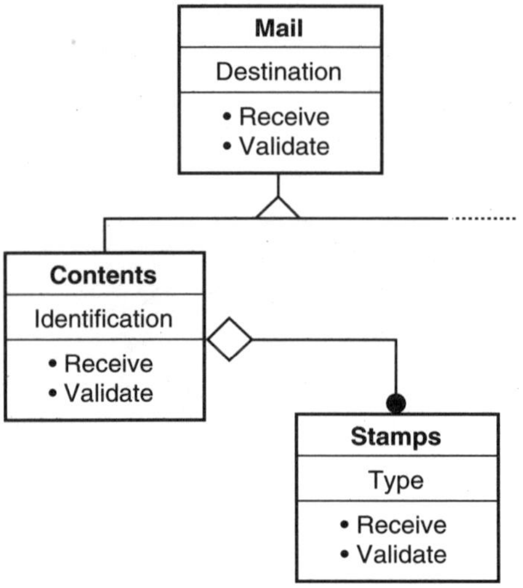

Figure 19.8 Object model of postal mail system.

Example 3: System Service Desk

Bringing a new application to production marks the end of the development process. The guideline is to reuse the existing software as much as possible. In the environment of the distributed object, a system service desk needs to be created to help software developers and managers in application development.

The system service desk is a supporting process that lasts as long as the application lives. The system service desk is used to tap into distant databases and repositories in the enterprise, consolidate information about technology assets, and use the knowledge thus gained in marketing.

An important factor in success is defining the processes in an organization. Once business processes are in place to input, monitor, and modify data, the corporation can create links between the system service desk and other corporate functions, thus eliminating the need for multiple tracking functions and making the system service desk the repository for all information about computer assets.

Once the system service desk has access to information stored in other areas of the business, an organization can treat its computers as strategic assets rather than as trouble tickets to be resolved into closed-out status.

Figures 19.9 through 19.12 show sample domain analysis and design for this example.

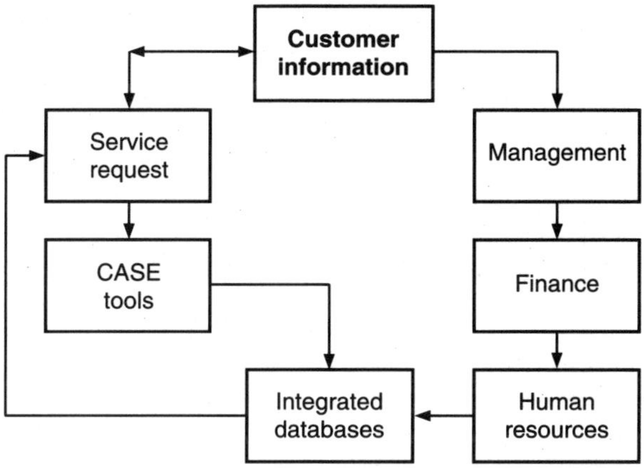

Figure 19.9 Architecture view of the system service desk.

Data dictionary

Asset description = {description + number + source}
Customer info = [complaint | suggestion]
Defects tracing = [metric | matrix]
Management = [manager | engineer | programmer]
PPS = {organization guidelines}
Resolution = [defects solution | repair | purchase]
Update assets = {necessary changes}
Update info = [repository | database]

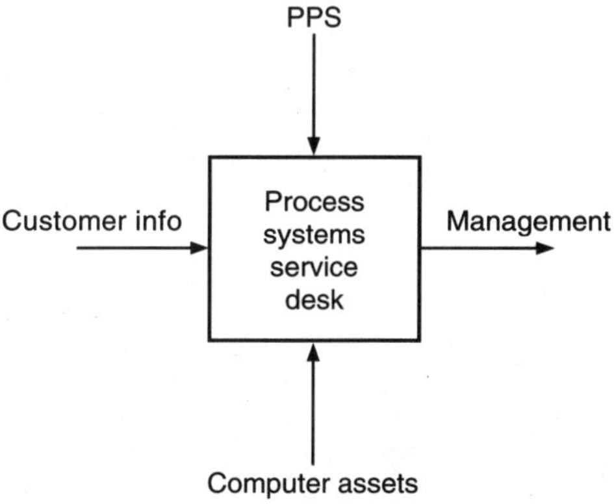

Figure 19.10 Context diagram of the system service desk.

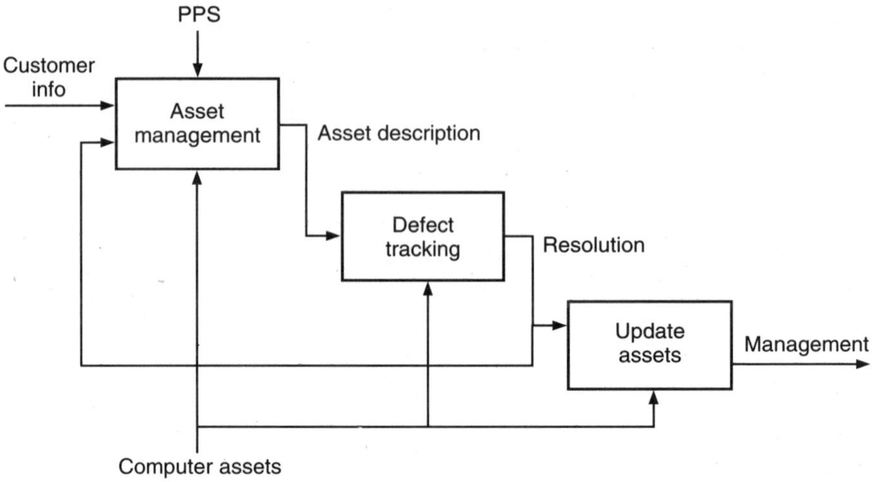

Figure 19.11 IDEFo model of the system service desk.

Discussion. The system service desk is useful and a company that employs such a system can reap significant ROI. A system service desk employee pulls up a record with an exact description of the asset on a caller's desktop that provides the following data:

- What kind of system it is
- How much memory it has
- What applications are running
- How it is connected to the network

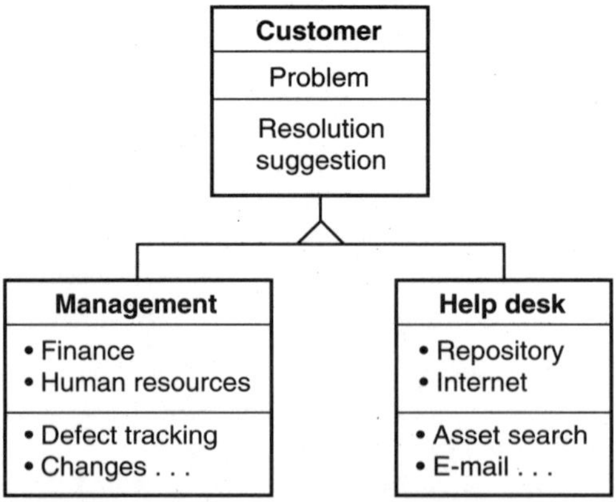

Figure 19.12 Object model of the system service desk.

The system service desk personnel are more likely to be able to resolve the problem on the first call.

An organization that automates the process of picking up changes and repopulating its assets system from the system service desk can also track the costs of those assets accurately. The payoff comes in the form of detailed information that the organization needs to make good technology decisions.

An organization should keep a full-time developer on staff who accommodates changes in the system service desk and develops a simple link to the organization's e-mail system to generate automated mail messages. It has been observed that this system service desk process has saved as many as four calls to the help desk per trouble ticket.

Asset management should also get real-time updates. The system service desk has traditionally been known as the *help desk*. Help desks have often been poor at identifying when to replace, rather than fix, an asset. With the help of an automated system service desk, clients can really begin to manage the requirements of a dynamic information technology infrastructure.

Fundamentally, this concept of a system service desk can fit any organization. Obviously, system service desks are all dealing with managing the same object. The system service desk integrates enterprisewide asset management with service and support functions. This concept is applicable in financial institutions and telecommunications organizations that use the technology to give them a competitive edge [Tris97].

Example 4: Information-Processing System

An information-processing system is typical for distributing and handling messages. A person inputs messages for processing. Outputs are the corrected messages. An organization's PPS and rules and regulations are the controlling factors. The mechanism that performs this activity is the computer information system. Like others in this chapter, this is a generic case study.

The input message is validated in accordance with the organization's PPS. The message is further compared for format and any error in the text. If an error is found, then it is corrected and the corrected text is sent back for validation. The repository is updated for future reference. The corrected message is then output from this process.

Figures 19.13 through 19.16 illustrate domain analysis and design of an information-processing system.

Data dictionary

C-Msg = [text correction | address correction]

Compare = {defects}

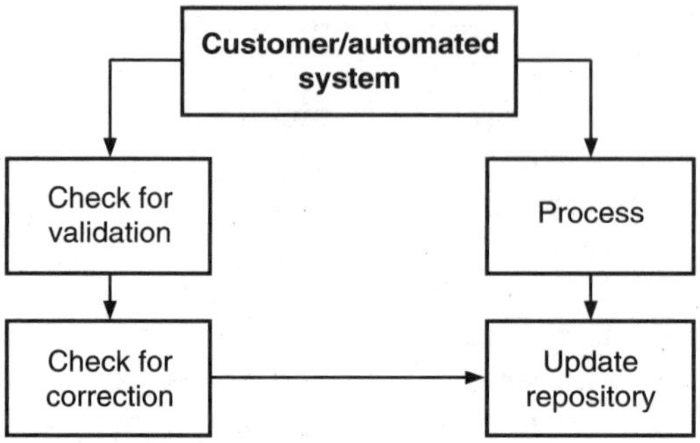

Figure 19.13 Architecture of an information-processing system.

Correct message = ** no error

Corrected message = send to destination

F-Msg = {formatted message}

Human message = {input message}

PPS = {policy, procedures, and standards}

Rules/regulations = {organization guidance}

U-Msg = {updated message}

Update repository = {future references}

V-Msg = {verified message}

Validate message = ** validated message

Discussion. This is a generic case study for handling and distributing messages with the help of a computer. This generic solution can fit any

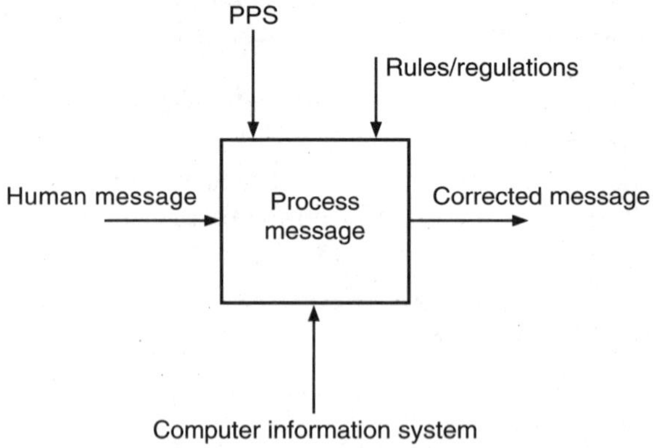

Figure 19.14 Context diagram of an information-processing system.

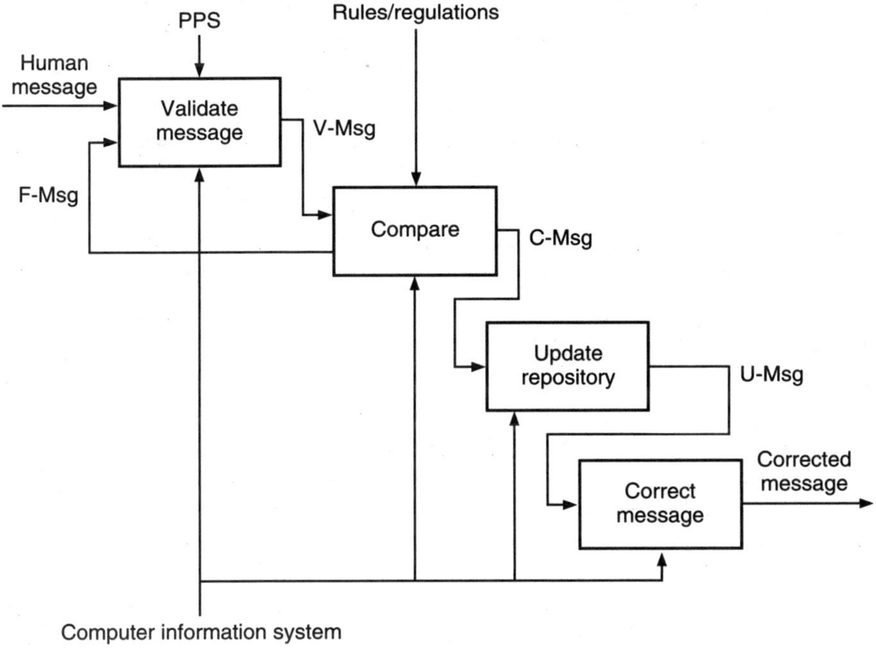

Figure 19.15 IDEFo model of an information-processing system.

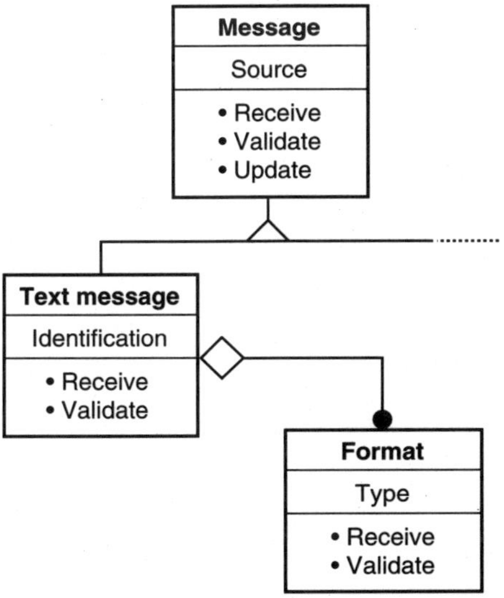

Figure 19.16 Object model of an information-processing system.

real-life situation. This is simply a template to be reused. There can be many methods for checking on the input message. An actual person does not have to deliver the input message; this process can be automated. The envelope that contains the message is thoroughly checked for accuracy. In some cases, time is a critical factor in sending a message.

Sometimes a message will need to be encrypted. You can expand this small, generic case study in many different directions.

Sample 5: Commercial Message-Processing System

This commercial message-processing system is typical for distributing and handling messages in the business community. A person inputs messages for processing. Outputs are the corrected messages. An organization's PPS and rules and regulations are the controlling factors. The mechanism that performs this activity is the computer information system. Like others in this chapter, this is a generic case study.

The input message is validated in accordance with the organization's PPS. The message is further compared for the format and any error in the text. If there is an error, it is corrected and the corrected text is sent back for validation. The repository is updated for future reference. The corrected message is the output from this process.

Figures 19.17 through 19.20 show the sample domain analysis and design for this example.

Data dictionary

C-Msg = [text correction | address correction]

Compare = {defects}

Correct message = ** no error

Corrected message = send to destination

F-Msg = {formatted message}

Human message = {input message}

PPS = {policy, procedures, and standards}

Rules/regulations = {organization guidance}

U-Msg = {updated message}

Update repository = {future references}

V-Msg = {verified message}

Validate message = ** validated message

Discussion. This is a generic case study for handling and distributing messages with the help of a computer. This generic solution can fit any

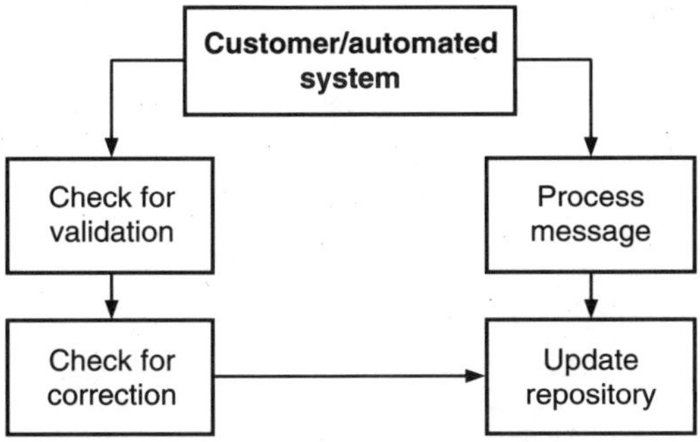

Figure 19.17 Architecture view of a commercial message-processing system.

real-life situation. This is simply a template to be reused. There can be many methods of checking on the input message. An actual person does not have to deliver the input message; this can be automated. The envelope that contains the message is thoroughly checked for accuracy. In some cases, time is a critical factor in sending a message.

Sometimes a message will need to be encrypted. You can expand this small, generic case study in many different directions.

Sample 6: Medical Hospital Information System

A medical hospital system consists of patients, employees, doctors, nurses, rooms, beds, and a medicine dispensary. There are also facili-

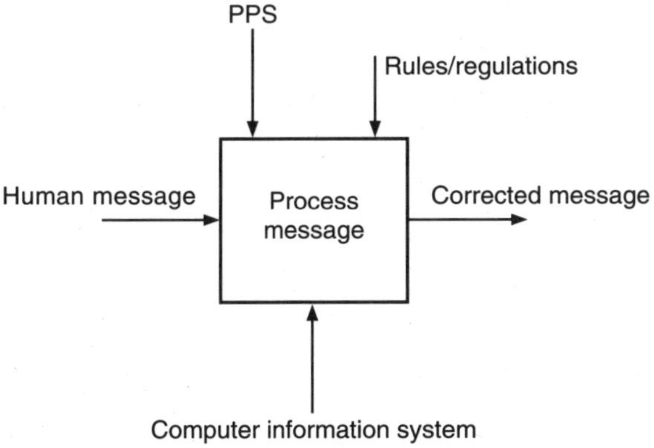

Figure 19.18 Context diagram for a commercial message-processing system.

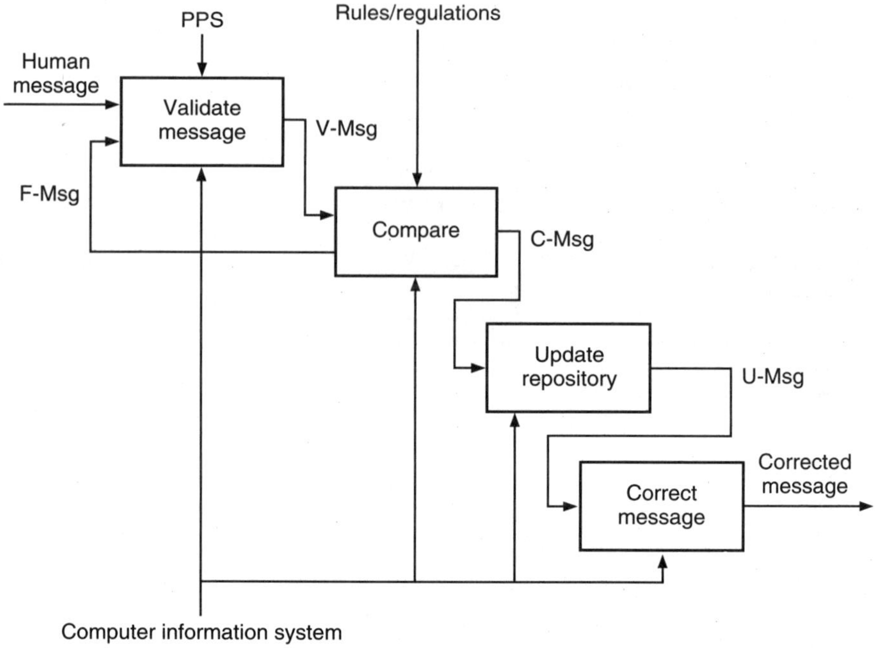

Figure 19.19 IDEFo model of a commercial message-processing system.

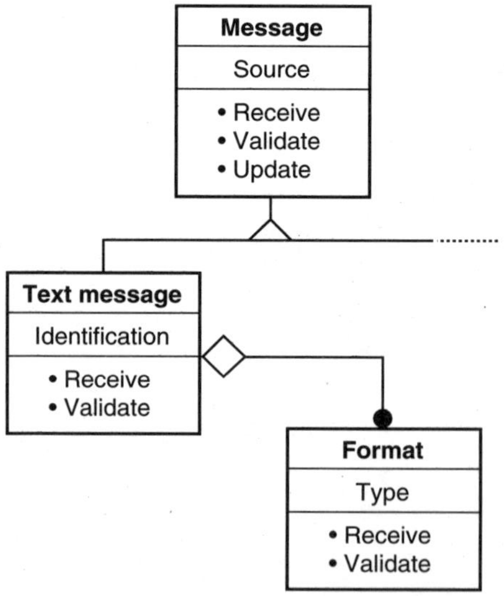

Figure 19.20 Object diagram of a commercial message-processing system.

ties for x rays, testing, and checking a patient with modern equipment. A patient is admitted into a hospital for a particular treatment or a checkup. There is also a laboratory for testing blood and so on.

Hospital records are kept on the computer for a long time. The patient may or may not have insurance. The patient pays for the services provided by the hospital. On release from the hospital, the patient is provided with complete guidelines, a medicine list, and precautions for the future.

The hospital hires doctors and nurses on salary, and it also hires part-time help. The hospital has many departments. The administrators manage the hospital with the help of automated systems.

Figures 19.21 through 19.24 show the sample domain analysis and design for this example.

Data dictionary

A-patient = {admitted patient}

Admit patient = {name + address + telephone + occupation + insurance}

D-patient = diagnosed patient

Diagnose ailment = {blood test + x ray + temperature + blood pressure + pulse rate}

Insurance = {name + address + telephone + insurance number}

Hospital PPS = {hospital policy, procedures, and standards}

Patient = {ailment + (doctor)}

Patient bill = guidance + (credit)

Patient doctor guidance = ** doctor advised patient for admission in the hospital

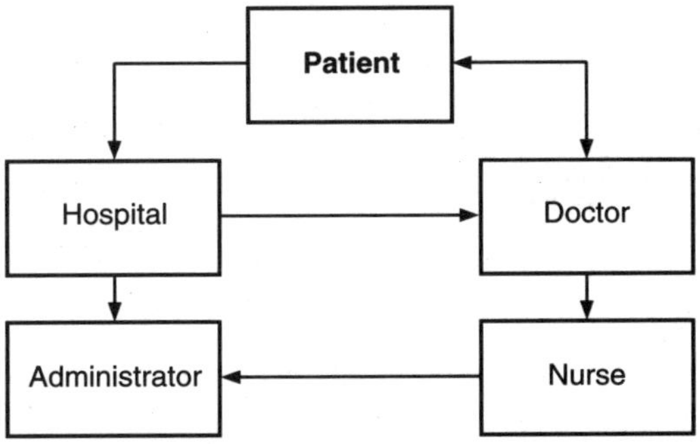

Figure 19.21 Architecture view of a medical hospital information system.

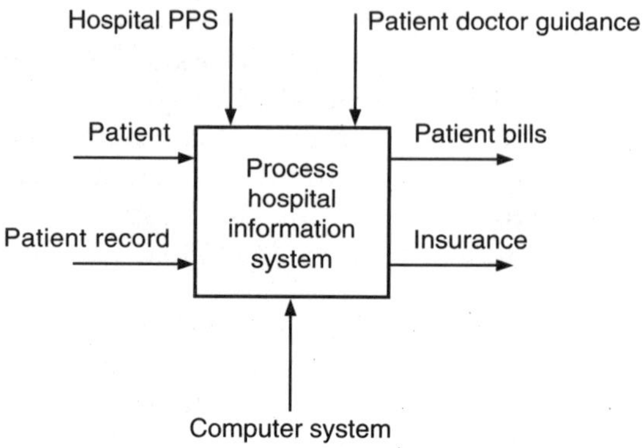

Figure 19.22 Context diagram for a medical hospital information system.

Release patient = {prescription + guidance} + bill payment + (finance office) + (update repository)

T-patient = treated patient

Treat patient = {medicine} + (doctor guidance)

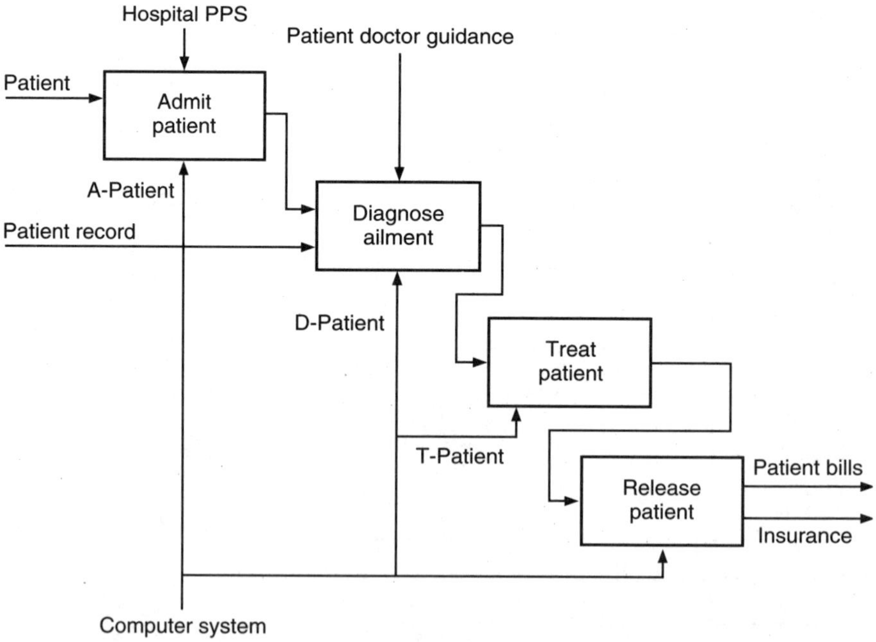

Figure 19.23 IDEFo model of a medical hospital information system.

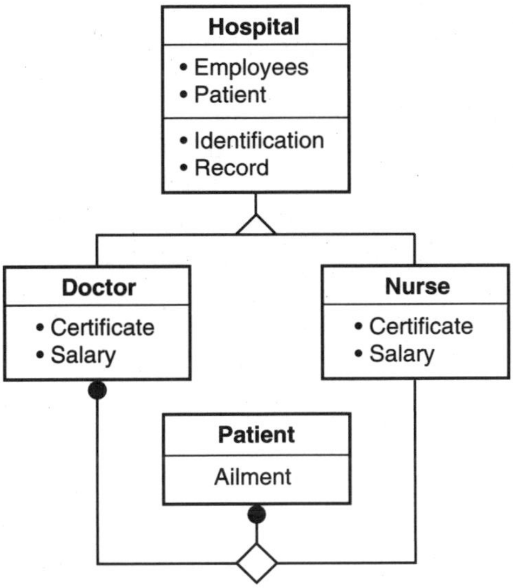

Figure 19.24 Object diagram of a medical hospital information system.

Discussion. This is a generic case study for a hospital. The patient can be an inpatient or an outpatient, but the process is practically the same. Normally, the doctor recommends that the patient be treated by a hospital. In an emergency, the patient goes directly to the hospital.

If the patient is admitted to the hospital, a room is allocated. The patient may have more than one doctor and more than one nurse, depending on the situation. How long a patient stays also depends on the ailment.

Bill payment is another concern of the hospital administration. Upon release of the patient, an administrator demands payment. The patient makes payment arrangements or directs the insurance company to pay the medical bills. The insurance company may not pay the full amount to the hospital. The patient is then responsible for paying the balance to the hospital.

Sample 7: Medical Clinic System

A medical clinic system consists of patients, employees, doctors, nurses, rooms, and examination beds. There is also modern equipment for checking patients. A patient calls to set up an appointment to see a doctor. The patient comes on time and discusses the situation with an employee at the front desk. If this is the patient's first visit, the desk receptionist asks the patient to fill out a form to provide a detailed life history and preferred mode of payment. The patient may or may not have insurance. The patient pays for the services provided by the doctor.

The doctor's office maintains the patient's records on a computer. After the examination, the doctor discusses with the patient complete guidelines, the medical prescription, tests, and precautions.

The patient again stops at the front desk to make a future appointment to see the doctor and to settle the payment. The doctor's office files the insurance claims and bills the patient for the balance amount.

Figures 19.25 through 19.28 show sample domain analysis and design for a medical clinic system.

Data dictionary

A-patient = {visiting patient}

Admit patient = {name + address + telephone + occupation + insurance}

D-patient = diagnosed patient

Diagnose ailment = {blood test + x ray + temperature + blood pressure + pulse rate}

Insurance = {name + address + telephone + insurance number}

Doctor PPS = {doctor policy, procedures, and standards}

Patient = {ailment + (previous doctor)}

Patient bill = guidance + (credit)

Patient doctor guidance = ** doctor advised patient for admission in the hospital

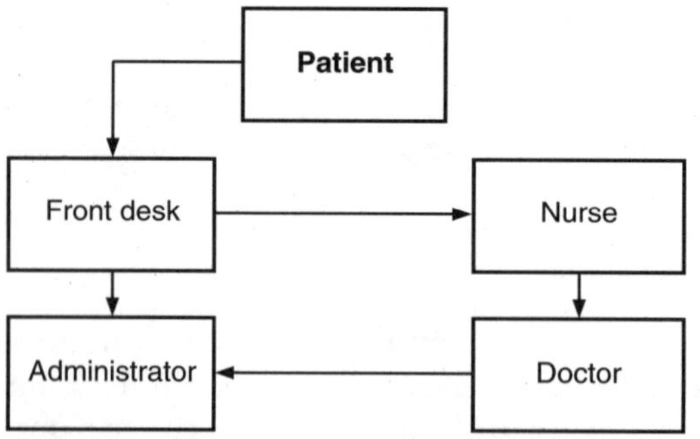

Figure 19.25 Architecture of a medical clinic system.

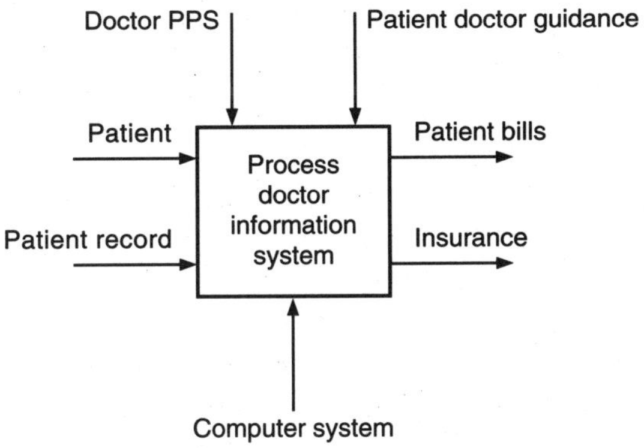

Figure 19.26 Context diagram for a medical clinic system.

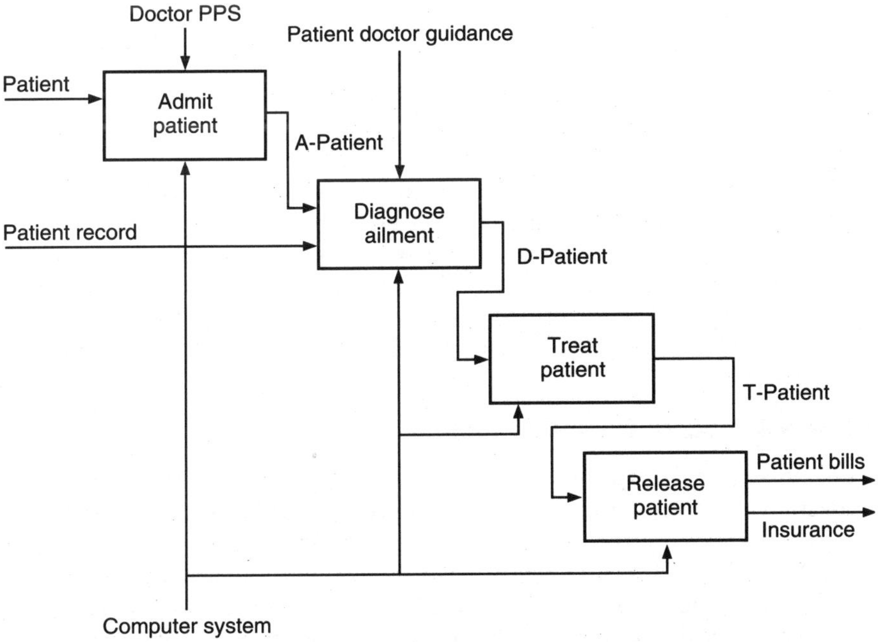

Figure 19.27 IDEFo model of a medical clinic system.

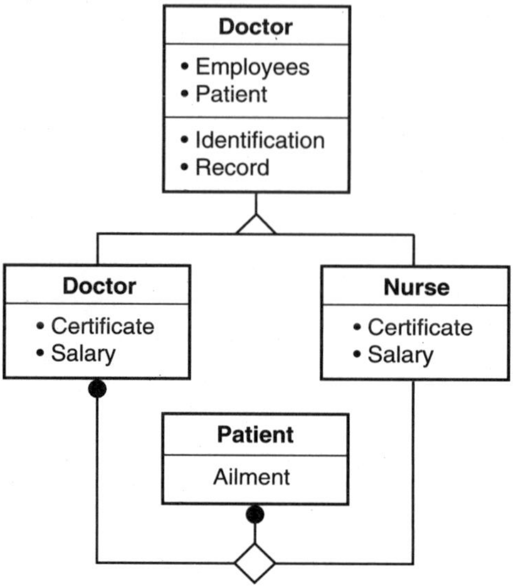

Figure 19.28 Object diagram of a medical clinic system.

Release patient = {prescription + guidance} + bill payment + (finance office) + (update repository)

T-patient = treated patient

Treat patient = {medicine} + (doctor guidance)

Discussion. This case study is a subset of the hospital domain. A patient visits a doctor's office. The patient might see a doctor that he or she has seen previously. The patient makes payment arrangements or directs the insurance company to pay the medical bills. The insurance company may not pay the full amount to the hospital. The patient is responsible for paying the balance to the doctor's office.

Sample 8: Modern Computer Technology

The owner of the Superior Grocery chain of stores wants to convert the existing information system to modern computer technology. The management is looking into intelligent cash registers that read bar codes, provide online sales, and print receipts for customers. Customers can pay by cash, check, charge card, coupon, or government draft. The cash registers should record the mode of customer payment and any balance amount for refund. The cash registers should be user-friendly and provide real-time response.

All the stores' computers are linked via a network to the central headquarters computer in a client/server relationship. The central management provides information such as policy, procedures, and standards for markup, taxes, sale prices, inventory control, advertisement, and profit margin to all the stores.

There is a store-by-store incentive program to reward employees for good behavior, helpful attitude, most sales, and team work.

All purchasing is conducted at the central headquarters and goods are distributed to each store as needed. All the stores update the central repository with each sale.

Figures 19.29 through 19.32 show the sample domain analysis and design process for this example.

Data dictionary:

C-inv = {sold items + returned items | damaged items}

Central PPS = *** organization policy, procedures, and standards

Computer network = *** client/server network, online, real-time system, batch system

Customer = {items + payment}

Items = *** any items in the store

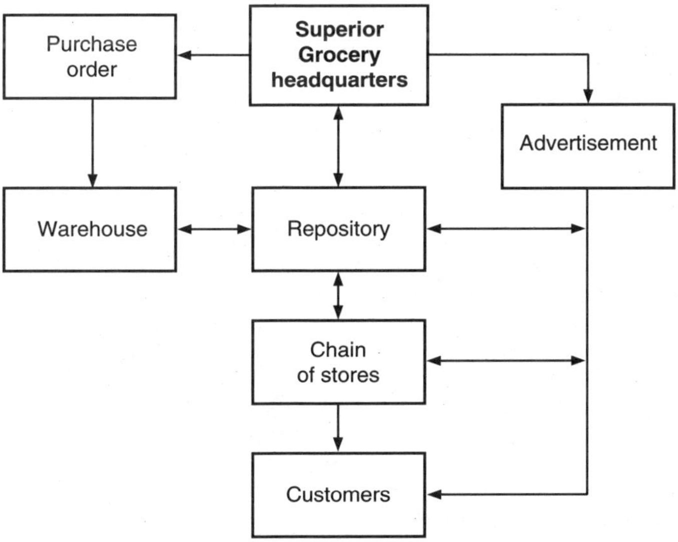

Figure 19.29 Architecture view of processing for the Superior Grocery chain of stores.

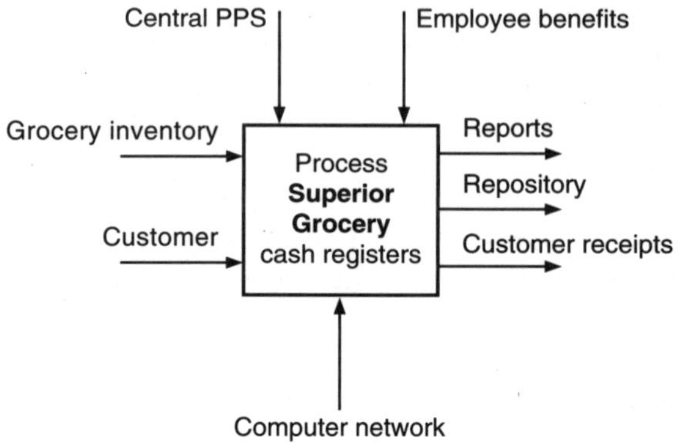

Figure 19.30 Context diagram for Superior Grocery.

Payment = [cash | check + ID | traveler's checks + ID | charge cards | coupons]

Customer receipts = [change back | refund | items cancelled]

Employee benefits = {bonus + recognition + retirement}

Grocery inventory = *** all items for sale in the stores

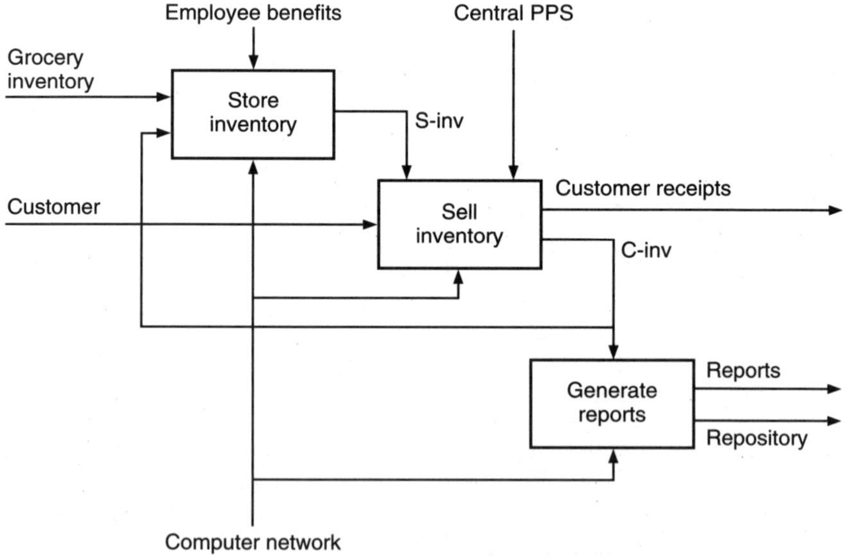

Figure 19.31 IDEFo model of processing for Superior Grocery stores.

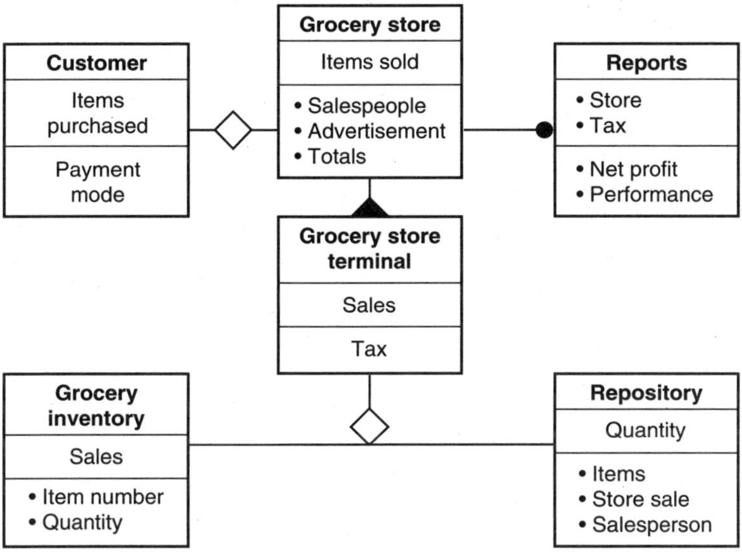

Figure 19.32 Object model of processing for Superior Grocery stores.

Reports = [daily sales + salesperson sales + inventory + taxes + weekly sales + monthly sales + yearly sales + gross profits + net profits]

Repository = ** all items, sale items, inventory

Discussion. This is a generic case study that can apply to hundreds of grocery stores—the principle is the same for any grocery store. There is always ground for modification if this solution does not fit the reuse situation.

Chapter

20

Case Study: Distributed Object Technology in a Three-Tier Client/Server Environment

This chapter presents a case study of an airline reservation system using distributed object technology in a three-tier client/server environment. The discussion of the case study focuses on distributed object technology, three-tier client/server environments, the service object, service object replication, partitioning, load balancing, and failover. A distributed object, three-tier, client/server development tool called Forté® will be referenced throughout this chapter. For more information concerning Forté and the associated product line, please refer to the Forté Internet site at http://www.forte.com.

An Airline Reservation System

- *Customer:* OnTime Airlines
- *Requirements and constraints:* To create a program to handle flight reservations and accept customer complaints. This system will also provide each customer service representative with an inbox for the purpose of receiving internal memos from another application. A note window will be developed in order to handle any special customer needs such as wheelchair access or a child traveling alone. A complaint window will allow any customers to register informal and formal complaints, the distinction being that a formal complaint must be in writing. The system must be able to handle up to 100 customer service representatives making airline reservations for customers who phone in requests. Note that there is currently no legacy system, but a flight schedule and fare information database exists. See Fig. 20.1 for the window flow diagram.

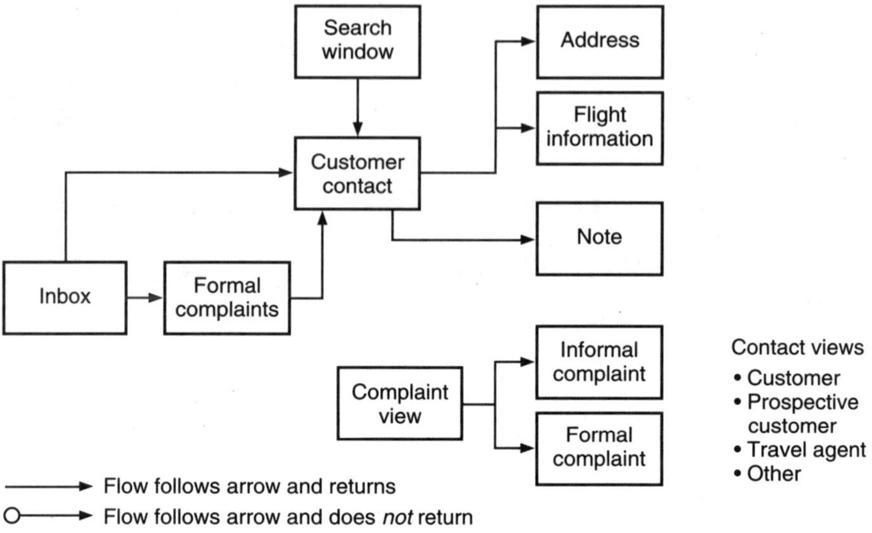

Figure 20.1 Window flow diagram.

Distributed objects

Distributed objects have the same properties as nondistributed objects, such as inheritance, abstraction, encapsulation, and polymorphism (overloading and overriding). However, distributed object technology allows objects to be distributed over many computers within a single environment. Objects in either a distributed or a nondistributed application have a single location. A distributed application can provide access to many computers and external connections through a single integrated system. In order to interact with a particular object in a distributed environment, the application must go to the computer at which the object is located; normally the object is located on the machine where it was created. For example, if developer A builds the complaint component and developer B builds the customer contact component, then the code that developer B constructs must go to developer A's computer in order to access the complaint component.

Three-tier client/server environment

An application environment is a combination of both hardware and software located at development and deployment sites. A two-tier client/server environment consists of the client (tier one) and server (tier two). A simple client/server application runs on two computers: a desktop computer (the client) and a database (the server), as shown in Fig. 20.2. For example Forté can access multiple databases residing on the same

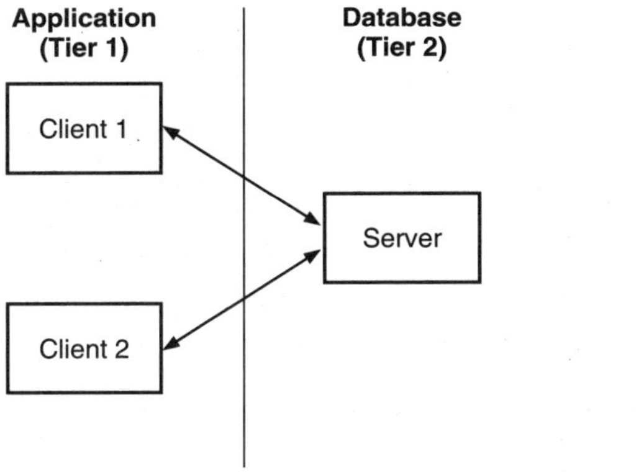

Figure 20.2 Two-tier client/server application.

server, using a single database resource manager. One method to accomplish this task is to create a file on the server, consisting of environment variables, then access these environment variables as needed. Other examples consist of third-generation language applications and API. The phrase "three-tier client/server" environment refers to a client (tier one), a business layer (tier two), and a server (tier three), as shown in Fig. 20.3. The business class logic for this case study is shown in Fig. 20.4.

Service object

A service object is a global object. It can be accessed from any method within a program and it is accessed in the same way as other objects. It is the means whereby an application communicates with external systems such as databases or other applications. For example, a single

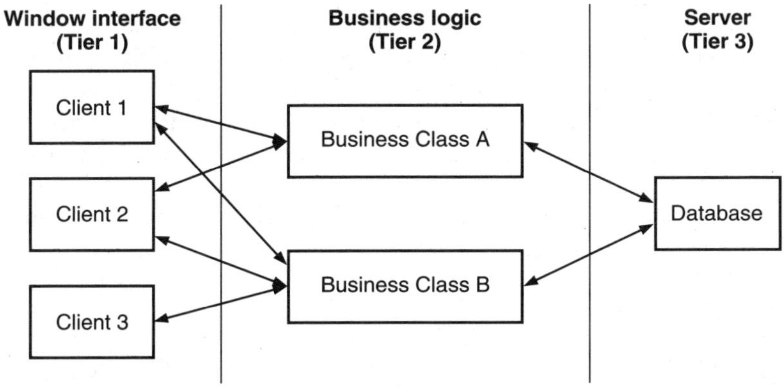

Figure 20.3 Three-tier client/server environment.

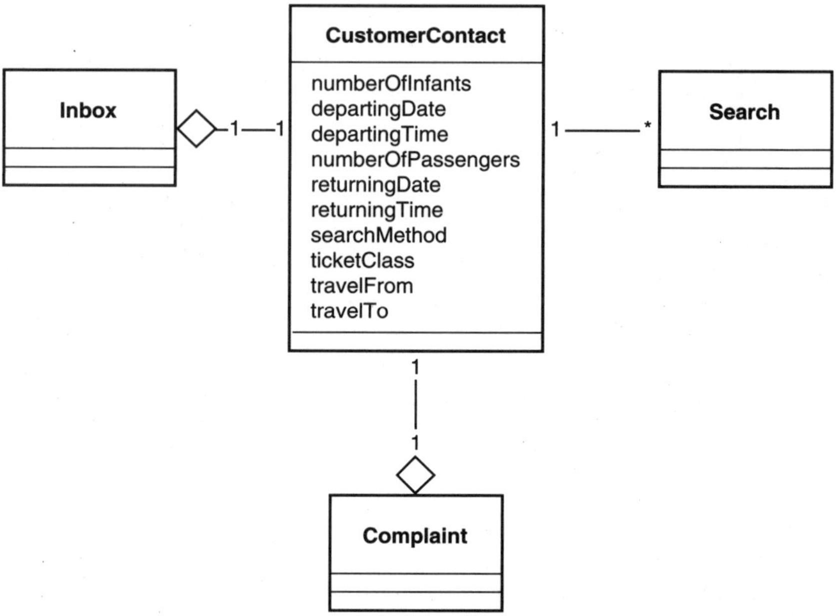

Figure 20.4 Business class logic.

database service object can be used to invoke multiple database sessions asynchronously.

Service objects are the objects that can be replicated and distributed on multiple computers in the environment. For instance, the Customer Contact window is displayed on up to 100 computers, and each computer can search the flight reservation database. Also, each computer must be able to register complaints on the Complaint database, located on the same server computer. The two objects used to interact with each database can reside on two different computers, thus reducing network traffic.

Shared objects have an automatic locking mechanism, which is necessary to prevent conflicts when multiple tasks attempt to access or change an object's state. Note that the object is locked until the transaction is complete. Thus, if two customer contact representatives were viewing the availability of seats on a flight, then whichever one clicked the Complete button first would hold the lock until the commit sequence was completed.

Replication

Replicating an object is the process of making a copy of an object in order to use it for failover and load balancing asynchronously. Once the object is replicated, it can be partitioned onto other computers—either client systems or servers in the environment. The objects to be replicated are service objects, such as the connection to an external corporate messaging application, and shared business services, such as the flight reservation database. Server partitions can also be replicated and applied for failover and load balancing synchronously.

Partitioning

A partition is made up of one or more service objects; it serves to decouple a distributed application from the details of its deployment in a runtime environment. In the partitioning process for this case study, the airline reservation application is configured for a specific target deployment environment. First, the application is divided into separate logical sections called (logical) *partitions*. Next, these partitions are assigned to the different computers in the specified deployment environment. Each partition is an independent process that can run on some computer. For example, this application has a client partition on the desktop that provides the graphical user interface. Other partitions include the DBMS server, where flight reservation and customer databases reside, which runs on a server machine. The 3GL-message system service is also partitioned onto a different computer. Forté automatically coordinates all communication between the partitions. As new hardware architectures or additional machines are added to the environment, Forté can repartition an application to take advantage of the new capabilities—without requiring an application rewrite. When a Forté runtime system starts up a partition, it creates a number of system objects that coexist with all the application objects within the partition. These runtime system objects support the running of each partition on its respective platform and the functioning of distributed objects as a single application. If a service object creates other objects, they will all be located in the same partition. For instance if a service object is used to fetch flight information from the flight reservation database, then the object that was created to hold this information will be on the same partition as the service object that created it.

Load balancing

A service object, such as the flight reservation database manager object, can be replicated any number of times for the purpose of load balancing. Load balancing means using multiple copies of a service object located on different computers for simultaneous usage by multiple clients. To provide load balancing, a service object must be replicated, then that replicate can be installed either on the computer on which it was created or on a different computer in the environment. By placing the flight reservation database service object on several computers, bottlenecks are reduced. Forté automatically provides a router partition that coordinates the requests for a service to the next available object, uses parallel processing, and coordinates to connections to all copies of a service object. For load balancing, parallel processing can be provided by distributing the demand for a service among a number of replicates of the partition that provides the service.

Failover

A service object can also be replicated any number of times for the purpose of failover, which is a means to provide a backup service object to be used if the primary object fails. Failover provides built-in fault tolerance for an application. The process for locating replicates of a service object onto different computers is the same for failover and load balancing. However, Forté will maintain a connection only to the primary service object and, if that fails, then the secondary replicate will be accessed. Until then, the secondary service object will not be used. In the case of combined failover and load balancing, the router partition is replicated, whereby one is the primary router and the replicate is the secondary router. If the primary router partition fails, then the secondary router partition automatically becomes active.

A sample use case has been added for generating a flight confirmation number. This use case has three parts: general information, analysis information, and design information.

Use case general information

- *Title:* Handle customer phone call
- *Functional area:* Contact management
- *Author:* Bob Jones
- *Business contact:* Joe Smith
- *Update date:* 3/11/98
- *Business context:* A customer calls an OnTime Airline customer service representative to book a ticket for a flight.
- *Actors:* Customer service representative; Supervisor
- *Overview:* The actor enters all relevant information needed to book a flight.

Use case analysis information

- *Preconditions:* The actor wishes to reserve a seat for a customer using the customer's desired flight destination, date, and time.
- *Basic course:* The actor provides the customer flight destination, date, and time to the system, then searches the system to confirm that the flight date and time exist. If the flight exists, then the system will return all available seat numbers. Based on customer preferences, the actor reserves the desired seat number. The system issues an associated confirmation number.
- *Postconditions:* The actor has reserved a seat number for the customer.
- *Alternate course:* If the flight destination, date, and time are cross-referenced and no flights are found, then the system returns a message asking the actor to re-enter flight information.
- *Business rules:* If three unsuccessful attempts to reserve a seat on a flight are made, then the system suggests alternative routes using connecting flights.

Use case design information

- *Interface elements:* Customer Contact window
- *Preconditions:* The actor intends to search the flight reservations systems database.
- *Basic course:* The Customer Contact window is displayed on the screen. The Customer Contact window has a File menu bar at the top and a toolbar at the bottom of the screen.

The File menu has the following items:

Save: Saves the data on the current active screen.

Print: Prints the data on the current active screen. The windows default printer is used to print a bitmap image of the window.

Close: Closes the current active screen.

The toolbar provides shortcuts to other windows or menu items.

When the Customer Contact window is being displayed, there are validations for the following fields:

Departing date and time:	This date should be the same as today or later than today.
Arriving date and time:	This date should be the same as or later than the departing date.
Destination information:	Both cities and states must exist in the database.

- *Postconditions:* The actor returns a confirmation number to the customer.
- *Alternate course:* The actor searches for flight information with the given information. The database returns more than one possible match. The actor redefines the search criteria, then selects a flight that is suitable to the customer.

Field:	*Field Name:*	*Type:*
Requirements	First name	String
	Middle	String
	Last name	String
	Address	String
	City	String
	State	String
	Zip	TextData
	Home phone	TextData
	Returning date	DateTimeData
	Travel from	String
	Travel to	String
	Search criteria	Integer
	Office phone	TextData
	Total number of passengers	Integer
	Number of infants	Integer
	Departing date	DateTimeData
	Travel class	Integer

Figure 20.5 shows the Customer Contact window. From this window, the actor can navigate to any of the other windows. Figure 20.6 is the Customer Contact window with customer information and a flight confirmation number filled in.

Discussion. The flight reservation system application is platform-independent; the same program can run on any supported client system. Thus, this distributed application can be deployed in either a

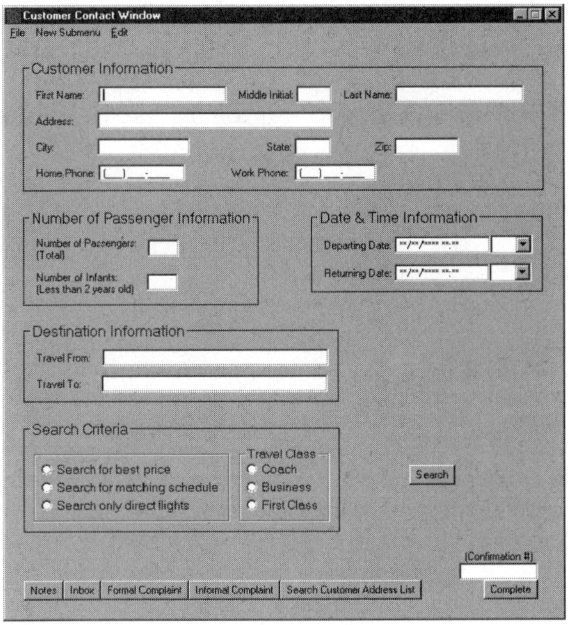

Figure 20.5 Customer Contact Window.

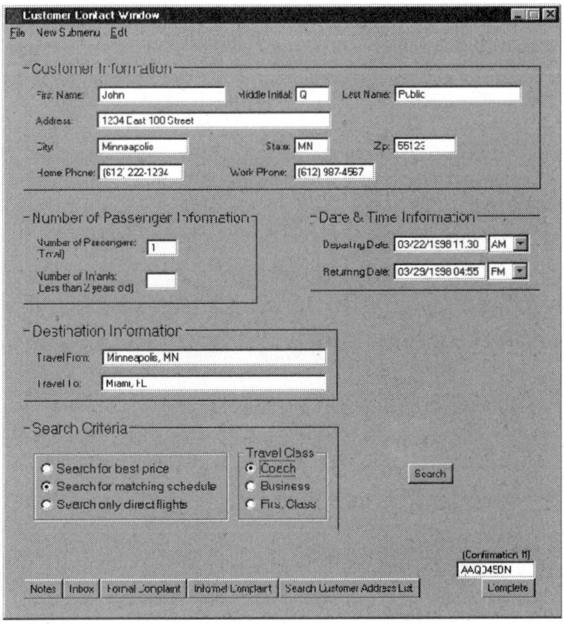

Figure 20.6 Flight information.

single environment or multiple environments, where the effort in deploying in multiple environments consists of system administrative overhead. (*Sources:* Forté Software, Inc., 1800 Harrison St., Oakland, CA 94612; Born Information Services Group, 445 East Lake St., Suite 120, Wayzata, MN 55391.)

Appendix A

Acronyms

ACAP	Analyst Capability
ADL	Ada Design Language
ADS	Aion Development System
AEXP	Application Experience
AI	Artificial Intelligence
ANSI	American National Standards Institute
API	Application Program Interface
CASE	Computer-Aided Software Engineering
CCSOM	*Computer Center Software Operational Manual*
CDR	Critical Design Review
CDRL	Contract Data Requirements List
CFD	Control Flow Diagram
CISAM	Computer Instruction Set Architecture Manual
CLIN	Contract Line Item Number
CM	Configuration Management
CMM	Capability Maturity Model
COCOMO	Constructive Cost Model
COM	Common Object Model
CORBA	Common Object Request Broker Architecture
COTS	Commercial Off-The-Shelf
CPM	Critical Path Method
CPU	Central Processing Unit
CSC	Computer Software Component
CSCI	Computer Software Configuration Item
CSDM	Computer Software Development Methodology

CSOM	Computer System Operator Manual
CSU	Computer Software Unit
DADP	Domain Analysis and Design Process
DBDD	Database Design Document
DBMS	Database Management System
DCE	Distributed Computing Environment
DCI	Distributed Computing Infrastructure
DCOM	Distributed Common Object Model
DD	Data Dictionary
DDD	Domain Data Dictionary
DDL	Data Definition Language
DDM	Domain Dynamic Model
DE	Domain Engineering
DFD	Data Flow Diagram
DFM	Domain Functional Model
DID	Data Item Description
DII	Dynamic Invocation Interface
DIM	Domain Information Model
DML	Data Manipulation Language
DOD	Department of Defense
DOE	Distributed Object Environment
DOI	Distributed Object Infrastructure
DOM	Distributed Object Model
DOT	Distributed Object Technology
DPM	Domain Prototype Model
DSD	Data Structure Diagram
DSOM	Distributed System Object Model
DSSA	Domain-Specific Software Architecture
EC	Estimated Cost
ELOC	Estimated Line of Code
ER	Entity Relationship
EST	Eastern Standard Time
EV	Earned Value
FCA	Functional Configuration Audit
FODA	Feature-Oriented Domain Analysis
FQT	Formal Qualification Testing
FSE	Forward Software Engineering
GA	Generic Architecture

GFS	Government-Furnished Software
GSA	Generic Solution Architecture
GUI	Graphic User Interface
HOOD	Hierarchical Object-Oriented Design
HPO	High-Performance Option
HWCI	Hardware Configuration Item
ICAM	Integrated Computer-Aided Manufacturing
ICT	Intelligent CASE Tools
IDD	Interface Design Document
IDEF	CAM Definition
IDL	Interface Definition Language
IEEE	Institute of Electrical and Electronics Engineers
IIOP	Internet Inter-ORB Protocol
I/O	Input/Output
IORL	Input/Output Requirements Language
IORTD	Input/Output Relationships and Timing Diagram
IRD	International Resources Dictionary
IRP	Iterative Refinement Process
IRS	Interface Requirements Specification
ISO	International Standards Organization
IV&V	Independent Verification and Validation
JODA	Joint Object-Oriented Domain Analysis
JSD	Jackson System Development
JSP	Jackson Structured Programming
KBMS	Knowledge-Based Management System
KBS	Knowledge-Based System
LOE	Labor of Efforts
LRM	Language Reference Manual
MAGEC	Mask and Application Generator and Environment Controller
MANPRINT	Manpower and Personnel Integration
MM	Man-month
MMI	Man-Machine Interfaces
MODSIM	Modular Simulation Language
MRE	Magnitude of Relative Error
NATO	North Atlantic Treaty Organization
NDS	Nondevelopment Software
OAM	Object Analysis Model

OBM	Object Behavior Model
OCD	Operational Concept Document
ODF	Object Definition Language
OIM	Object Information Model
OLE	Object Linking and Embedding
OMA	Object Management Architecture
OMG	Object Management Group
OML	Object Management Library
OO	Object-Oriented
OOD	Object-Oriented Design
OODB	Object-Oriented Database
OODBMS	Object-Oriented Database Management System
OODM	Object-Oriented Design Method
OOM	Object-Oriented Methodology
OOP	Object-Oriented Programming
OPM	Object Process Model
OOSD	Object-Oriented Structured Design
OSF	Open Software Foundation
OSI	Open System Interconnection
OTS	Off-the-Shelf
P-Spec	Process Specification
PC	Personal Computer
PCA	Physical Configuration Audit
PCAP	Programmer Capability
PDL	Program Design Language
PDR	Preliminary Design Review
PERT	Program Evaluation and Review Technique
PPD	Predefined Process Diagram
PSA	Program Statement Analyzer
PSL	Program Statement Language
PST	Pacific Standard Time
QA	Quality Assurance
QAS	Quality Assurance Section
RDM	Requirements Definition Model
RE	Re-software Engineering
RELY	Required Software Reliability
RFP	Request For Proposal
ROM	Read-Only Memory

RM	Refinement Method
RPC	Remote Procedure Call
RSE	Reverse Software Engineering
RSI	Report Specification Interface
RSL	Requirements Statement Language
RSO	Reusable Software Objects
RT	Requirements Tracer
RTE	Runtime Environment
RTL	Runtime Library
RUSE	Required Reusability
SA	Structured Analysis
SADT	Structured Analysis and Design Technique
SBD	Schematic Block Diagram
SCR	Software Cost Reduction
SD	Structured Design
SDD	Software Design Document
SDF	Software Development File
SDL	Software Development Library
SDP	Software Development Plan
SDR	System Design Review
SECP	Software Engineering Conversion Plan
SED	Software Engineering Design
SEDD	System Engineering Design Document
SEDP	Software Engineering Development Plan
SEI	Software Engineering Institute
SEMP	Software Engineering Maintenance Plan
SERA	Software Engineering Requirements Analysis
SII	Static Invocation Interface
SIOM	Software Input/Output Manual
SIP	Software Installation Plan
SOM	System Object Model
SOW	Statement of Work
Spec	Specification
SPM	Software Programmer's Manual
SPS	Software Product Specification
SQL	Structured Query Language
SREM	Software Requirements Engineering Methodology
SRP	Software Reuse Plan

SRR	System Requirements Review
SRS	Software Requirements Specification
SSA	Structured System Analysis
SSD	Strategies for System Development
SSDD	System/Segment Design Document
SSP	Software Support Plan
SSR	Software Specification Review
SSS	System/Segment Specification
STD	State Transition Diagram
StP	Software through Pictures
STR	Software Test Report
STT	State Transition Table
SUM	Software User's Manual
TAGS	Technology for the Automated Generation of Systems
TRR	Test Readiness Review
UCRA	User-Centered Requirements Analysis
UI	User Interface
UC	User Cases
VDD	Version Description Document
VDM	Vienna Development Methodology
VMVT	Virtual Machine Volatility Target
VEXP	Virtual Machine Experience
WBS	Work Breakdown Structure
WWW	World Wide Web

Appendix

B

Vendors for CASE Tools, Domain Analysis, and Design Methods

Vendors	*Products*
Aion Corporation 101 University Avenue Palo Alto, CA 94301	ADS
AI Corp 138 Technology Drive Waltham, MA 02254 617-891-6500	KBMS
American Management Systems 1777 North Kent Street Arlington, VA 22209 703-841-5507	Logiscope
Applied Business Technology Corp. 361 Broadway New York, NY 10013 212-219-8945	ABT Project Bridge, Workbench, Graphics, Metrics Manager
Ascent Logic Corporation 180 Rose Orchard Way, Suite 200 San Jose, CA 95134 408-943-0630	RDD-100
Berard Software Engineering 301-417-9884	BOCS

Business Objects, Inc. 2500 Sand Hill Road, Suite 240 Menlo Park, CA 94025 415-854-1500	BusinessObjects
CACI 3333 North Torrey Pines Court La Jolla, CA 92037 619-457-9681	MODSIM II
Cadre Technologies 222 Richmond Street Providence, RI 02903 401-351-5950	ObjectTeam, Teamwork/OOA, Teamwork/OOD, RqT
Chen & Associates 504-926-5765	ObjectModeler
Cisi-Ingenierie 2, rue Jules Vedrine 31400 Toulouse France (33) 6120 4324	HOOD
Dansk Datamatik Center Lundtoftevej 1 C DK-2800 Lyngby Denmark	VDM
Dynamics Research Corp. 60 Frontage Road Andover, MA 01810 508-475-9090	AdaMAT
Evergreen CASE Tools 8522 154th Avenue NE Redmond, WA 98052	Easy CASE Plus
GEC-Marconi 12110 Sunset Hills Road Reston, VA 22090 703-648-1551	GECOMO PLUS
Goddard Space Flight Center Greenbelt, MD 20771 301-286-7631	GOOD
Grady Booch c/o Rational 835 S. Moore Street	OOD

Lakewood, CO 80226 303-986-2405	
i-Logix Inc. 22 Third Avenue Burlington, MA 01803 617-332-8678	STATEMENT
IBM Corporation P.O. Box 700 Suffern, NY 10901 914-578-3535	S-JAD AD/Cycle
Interactive Development Environments, Inc. 595 Market Street, 12th Floor San Francisco, CA 94105 415-543-0900	StP
MAGEC Al Lee & Associates P.O. Box 260319 Plano, TX 75026 214-248-0823	MAGEC
MARK V Systems Limited 16400 Venture Blvd., Suite 303 Encino, CA 91436 510-658-9404	ObjectMaker, ProcessMaker, MethodMaker, Ada Code Generation, C++ Code Generation
Meridian/Verdix Co. 10 Pasteur Street Irvine, CA 92718 714-727-0700	Ada Compiler C++ CASE Tools
Meta Systems, Ltd. 315 E. Eisenhower, Suite 200 Ann Arbor, Michigan 48108 313-663-6027	PSL/PSA
Michael Jackson Systems Ltd. 22 Little Portland Street London WIN 5AF United Kingdom (01) 499 6655	JSD
Objectivity Inc. 800 El Camino Real Menlo Park, CA 94025 415-688-8000	Objectivity/DB

Object Design One New England Executive Park Burlington, MA 01803	ObjectDesign, ObjectStore
Palladio Software Corp. 16535 W. Bluemound Road, Suite 360 Brookfield, WI 53005 414-789-5253	Palladio Software
Project Technology, Inc. 2560 Ninth Street, Suite 214 Berkeley, CA 94710 415-845-1484	OOA
Software Development Concepts 424 West End Avenue, 11 E New York, NY 10024	WARD/MELLOR
Software Productivity Solutions 122 N. Fourth Avenue Indialantic, FL 32903 407-984-3370	Ali, Classic-Ada/ONTOS
Stepstone Corp. 75 Glenn Road Sandy Hook, CT 06482	Objective-C
Synthesis Computer Technologies 5199 E. Pacific Coast Highway Long Beach, CA 90804 213-494-4069	case/ap
Teledyne Brown Engineering Cumming Research Park 300 Sparkman Drive NW P.O. Box 070007 Huntsville, Alabama 35807 800-633-4675	RT TAGS
Transform Logic Corp. 8502 East Viade Venture Scottsdale, AZ 85258 800-872-8296	DesignAid II
Venue 1549 Industrial Road San Carlos, CA 94070 800-228-5352	Medley

Verilog Inc. 3010 LBJ Freeway, Suite 900 Dallas, TX 75234 214-241-6595	Verilog Object
Westinghouse Electric Corp. P.O. Box 17319-MS A455 Baltimore, MD 21203 410-765-9966	ReuSE

Appendix

C

Software Reuse Repositories

Vendors	*Products*
Apiary Inc. 501-376-3600 http://www.apiary.com	Developer Suite for NetWare
Austin Software Foundry 512-329-6697 http://www.foundry.com	AdAPT Advanced Application
Bits & Pixels 512-335-7315 http://www.bitpix.com	Java Intelligent Agent Library
Black Ice Software Inc. 603-673-1019 http://www.blackice.sendfax.com	Image SDK Plus, Monochrome Generic Printer, TIFF SDK
Channel Inc. 617-861-7824 http://www.dbcad.it	DB CAD DEV Partitioning Toolkit
ChipChat 313-565-4000 http://www.chipchat.com	ChipChat Communications Objects
Cimmetry Systems Inc. 514-735-3219 http://www.cimmetry.com	VCET, EDAT
Code Farms Inc. 613-838-4819 http://www.codefarms.com	Pattern Template Library

Digital/Cushing Group 110 Spit Brook Road Nashua, NH 03062 800-392-0071	ObjectBroker
Egerter Software 519-641-7542 http://www.egerter.com	Power Render
Expersoft 5825 Oberlin Drive San Diego, CA 92121 619-824-4100	CORBAplus
FarPoint Technologies 919-460-4551 http://www.fpoint.com	Calendar ObjX
Front Desk Source Code 514-597-1692 http://www.iti-logical.com	Front Desk Source Code
Genitor Corp. 888-436-4867 http://www.genitor.com	Genitor Skeleton Classes
Greenleaf Software Inc. 972-248-2561 http://www.gleaf.com/~gleaf	Comm++ For MFC
Griffin Technologies 913-832-2070 http://www.griftech.com	Langner Universal Communications API
ILOG Inc. 415-390-9000 http://www.ilog.com	ILOG Views, ILOG Vision, ILOG Rules, ILOG Server
Interactive Network Technologies Inc. 703-975-7434 http://www.int.com	Carnac
Intelligent Documents Inc. 403-434-2600 http://www.intelligentdoc.com	Document Workbench
IONA Technologies 201 Broadway, Floor 3 Cambridge, MA 02139 617-679-0900	Orbix

LEAD Technologies Inc. 704-332-5532 http://www.leadtools.com	LEADTOOLS ActiveX
Netronic +49 24 08 1410 http://www.netronic.de	VARCHART Diagram
Netron Inc. 416-636-8333 http://www.netron.com	Netron Fusion
ObjectSpace 972-934-2496 http://www.objectspace.com	Standards<ToolKit> (OCX) 16/32 Pro
Objects Arts Inc., Software Div. http://www.objectarts.com/software	Object Text
ObjectSpace 972-934-2496 http://www.objectspace.com	Communications<toolKit>, Internet<ToolKit>, Web<ToolKit>, Foundations<ToolKit>
Okino Computer Graphics 905-672-9328 http://www.okino.com	NuGraf Developer's 3D Toolkit
OMG 492 Old Connecticut Path Framingham, MA 01701 508-820-4300	CORBA
Page Technology Marketing Inc. 619-658-0191 http://www.tfb.com/pagetech/	PCLTool SDK
Prentice Hall Professional Technical Reference 201-236-7000 http://www.prenhall.com	*Not Just Java*
Quadbase Systems Inc. 408-982-0835 http://www.quadbase.com	CyberChart
Raima Corp. 206-515-9477 http://www.raima.com	Raima Object Manager
Rogue Wave Software Inc. 541-754-3010 http://www.roguewave.com	Inter.Net.h++, Math.h++, Net.h++, Threads.h++, Tools.h++, Standard C++ Library

Sheridan Software Systems Inc. 516-753-0985 http://www.shersoft.com	ActiveListBar, ClassAssist, WinAPI Oblets
SunSoft 2550 Garcia Avenue Mountain View, CA 94043 1-800-sunsoft	NEO, Joe
TeraTech-Tools for Programmers 800-447-9120 http://www.teratech.com/teratech	Dazzle/VB
Videotex Systems Inc. 800-888-4336 http://www.videotexsystems.com	T-BASE
Vireo Software 508-264-9200 http://www.vireo.com	Driver::Works for Windows NT/WDM
Visigenic 800-632-2864 www.visigenic.com	VisiBroker

Appendix

D

References

Association for Computing Machinery (ACM), *Ada Letters,* July/August 1997.
Association for Computing Machinery (ACM), *Ada Letters,* May/June 1992.
Association for Computing Machinery (ACM), *Software Engineering Notes,* January 1993.
Association for Computing Machinery (ACM), *Communications,* December 1997.
Ada Information Clearing House, Fall 1997.
Agresti, W. W., *Tutorial: New Paradigms for Software Development,* The Computer Society Press, Los Angeles, 1986.
Allworth, S.T., Zobel, R.N., *Introduction to Real-Time Software Design,* Springer-Verlag, New York, 1987.
Application Development Trends, An SPG/ULLO Publication (papers), June 1997.
Arango, G., Prieto-Diaz, R., *Domain Analysis: Concepts and Research Directions,* 1990.
Arango, Guillermo, "Domain Engineering for Software Reuse," Ph.D thesis, University of California at Irvine, 1988.
Ardis, Mark A., Berztiss, Alfs T., Formal Verification of Programs, SEI Curriculum Modules, Pittsburgh, Pennsylvania, 1988.
Bailin, S., *Domain Analysis with KAPTURE,* CTA Inc., Rockville, Maryland, 1992.
Bailin, S., Moore, J., *The KAPTURE Environment: An Operation Concept,* CTA Inc., Rockville, Maryland, 1992.
Baldo, James, *Reuse in Practice Workshop Summary,* IDA, PA, 1989.
Balzer, R., Cheathm, T., and Green, C., "Software Technology in the 1990's: Using a New Paradigm," *Computer,* vol. 16, no. 11, November 1983, pp. 39–46.
Basili, V., "Viewing Maintenance as Reuse-Oriented Software Development," *IEEE Software,* January 1990, pp. 19–25.
Bauer, F.L., "Programming as an Evolutionary Process," *Proceedings 2nd International Conference on Software Engineering,* IEEE Computer Society, New York, January 1976, pp. 222–234.
Berard, V. Edward, *Essays on Object-Oriented Software Engineering,* vol. 1, Prentice Hall, Englewood Cliffs, New Jersey, 1993.
Bergland, G.D., Gordon, R.D., *Software Design Strategies,* IEEE Computer Society Press, Washington, D.C., 1981.
Birrell, N.D., Ould, M.A., *A Practical Handbook for Software Development,* Cambridge University Press, New York, 1985.
Bjorner, D., Jones, C.B., *Formal Specifications and Software Development,* Prentice Hall, Englewood Cliffs, New Jersey, 1982.
Blank, J., Krijger, M. J., *Software Engineering: Methods and Techniques,* Wiley Interscience, New York, 1983.
Boehm, B., "Software Engineering," *IEEE Transactions on Computers,* vol. C-25, no. 12, December 1976, pp. 1226–1241.

Boehm, B., *Software Engineering Economics,* Prentice Hall, Englewood Cliffs, New Jersey, 1981.

Boehm, B., "A Spiral Model of Software Development and Enhancement," *IEEE Computer,* vol. 21, no. 5, May 1988.

Bohm, C., Jacopini, G., "Flow Diagrams, Turing Machines and Languages with only Two Formation Rules," *Communications of the ACM,* vol. 9, no. 4, May 1966.

Booch, G., *Object-Oriented Analysis and Design with Applications,* Addison-Wesley, Reading, Massachusetts, 1994.

Booch, G., "Object-Oriented Development," *IEEE Transactions on Software Development,* vol. SE-12, no. 2, February 1986, pp. 211–221.

Booch, G., *Software Engineering with Ada,* Benjamin/Cummings, Menlo Park, California, 1982.

Brackett, John W., "Software Requirements," *SEI Curriculum Module SEI-CM-19-1.0,* December 1988.

Braun, Christian, "Software Reuse," presentation, GTE Federal Systems, University of Southern California, Information Sciences Institute, 1992.

Braun, Christian, Hatch, William, Ruegsegger, Theodore, "Domain Specific Software Architectures—Command & Control," GTE Federal Systems, University of Southern California, Information Sciences Institute.

SEI Bridge, Software Engineering Institute, Carnegie Mellon University, Pittsburgh, Pennsylvania, December 1992.

Bruns, Glenn, Potts, Colin, *Domain Modeling Approaches to Software Development,* technical report, Microelectronics Computer Technology Corp., Texas, 1988.

Budde, R., Kuhlenkamp, K., Mathiassen, L., and Zullighoven, H., *Approaches to Prototyping,* Springer-Verlag, New York, 1984.

Budgen, David, Sincovec, Richard, "Introduction to Software Design," *SEI Curriculum Module SEI-CM-2-1.2* (Preliminary), July 1987.

Buhr, R.J.A., *System Design with Ada,* Prentice Hall, Englewood Cliffs, New Jersey, 1984.

Cameron, John, *JSP & JSD: The Jackson Approach to Software Development,* IEEE Computer Society Press, Washington, D.C., 1989.

Carmichael, A., *Object Development Methods,* SIGS Publication, New York, 1994.

Case, A., *Team System Analysis,* Prentice Hall, Englewood Cliffs, New Jersey.

Central Archive for Reusable Defense Software (CARDS), draft, 1992.

Chen, P.P., "The Entity-Relationship Model—Toward a Unified View of Data," *ACM Transactions on Database Systems,* vol. 1, March 1976, pp. 9–36.

CIO magazine, Section 1, October 15, 1997, pp. 55–62.

Clement, P.C., Parker, R.A., Parnas, D.L., Shore, J.E., and Brit, K.H., *A Standard Organization for Specifying Abstract Interfaces,* Naval Research Laboratory, Washington, D.C.

Coad, Peter, *Object Models: Strategies, Pattern & Applications,* Prentice Hall, Englewood Cliffs, New Jersey, 1994.

Coad, Peter, Nocola, J., *Object-Oriented Programming,* Prentice Hall, Englewood Cliffs, New Jersey, 1993.

Coad, Peter, Yourdon, Edward, *Object-Oriented Analysis,* Prentice Hall, Englewood Cliffs, New Jersey, 1990.

Cohen, Sholom, "A Model Base for Software Engineering," Software Engineering Institute, Carnegie Mellon University, Pittsburgh, Pennsylvania, 1992.

Coleman, Derek, *Object-Oriented Development: The Fusion Method,* Prentice Hall, Englewood Cliffs, New Jersey, 1994.

Collofello, James S., "Introduction to Software Verification and Validation," *SEI Curriculum Module,* 1988.

Collofello, James S., "The Software Technical Review Process," *SEI Curriculum Module SEI-CM-3-1.2* (Preliminary), July 1987.

Communications Week, July 1992.

Computer Design, A Pennwell Publication, April 1993.

Computer Design, A Pennwell Publication, August 1993.

Computerworld, May 1992.

Connor, M.F., "Structured Analysis and Design Technique (SADT) Introduction," *Engineering Management Conference Record,* IEEE, May 1980, pp. 138–143.

Cook, Capt. David, *Object Oriented Development & Object Oriented Programming in Ada and Ada 9X,* U.S. Air Force Academy, 1992.
Cross, N., *Development in Design Methodology,* John Wiley, New York, 1984.
CrossTalk, The Journal of Defense Software Engineering, Software Technology Support Center, August and October 1992.
CTA Inc., JIAWG Reuse System Description, Ridgecrest, California, 1990.
Dabrowski, Christopher, Kirkendall, Thomasin, *Preliminary Report on Domain Analysis Methods,* Computer Systems Lab, NIST, 1992.
Danforth, Scott, Koenen, Paul, and Tate, Bruce, *Objects for OS/2,* Van Nostrand Reinhold, New York, 1994.
Datamation, A Cahners Publication, October 1992.
Davis, C.G., Jajodia, S., Ng, P.A., and Yeh, R.T., *Entity-Relationship Approach to Software Engineering,* North Holland, New York, 1983.
DBMS Client/Server Computing, An M&T Publication, January 1993.
DEC Professional, April 1992.
Defense Electronics, A Cardiff Publication, February 1993.
DeMarco, T., *Structured Analysis and System Specification,* Prentice Hall, Englewood Cliffs, New Jersey, 1979.
Dijkstra, E.W., Dahl, F., and Hoare, C.A.R., *Structured Programming,* Academic Press, New York, 1972.
Domain Analysis Guidelines, draft, DOD Software Reuse Initiative, 1992.
Domain Engineering Guidebook, Software Productivity Consortium, 1992.
Druffel, L., "Software Technology for Adaptable, Reliable Systems—Program Strategy," *SIGSOFT Software Engineering Notes,* vol. 8, April 1983.
Dusink, E.M., Van Katwijk, J., "Reflections on Reusable Software and Software Components," Technical University, Delft, The Netherlands, 1992.
Embedded Systems, A Miller Freeman Publication, April 1991.
Embedded Systems, A Miller Freeman Publication, March 1992.
"Entering ORB-it," *Software Magazine,* January 1997.
Ewald, Alan, Roy, Mark, "Distributed Objects," *Object Magazine,* January 1997.
Fairly, R., *Software Engineering Concepts,* McGraw-Hill, New York, 1985.
Federal Computer Week, August 1992.
Federal Computer Week, August 1993.
Firth, Robert, Wood, Bill, Pethia, Rich, Roberts, Lauren, Mosley, Vickey, and Doice, Tom, *A Classification Scheme for Software Development Methods,* technical report, Software Engineering Institute, Carnegie Mellon University, Pittsburgh, Pennsylvania, November 1987.
Fox, J.M., *Software and Its Development,* Prentice Hall, Englewood Cliffs, New Jersey, 1982.
Freeman, Peter, Wasserman, Anthony, *Tutorial on Software Design Techniques,* IEEE Computer Society, Washington, D.C., 1983.
Gane, C., Sarson, T., "Structured Systems Analysis: Tools and Techniques," *Computer,* July 1977.
Gommaa, H., "Software Development of Real-Time Systems," *Communication,* ACM 29, July 1986, pp. 657–668.
Goodenough, John B., Borger, Mark W., Ada Usage/Performance Specification, Software Engineering Institute, *ACM Ada Letters,* Fall 1990.
Government Computer News, August, October, and November 1992.
Government Computer News, Technology Report, March 31, 1997.
Gries, D., "A Note on a Standard Strategy for Development Loop Invariants and Loops," *Science of Computer Programming,* 1982.
Guttman, Michael, Matthews, Jason, *The Object Technology Revolution,* John Wiley, New York, 1995.
Harel D., *STATEMATE: A Working Environment for the Development of Complex Reactive Systems,* IEEE Press, New York, 1988, pp. 396–406.
Harel, D., Pnueli, A., and Sherman, R., "On the Formal Semantics of Statecharts," *Proceedings of the 2nd IEEE Symposium on Logic in Computer Science,* Ithaca, New York, June 22–24, 1987, IEEE Press, New York, 1987.
Henderson-Sellers, B., Edwards, J.M., *Object-Oriented Knowledge, Book Two: The Working Object,* Prentice Hall, Englewood Cliffs, New Jersey, 1994.

Hoare, C.A.R., "An Overview of Some Formal Methods for Program Design," *Computer,* September 1987.
Holibaugh, R., *JODA Method,* Software Engineering Institute, Carnegie Mellon University, Pittsburgh, Pennsylvania, 1992.
Hori, S., *CAM-I Long Range Planning Final Report for 1972,* Illinois Institute of Technology Research, Chicago, 1972.
HP Professional, November 1990.
Humphrey, Watts S., *CASE Planning and the Software Process,* technical report, CMU/SEI-89-TR-26.
Husa, J.D., "Stimulating Software Engineering Process—A Report of the Software Engineering Planning Group," *ACM SIGSOFT Software Engineering Notes,* vol. 8, no. 2, April 1983.
Hutt, A., *Object Analysis and Design: Description of Methods,* Irwin Professional Publishing, Burr Ridge, Illinois, 1994.
IBM, *SOM Objects Developer Toolkit, User Guide,* IBM, 1994.
IEEE, *Computer,* February 1991.
IEEE, *Computer,* August 1992.
IEEE, *Computer,* December 1992.
IEEE, *Computer,* June 1993.
IEEE, *Software,* September 1993.
IEEE, *Spectrum,* October 1990.
IEEE, *Spectrum,* January 1991.
IEEE, *Spectrum,* July 1992.
IEEE, *Spectrum,* September 1992.
IEEE, *Spectrum,* Annual Review, 1993.
IEEE, *IEEE Transactions on Software Engineering,* March 1991.
IEEE, *IEEE Transactions on Software Engineering,* December 1991.
IEEE, *IEEE Transactions on Software Engineering,* July 1992.
IEEE, *IEEE Transactions on Software Engineering,* April 1993.
Information Week, A CMP Publication, August 1992.
Information Week, A CMP Publication, January 1993.
Information Week, A CMP Publication, May 1993.
Information World, vol. 19, no. 27, July 7, 1997, p. 1.
Jackson, M., "The Jackson Design Methodology," *Infotec State of the Art Report, Structured Programming,* 1978.
Jacobson, Ivar, *Object-Oriented Software Engineering,* Addison-Wesley, Reading, Massachusetts, 1992.
Johnson, A.L., "Software Engineering Combines Management and Technical Skills," *SEI Bridge,* Software Engineering Institute, Carnegie Mellon University, Pittsburgh, Pennsylvania, August/September 1986.
Jorgensen, Paul C., "Requirements Specification Overview," *SEI Curriculum Module SEI-CM-1-1.2* (Preliminary), July 1987.
Journal of Object-Oriented Programming, A SIGS Publication, June 1991.
Kang, Kyo, Cohen, Sholom, Hess, James, Novak, William, and Peterson, Spencer, *Featured-Oriented Domain Analysis Feasibility Study,* Software Engineering Institute, Carnegie Mellon University, Pittsburgh, Pennsylvania, 1990.
Kasperson, Donna, *IEEE Software,* September 1994, p. 12.
Katzan, Harry, *Systems Design and Documentation,* Van Nostrand Reinhold, New York, 1976.
Khoshafian, Setrag, *Intelligent Offices: Object-Oriented, Multi-Media Information Management in Client / Server Architectures,* John Wiley, New York, 1992.
Lau, Christiana, *Object-Oriented Programming Using SOM and DSOM,* Van Nostrand Reinhold, New York, 1994.
Lee, Kenneth J., Rissman, Michael S., "An Object-Oriented Solution Example: A Flight Simulator Electrical System," *SEI Technical Report,* 1989.
Leveson, N.G. "Software Safety: Why, What, and How," *ACM Computing Surveys,* June 1986.
Liskov, B., Zilles, S.N., "Programming with Abstract Data Types," *ACM SIGPLAN Notices,* vol. 9, no. 4, April, 1974, pp. 50–60.

Love, T., *Object Lessons,* A SIGS Publication, 1993.
Lubars, Mitchell, "Wide-Spectrum Support for Software Reusability," *Proceedings of the Workshop on Software Reusability and Maintainability,* National Institute of Software Quality and Productivity, Washington, D.C., 1987.
Martin, Charles F., *User-Centered Requirements Analysis,* Prentice Hall, Englewood Cliffs, New Jersey.
Martin, James, Odell, James, *Object-Oriented Methods,* Prentice Hall, Englewood Cliffs, New Jersey, 1994.
Martin, James, Odell, James, *Principles of Object-Oriented Analysis and Design,* Prentice Hall, Englewood Cliffs, New Jersey, 1993.
Mattison, R., *The Object-Oriented Enterprise: Making Corporate Information Systems Work,* McGraw-Hill, New York, 1994.
McMenamin, S.M., Palmer, J.F., *Essential Systems Analysis,* Yourdon Press, New York, 1984.
Meyer, Bertrand, *Object-Oriented Software Construction,* Prentice Hall, Englewood Cliffs, New Jersey, 1988.
Mills, Everald E., "Software Metrics," *SEI Curriculum Module SEI-CM-12-1.0,* October 1987.
Mills, H.D., "Stepwise Refinement and Verification in Box-Structured Systems," *IEEE Computer,* vol. 21, no. 6, June 1988, pp. 23–36.
Mills, H.D., Dyer, M., and Linger, R.C., "Cleanroom Software Engineering," *IEEE Software,* September 1987.
Moore, J., Bailin, S., "Domain Analysis: Framework for Reuse," in R. Prieto-Diaz and G. Arango, *Domain Analysis and Software Systems Modeling,* Ieee Computer Society Press, Los Alamitos, California, 1991.
More, Jorge J., Wright, Stephen J., *Optimization Software Guide,* SIAM, Philadelphia, 1993.
Mowbray, T., "An Introduction to CORBA," *CROSSTALK,* February 1997.
Network Computing, DCE, March 1, 1997, p. 109.
Network World, March 1993.
Nielsen, Kjell, *Object-Oriented Design with Ada,* Bantam Books, New York, 1992.
Object Magazine, A SIGS Publication, May 1991.
Object Management Group, "What is CORBA?," August 1997.
Objectivity, Inc., *Objectivity/DB, Documentation I & II,* 1991.
Palmer, J.F., "Integrating the Structured Techniques with JAD: Leveled Systems Development," *Working Paper Presented at the 12th Structured Methods Conference,* August 1987.
Parnas, D., "On the Criteria to be Used in Decomposing Systems into Modules," *Communication of the ACM,* vol. 15, December 1972.
Parnas, D.L., Clements, P.C., and Weiss, D.M., "The Modular Structure of Complex Systems," *IEEE Transactions on Software Engineering,* vol. SE-11, no. 3, March 1985.
Partsch, H., Steinbruggen, R., "Program Transaction Systems," *Computing Surveys,* vol. 15, no. 3, September 1983, pp. 199–236.
Peterson, James, *Design for Windows managers,* technical report, MCT, Texas 1986.
Peterson, Spencer, "Coming to Terms with Software Reuse Terminology: A Model-Based Approach," *SEI, ACM Software Engineering Notes,* April 1991.
Pohl, I., *C++ for Pascal Programmers,* Benjamin/Cummings, Menlo Park, California, 1991.
Prieto-Diaz, Ruben, "Domain Analysis: An Introduction," *ACM SIGSOFT Software Engineering Notes,* April 1990.
Prieto-Diaz, Ruben, "The Reuse Library Process Model," *STARS Reuse Library Program,* New York, March 1991.
Pyster, Arthur, Barnes, Bruce, *The Software Productivity Consortium Reuse Program,* IEEE, 1988.
Reuse Driven Software Processes Guide Book, Software Productivity Consortium, 1993.
Reuse Library Process Model, STARS Program, 1991.
RIG Technical Report, RTR-0001 RIG Glossary, 1993.
Rombach, H. Dieter, "Software Specification: A Framework," *SEI Curriculum Module SEI-CM-11-1.0,* October 1987.

Ross, D.T., "Applications and Extensions of SADT," *IEEE Computer,* vol. 18, no. 4, April 1985, pp. 25–34.
Ross, D.T., "Douglas Ross Talks about Structured Analysis," *IEEE Computer,* vol. 18, no. 7, July 1985, pp. 80–88.
Royce, W.W., "Managing the Development of Large Software Systems," *Proceedings 9th International Conference on Software Engineering,* IEEE Computer Society, 1987, pp. 328–338.
Rumbaugh, James, Blaha, Michael, Premerlani, William, Eddy, Frederick, and Lorensen, William, *Object-Oriented Modeling and Design,* Prentice Hall, Englewood Cliffs, New Jersey, 1991.
Rush, G., "A Fast Way to Define System Requirements," *Computerworld,* October 7, 1985.
Sathi, A., Morton, T., and Roth, S., "Callisto: An Intelligent Project Management System," *AI Magazine* vol. 7, no. 5, 1986, pp. 34–52.
Scacchi, Walt, "Models of Software Evolution: Life Cycle and Process," *SEI Curriculum Module SEI-CM-10-1.0,* October 1987.
Shlaer, Sally, Mellor, Stephen, *Object-Lifecycles: Modelling the World in States,* Prentice Hall, Englewood Cliffs, New Jersey, 1992.
Shlaer, Sally, Mellor, Stephen J., *Object Oriented Systems Analysis, Modelling the World in Data,* Yourdon Press, Englewood Cliffs, New Jersey, 1988.
Siegel, J., *CORBA Fundamentals and Programming,* OMG, John Wiley, New York, 1996.
Sodhi, Jag, *Computer Systems Techniques: Development, Implementation, and Software Maintenance,* TAB Professional and Reference, TAB Books, Blue Ridge Summit, Pennsylvania, 1990.
Sodhi, Jag, "Evaluation of Teaching SERA," *Seventh Annual National Conference for Ada Technology,* 1989.
Sodhi, Jag, *Managing Ada Projects Using Software Engineering,* TAB Professional and Reference, TAB Books, Blue Ridge Summit, Pennsylvania, 1990.
Sodhi, Jag, "Overview of Ada Features for Real-Time Systems," *Defense Science,* November 1988.
Sodhi, Jag, *Software Engineering Methods, Management, and CASE Tools,* McGraw-Hill, TPR, New York, 1991.
Sodhi, Jag, *Software Requirements Analysis and Specification,* McGraw-Hill, New York, 1992.
Sodhi, Jag, George, K.M., "Objects with Multiple Representations in Ada," *Seventh Annual National Conference for Ada Technology,* 1989.
Sodhi, Jag, Sodhi, Prince, *Object-Oriented Methods for Software Development,* McGraw-Hill, New York, 1996.
Software, A Sentry Publication, January 1992.
Software, A Sentry Publication, May 1992.
Software, A Sentry Publication, September 1992.
Software Development, A Miller Publication, October 1997.
Software Development, A Miller Publication, January 1998.
Spurr, Kathy, et al., *Software Assistance for Business Reengineering,* John Wiley, New York, 1994.
Stikeleather, J., Clarke, J., and Fingar, P, "Distributed Computing for Business," Technical Resource Connection.
Taylor, D., *Object-Oriented Information Systems,* John Wiley, New York, 1992.
Technical Review 1992, Software Engineering Institute, Carnegie Mellon University, Pittsburgh, Pennsylvania.
Teichrow, D., "PSL/PSA: A Computer Aided Technique for Structured Documentation and Analysis of Information Processing Systems," *IEEE Transaction Software Engineering,* vol. SE-3, no. 1, January 1977, pp. 41–48.
Tristram, Claire, *Lantimes,* December 18, 1997, p. 26.
The Starts Guide, NCC, Manchester M1 7ED.
U.S. Department of Defense, Deputy Assistant Secretary of the Air Force, *Ada and C++: A Business Case Analysis,* 1991.
U.S. Department of Defense, *Military Standard, Defense System Software Development,* DOD-STD-2167A, Washington, D.C.

U.S. Department of Defense MIL-STD-SDD (498), draft, Military Standard for Software Development and Documentation, December 1992.

U.S. Department of Defense, Proceedings of Software Technology Conference, U.S. Air Force Software Technology Support Center (STSC), September 1994.

U.S. Department of Defense Software Reuse Initiative Vision and Strategy, 1992.

U.S. Department of Defense, *U.S. Department of Air Force ESD Implementation Guide for DOD-STD-2167A System Software Development Standard,* MA, January 30, 1989.

U.S. Department of Defense Ada Joint Office, "Ada Methodologies: Concepts and Requirements" (Methodman Document), November 1982.

U.S. Department of Defense Global Protection Against Limited Strikes Software Reuse Strategy, 1992.

Van Warren, L., Beckman, B.C., *System for Retrieving Reusable Software,* NASA Tech. Briefs, 1993.

Ward, T. Paul, Bracket, W. John, *Object-Oriented Requirements Definition and Software Design,* Boston University, 1991.

Ward, T. Paul, Mellor, Stephen J., *Structured Development for Real-Time Systems,* vols. I, II, III, Yourdon Press, Englewood Cliffs, New Jersey, Prentice Hall, 1985.

Warnier, J.D., Orr, Kenneth T., *Structured Systems Development,* Yourdon Press, New York, 1977.

Wasserman, A.I., Pircher, P.A., and Muller, R.J., "An Object-Oriented Structured Design Method for Code Generation," *SIGSOFT Software Engineering Notes,* vol. 14, no. 1, January 1989, pp. 32–55.

Wirfs-Brock, Rebecca Wilkerson, Wiener, Lauren, *Designing Object-Oriented Software,* Prentice Hall, Englewood Cliffs, New Jersey, 1990.

Wirth, N., "Program Development by Stepwise Refinement," *Communications of the ACM,* vol. 14, no. 4, April 1971, pp. 221–227.

Wood, William, G., Long, John P., Wood, David P., *Classifying Software Design Methods,* technical report, CMU/SEI-89-TR-25.

Yourdon, E., ed., *Classics in Software Engineering,* Yourdon Press, New York, 1979.

Yourdon, Edward, Constantine, L. Larry, *Structured Design,* Yourdon Press, New York, 1978.

Zave, P., "An Operational Approach to Requirements Specification for Embedded Systems," *IEEE Transactions on Software Engineering,* vol. 8, no. 3, May 1982, pp. 250–269.

Appendix E

CORBA Success Stories

(*Source:* John Weiler and Nicole J. Glinski, Object Management Group, 492 Old Connecticut Path, Framingham, MA 01701; e-mail: *nicole@omg.org,* http://www.corba.org.)

AlliedSignal Engines Division

AlliedSignal's Engines Division spent two years building reusable objects based on CORBA application programming interfaces and set up CORBA to serve as the plumbing that connects components, clients, and servers. Now the framework is done, and the first application built on it is complete.

"We're building the fundamental building blocks that developers will use as they build applications in the future," said Wayne Haughey, information systems group leader at AlliedSignal's Engines Division. "Every time we pick this up and build a new application, we're avoiding [about] five man-years of work—and that's very conservative." At Object World West '97 in San Francisco, Haughey said that the five man-years account for savings of $750,000 per new application. CORBA enables applications, components, and databases to communicate easily with one another across multiple operating systems.

Wayne Haughey, Group Leader
AlliedSignal/Engines Division
1944 E. Sky Harbor Circle
Phoenix, AZ 85034

Ascom Autelca Ltd.

Ascom is a leading manufacturer of transportation fare collection systems. The company provides terminals for the efficient sale of services such as transport tickets. These terminals, called *ticket vending machines* (TVMs), are interconnected, thus supporting the distribution of services. The distributed services are alarm handling, collection of sales data, accounting for cash or cards, software upgrades, maintenance functionality, and access to tariff information. TVMs are produced for customers in over 20 countries. Therefore, the software has to be adaptable to very different needs. Scalability, robustness, and maintainability are major concerns for an availability of 24 hours per day and a lifetime of more than 15 years per machine.

The object-oriented paradigm was applied throughout the whole development process, and the resulting application is a fully distributed, component-based system. An implementation of the CORBA standard was used to interconnect single components to build an application and to handle requests from and to the management center. These components offer a powerful approach for reusing both architecture and code, and the component-based architecture, with CORBA as its communication infrastructure, best meets the customer requirements.

Ascom Autelca Ltd.
Morgenstrasse 129
CH-Bern, Switzerland

Digital Equipment Corporation

Digital Equipment worked closely with one of its partners in Europe (Linkvest) to design a software layer called the Credit Risk Management (CRM) framework. The layer sits on top of ObjectBroker and provides additional services for the application and BEA ObjectBroker itself.

The CRM framework deals primarily with three functions important to investment banking: fault management, interface implementation management to the customer, and type of investment management.

BEA ObjectBroker was used to construct a standard producer/consumer library. Risk calculation is layered into a tree-like structure of servers, so those users can access information quickly. *Producer servers* at lower levels provide partially computed data to *consumer servers* at higher levels in the tree.

BEA ObjectBroker enables staff to integrate existing applications and develop new distributed applications across heterogeneous platforms. It also connects seamlessly to the Microsoft Distributed COM OLE-based desktop community.

Paulette Rio
110 Spitbrook Road
Nashua, NH 03062

603-881-1650
Fax: 603-881-2550
E-mail: paulette.rio@zko.mts.dec.com

Baptist Health Systems of Florida

Baptist Health Systems (BHS) of South Florida has embarked on a long-term journey toward computerized patient records (CPR). As part of its "continuum of care" effort, Baptist Health Systems will evolve from a series of hospitals to an integrated delivery system that also provides well care. As a result, it will need to manage all clinical information generated as its organization(s) interacts with its patients and other customers.

During its growth, Baptist is required to manage diverse information across very distinct clinical disciplines, including diabetes, radiology, pharmacology, and pathology. Typically, different vendors specialize in different aspects of health care informatics. Although this provides very good departmental solutions, it fosters suboptimal enterprise functionality—for example, failing to produce consistent identification of a patient across multiple hospitals (or even across different departments within a hospital). Direct access to clinical information is nonexistent in these stovepipe systems. Data is repopulated across the different stovepipe systems through message exchange. The end result is an inefficient and nonscalable solution for creating computerized patient records.

Unfortunately, there is not a single information system vendor that covers the full spectrum of managing information throughout the continuum of care. The Baptist Health Systems approach allows the best vendor solution to be implemented for a particular clinical discipline, provided that the solution adheres to an information architecture that addresses the shortcomings of the previous generation of information systems.

The information architecture is equivalent to a blueprint that enforces components of a building to be constructed in a predefined, consistent fashion. Just as each of these building components is guided by standards and standard interfaces, components in the information architecture of a health care organization must be defined by a set of standard interfaces.

Baptist Health Systems is basing its computerized patient record systems on CORBA and, in turn, is actively promoting the standardization of its interfaces through the OMG process. Thus far, BHS has signed two contracts for OMA-compliant information systems with two separate vendors. BHS has direct access to the CORBA interfaces (IDL) of these systems and expects the CPR to be built as a collection of services/components, each with a set of interfaces. BHS has made OMG conformance an absolute requirement in its information selection process, and it expects to sign several more multimillion-dollar vendor contracts in the near future.

Kent Wreder, Corporate Director
CPR Architecture/Object Technology Group
8900 North Kendall Drive
Miami, FL 33176
305-596-6515
Fax: 603-881-2550
E-mail: kentw@bhssf.org

British Aerospace Airbus/ICL

ICL, the European computer giant, in partnership with Computer Science Corporation Ltd. (CSC), is set to roll out the world's biggest single deployment of CORBA-compliant object request broker technology at British Aerospace Airbus. The five-year contract is worth 2.5 million dollars.

Based on ICL's Dais object request broker (ORB), the technology will eventually be used by up to 4000 employees as part of the company's five-year information management strategy, following successful completion of a three-month pilot study.

British Aerospace Airbus has contracted the partnership for the integration of its legacy business systems and applications into a unified information infrastructure linked with new object-based applications. British Aerospace Airbus is the wing design and manufacturing component of the pan-European Airbus Industrie consortium, recognized as Boeing's competition in Europe.

ICL is working in partnership with CSC and British Aerospace Airbus to provide consultancy and implementation skills to prove the technology using SELECT Software's Object Modeling tool and the Dais ORB. It is also working closely with CSC, British Aerospace's information technology (IT) outsourcing partner, on providing skill transfer to implement and deploy the object technology.

"We chose distributed object technology for its high degree of flexibility in managing rapid change within the organization without compromising the quality of our IT support systems," said Francis Hayden, British Aerospace Airbus object strategy consultant. "Only ICL offered the combination of an in-depth knowledge of our industry with a strategic commitment to CORBA technology and an understanding of the organizational challenges arising from their implementation."

The pilot phase will enable British Aerospace Airbus to prove that object technology will work successfully in a distributed computing environment, linking new object-based applications with legacy systems. The pilot will be used to implement i500, ICL's X.500 product, directory service, initially for 380 users with a goal to roll it out to 3800 users.

New business applications will be developed using object technology. The objects are first modeled using the Select Object Modeling tool, developed using languages such as Java and C++, and distributed by the object request broker. In effect, Dais will form the hub of all future integrated applications by creating an environment in which objects are managed independently of the hardware and network in use.

Dais is based on the Object Management Group's Common Object Request Broker Architecture (CORBA) standard. ICL is an active member of the OMG and has provided several reference implementations of the CORBA standard.

ICL is a leading European information technology company. Operating in over 80 countries, it supplies integrated systems and services, which improve the performance of its customers' businesses.

ICL Inc., headquartered in Reston, Virginia, is responsible for expanding the company's North American market share by developing strategic technology partnerships and channels of distribution for ICL's leading-edge enterprise software products.

Anne Prine
11490 Commerce Park Drive
Reston, VA 22091
703-648-3300
Fax: 703-648-3350
E-mail: aprine@iclretail.com

Capitol One Financial Corporation/IONA Technologies

Are today's object technologies ready to handle huge, crucial, transaction-intensive applications? Capitol One Financial Corporation answered that in September 1997, as the company went live with an object-based business application to process all daily transactions of its nearly 10 million cardholders.

The system, expected to handle millions of transactions on a daily basis, is the first in a series of events representing a complete overhaul of the company's core business systems. The hodgepodge of IBM and Unisys mainframes and client/server and desktop applications are being replaced by a distributed, three-tier architecture based on standards: the Common Object Request Broker Architecture (CORBA), UNIX, C++, Java, and Web browsers.

Formed in 1989 when Signet Bank spun out its credit card business, Capitol One has rapidly become one of the nation's top ten credit card issuers. Last year alone, its customer base grew 40 percent. But the company's existing technology "was a barrier to further growth," says Tal Elyashiv, a Capitol One IT director. The company didn't see itself as only a credit card company. Capitol One also has a fledgling cellular phone business and expects to expand into other businesses, too. "We are a company wrapped around strategy," says Matt Cooper, Capitol One's senior vice president of business development.

The strategy is collecting, analyzing, and acting on information. Capitol One focuses heavily on what it calls "testing," or devising new financial products—typically credit cards with some new twist, such as a different interest rate—then mailing a sample to potential customers. The tests are usually devised by mining the company's data warehouse for trends. The response to each test helps Capitol One decide which products to develop and use more widely. The strategy has been extraordinarily successful: in the maturing credit card business, Capitol One grew from about $1 billion in customer accounts in 1989 to almost $12 billion in 1996.

However, the company's existing IT strategy was running out of steam. In 1989, Capitol One conducted 300 tests of new financial products. By 1996, the number had grown to more than 10,000. The existing systems weren't flexible enough to deal with anticipated increases in testing. "If one of the business parameters within which we operate changes, we can't wait a year to change our systems," Elyashiv says. "There's only a small window of opportunity in which we need to get new products to market."

It was clear that the existing systems needed to be replaced. But object technology wasn't Capitol One's first choice. Originally, IT staff tried to build a database-centric system, but that quickly proved unfeasible. "We realized that with a data-centric approach, we wouldn't get the kind of flexibility we wanted," Elyashiv says. The company decided that object technology, in contrast, would allow a move to a component-based architecture that would enable its systems to change rapidly with business conditions. The way ahead seemed clear. "Then reality set in," continues Elyashiv. "We realized that distributed objects were wonderful, but the state of the technology is such that there is a tremendous amount of risk."

To minimize the risk, Capitol One decided to build on object standards, such as CORBA, and build new applications using an iterative, incremental prototyping approach. As the project progressed, the prototypes gradually became production code. To further reduce the risk, the company built an "isolation layer"—software that separates its business objects from the supporting infrastructure while standards emerge.

Capitol One's software relies on Orbix, an object request broker from IONA Technologies in Dublin, Ireland, together with IONA-developed naming and security services. But Capitol One found it also needed other types of middleware: IBM's MQSeries messaging software for its guaranteed delivery between system components and a transaction monitor—Transarc Corporation's Encina—for transactional capabilities such as rollback. Linking these products meant more work. "These products are written with the assumption that you only need one of them," says Elyashiv.

Capitol One wrote the server-based software in C++ for deployment on Hewlett-Packard and Sun Microsystems application and database servers. It wrote the client software in Java. Users access the systems with Java-compatible Web browsers on Microsoft Windows clients. Capitol One plans to continue its iterative development process, whereby it keeps rebuilding prototypes and learning from them.

Even as the first application went into production, Capitol One planned four new iterations of its credit card processing application. The company has reused existing objects, especially those related to infrastructure, as it replaced all its core operational systems. In the meantime, some existing legacy applications were wrapped in object code to make them accessible to the new applications environment.

Capitol One Financial Corporation
2980 Fairview Park Drive
Falls Church, VA 22042

Continental Power Exchange/Salient Corporation

Once deregulation started in the electric industry with the passage of the Energy Policy Act (1992), the industry realized the need for real-time, continentwide transactions, made possible by CPEX. If these trends continue, and there is no reason to believe they won't, individual businesses and consumers may one day be able to select an energy provider in the same way that individuals shop for long-distance telephone service.

CPEX is a customized computer and dedicated telecommunications system that facilitates the efficient, cost-effective wholesale purchase, sale, and transmission of electric energy among its customers. Currently, over 60 participants from coast to coast use CPEX to trade electricity. CPEX is the first and only functional interactive electronic energy exchange based on competitive principles in North America.

The system overview is as follows: CPEX is the trading system that enables a trader to make offers and view the market. If an offer looks attractive, the trader simply accepts that offer to consummate a transaction. OpenAccess is the capacity reservation tool that CPEX uses to make reservations for the transmission of energy bought or sold, while the TransMail messaging system is used for disseminating information about each transaction to all involved parties. The service runs around the clock, seven days a week. At the top of every hour, a bell rings on a CPEX computer at a participant's site and announces that "the market is now open." Participating utilities enter their orders for the next hour or more into a computer and transmit them to CPEX. CPEX has the ability to display and rank the best 40 buy and sell offers at the same time.

Access to transmission lines is a key aspect of any system relying on competitive generation of electricity. OpenAccess allows users to zoom into any region of the country with a single mouse click; graphical displays immediately reveal transmission capacity and price. The buyer pays all costs associated with transmission; the fees are automatically calculated by CPEX and are included in the posted price. CPEX participants trade with each other confidentially. All offers to buy and sell are confidential until an offer has been accepted. At the end of each accounting period, participants settle their accounts via electronic funds transfer (EFT). Two days after the close of business each month, Continental provides a summary of purchases, sales, and transmission activity with all parties engaged in trades during the month.

Continental's decision to build CPEX on CORBA architecture was based on two primary considerations: performance and scalability. Since the people involved in the project had already used Smalltalk, they knew that objects could offer superior performance when accessing the unusual data structures of online electrical transactions. The nation's electrical grid is a complex and ever changing topography. Every CPEX transaction potentially represents a unique path through this system and thus cannot easily be made to fit into a relational, table-based structure. Each transaction has a life of its own that can best be effectively expressed using objects. The first release of CPEX was written in Smalltalk using the VisualWorks environment. This initial release operated on a single server and was based on an object-oriented database architecture that did not support distributed objects. While this worked in the initial phases, Continental felt that a federated system would be required to meet future demands.

Objectivity/DB was the database system settled on, because it is a truly distributed object database solution. The server runs on uniprocessors, symmetric multiprocessors, or networks of computers. A single database can be distributed among any number of computers. While each machine may manage a physical subset of the full database, each user connected to any machine has a logical view of the entire database. It also guarantees the ACID properties of databases: transactions are atomic and are enforced with two-phase commits; transactions are serialized to ensure consistency of data; both the integrity and durability of data are guaranteed.

This new version of CPEX consists of a client written in Visual C++ and a server written in Distributed Smalltalk, utilizing the federated Objectivity database; the communications interface is provided by Visigenic's CORBA-compliant ORB. The CPEX client is a PC running Windows NT 4.0. The server can run on Intel, Sun, or HP hardware using Windows NT 4.0 or one of several different flavors of UNIX.

With a federated software structure in place, CPEX will be ready to expand to more servers as growth demands. CPEX's hardware and server architecture is capable of supporting foreseeable changes that may be necessary when the client load arrives. Continental intends to stay at least one step ahead of the marketplace. (*Source:* D. Heise and D. Tuck, *Distributed Object Computing,* August/September 1997, pp. 30–36.)

Deutsche Presse Agentur (DPA)/ICL

Deutsche Presse Agentur (DPA), a leading global press agency based in Hamburg, Germany, has developed a multimedia information facility for its correspondents and customers worldwide. The completed facility enables immediate, integrated access to the variety of media input required to produce comprehensive, up-to-the-minute coverage of events taking place around the world.

ICL's Dais was selected to enable the integration of a news production system with the agency's photographic libraries and multimedia workstations. Responding to the ongoing need for quicker access to information in a variety of media, DPA knew that the technology supporting its new facility was a critical factor for success.

According to Klaus Sprick, senior vice president of technology for DPA, the use of a CORBA-based, object-oriented solution enables DPA to introduce true multimedia operations that improve its service for editors, reporters, and customers.

Sprick comments that ICL's Dais product set enables DPA to use a modern object-oriented design while exploiting its existing legacy systems. This was a primary consideration in the company's decision to choose Dais.

The service selected Dais over a competitive ORB product for its ability to integrate STRATUS, HP, and PC systems and its proven track record for supporting high-performance, mission-critical applications.

DPA assessed the performance of a Dais-enabled system prototype in November 1996 performance testing before confirming plans to offer its services to support more than 500 editors and 2000 reporters worldwide.

Indications

ICL's Dais is capable of delivering enterprise-level, multivendor systems integration in a mission-critical environment. With Deutsche Press Agentur, Dais established a third business case application for CORBA-based solutions for commercial customers. Due to its proven scalability, CORBA is appropriate and ready for high-end, high-volume, mission-critical applications.

Anne Prine
11490 Commerce Park Drive
Reston, VA 22091
703-648-3300
Fax: 703-648-3350
E-mail: aprine@iclretail.com

EIS International Incorporated

EIS International, a global leader in integrated call center management software, systems, and services, has announced it will adopt the CORBA as a platform for all future products.

As a Domain Contributing Member of the OMG, EIS will participate fully to develop standards for the telecommunications industry by "feeding requirements into the adoption process and voting on technologies for adoption with the Domain Technical Committee." EIS aligns itself with the world's top computing vendors, software developers, and end users that have selected CORBA as a platform standard. CORBA is aimed at addressing the need for interoperability among the generation of hardware and software products on the market today.

EIS International is a leading provider of advanced solutions for outbound and integrated inbound/outbound applications for the call center industry. With more than 76,000 workstations installed at more than 1350 locations, EIS provides systems for telemarketing, customer service, fund-raising, market research, and collections to increase productivity, enhance operational efficiency, and improve agent effectiveness in the call center.

EIS International
555 Herndon Parkway
Herndon, VA 20170
http://www.eisi.com

European BioInformatics Institute/Persistence Software, Inc.

Information technology managers at the European BioInformatics Institute in Cambridge, England, are giving scientists worldwide direct online access to the largest database of DNA information in existence. Scientists trying to find cures for cancer, heart disease, and Alzheimer's disease should be able to get needed research information faster with an object-based combination of CORBA and Java technologies.

Instead of the current practice of submitting queries and having workers at the institute sift through the information in the database, more than 10,000 scientists in academic, pharmaceutical, and biotechnology laboratories will be able to fire up their browsers and do more detailed searches themselves. They will have access to the information because developers are using the Java programming language and CORBA, which connects databases, clients, and servers to make the legacy information easily available.

The developers are using development tools and a server from Persistence Software in San Mateo, California, to make the transition easier. The institute mainly has Oracle databases but has many others from a slew of vendors. They hold information on about a billion different strands of DNA sequences. With so many databases, it is hard to access them if a user doesn't know exactly where the information is.

The developers at European BioInformatics Institute used Persistence's Object Builder to create wrappers that encapsulate chunks of the database information and enable them to be accessed and shipped to the front end. They also use Persistence's Object Server, which takes the query and does the digging. Object request brokers from IONA Technologies, Visigenic Software, and SunSoft ship the information to the client.

The institute also uses Java on the front end to ship the information across the Internet to the scientists. Because the Persistence tools, CORBA, and Java are all platform-independent, they can access information on any of the databases and ship it easily anywhere on the Internet.

"The Persistence technology makes it easier for them to transform an old legacy relational database into virtually an object-oriented database without actually having to build a whole new database," said Karen Boucher, director of The Standish Group International, Inc., in Dennis, Massachusetts. "With Persistence, they're throwing an extra layer over the database like a blanket. That helps wrap the information into usable objects."

Richard Browett, technical director at Valtech Ltd., an object-oriented consulting and training firm in London, said that changing the way scientists access information should speed up research. "By wrapping all the legacy information and letting scientists actually get their hands on it, we're serving them better," Browett said, "and that's the focus."

European BioInformatics Institute
Welcome Trust Genome Campus
Hinxton Cambridge CB10 1SD
United Kingdom
(*Source:* S. Gaudin, *Computerworld,* August 4, 1997, pp. 1, 55.)

Florida Power and Light, Information Management Division/DNS Technologies and Visigenic Software

Florida Power and Light, Miami, Florida, needs a flexible, powerful enterprise information system—that is, one that delivers a big-picture view of the business in real time. Like most companies, FPL doesn't have the luxury of starting over. It needs to build this new enterprise with existing 30-year legacy business systems and applications.

With utilities deregulation and the increased competition, FPL looks to distributed object technologies such as CORBA and object application servers as a way to re-architect the existing information systems into critical business tools. The Information Management group has developed a service-based enterprise architecture that will achieve a new level of performance, flexibility, and reuse.

The goals for FPL are to improve information flow, and thus operational efficiency, by integrating applications and data across the enterprise. Supporting management decision making by providing strategic information in real time is another goal. The final goal is to create flexible systems so that applications can be changed quickly to meet new business needs and opportunities, while the entire information system remains in sync.

FPL's ultimate decision is to use CORBA and object application servers to encapsulate business logic and data as services that can be used by an application. The existing applications and data stores are accessed via CORBA ORBs using IDL interfaces, which replace the in-house developed enabler interfaces.

The first project, a contractor time-sheet system, has successfully integrated new Java applications and clients that gather time-sheet and expense information and a mainframe application that performs account validation. The system has been developed to the pilot stage in a remarkably short amount of time, less than three months. Using CORBA, the project team was able to unite the new application with existing systems by simply creating a new interface, speeding development and minimizing impact on the production system. The project has also made several new business services available for reuse, including login validation and tracking contractors for security purposes.

Independence Blue Cross/IONA Technologies

Independence Blue Cross has announced the use of IONA's Orbix and CORBA in two mission-critical deployments, with plans for full enterprisewide deployment. Independence Blue Cross, an independent licensee of the Blue Cross/Blue Shield Association, administers contracts and claims covering hospital expenses, outpatient care, home care, and other institutional services. The initial CORBA-based system provides the underlying infrastructure to manage these contracts and the claims that come in through the Independence Blue Cross Electronic Data Interchange (EDI) system. Requirements for the business applications are supported for both Windows and UNIX. There is also a need to support clients built with Powersoft's PowerBuilder on Windows as well as clients built on UNIX. The ability of Orbix to integrate OLE and CORBA resolved these requirements. Independence Blue Cross provides health care to more than 2.8 million members. The company, with over 4700 employees, annually processes more than 5.7 million claims and responds to over 3.2 million customer inquiries.

Independence Blue Cross
1901 Market Street
Philadelphia, PA 19103

Nations Bank/Expersoft Corporation

Nations Bank was looking for standards-based architecture to provide the foundation with what could be an enterprisewide infrastructure for the direct-banking program, for the purpose of delivering world-class customer service through nontraditional channels. The industry appeared to be rallying around the OMG's CORBA 2.0 standard.

The CORBA 2.0–compliant ORB from ExperSoft, the CORBAPlus PowerBroker, will be used to support the Telephone Banking Project and Web Banking Project. In fact the same CORBA 2.0 infrastructure supports both projects.

The Telephone Banking Project encompasses voice response units and customer service centers. When fully deployed, Nations Bank will have three to five customer service centers, each with over 600 agents. Nations Bank is currently trying to stress-test the system at over 300 transactions per second. The Web Banking Project will provide bank customers with a Web browser interface to their accounts, as well as other financial services.

Nations Bank is using a Windows NT 3.51 environment (both desktop and server), with an Oracle database server running under HP-UX. The LAN topology is 100BaseT, even to the desktop. The customer service centers are interconnected using a backbone nodal network.

Both projects fall within the Direct Banking Program and were tested with a production implementation date of February 1997.

Lois Leslie
6620 Mesa Ridge Road, Suite 100
San Diego, CA 92121
619-824-4100
Fax: 619-824-4110
E-mail: lleslie@expersoft.com

Swiss Telecom PTT

Swiss Telecom went through the migration of a legacy application to CORBA. The application had emerged out of a legacy application (around 1980) heavily used for subscriber administration, which was already distributed in the first place. The system consisted of a centralized host base with decentralized terminal concentrators in the form of IBM Series/1 computers in the 17 regional offices of Swiss Telecom.

When the Windows desktop wave hit the enterprise, the desire to replace the user interface became a requirement. This was at the same time that CORBA entered the scene, and Swiss Telecom decided that this technology was not only the solution to solve this migration problem, but that it also was the strategy to make a component-based architecture in the heterogeneous environment of this enterprise.

The purpose of the project was to wrap the legacy application with a CORBA-IDL interface to make it accessible for the front end and also for other applications within the enterprise. The user interface was more comfortable for the user.

Postfach
CH-3029 Bern, Switzerland

The Gap, Inc./Visigenic Software

The Gap, Inc., has turned to an object-oriented architecture to provide its sales force with the information it needs to maintain the company's 20 percent annual growth rate. The Gap has 1900 stores around the world and posted $5.3 billion in sales last year. Its fast growth rate poses some serious issues for the international chain's 3000 users and its information technology department.

The challenge in that kind of growth environment is keeping everyone connected and giving them immediate access to the most up-to-date information available. At The Gap, that information is spread across a wide array of systems. Gap has IBM mainframes running on the back end, Sun Microsystems Solaris servers on the middle tier, and OS/2 and Windows NT–based desktops, which means that World Wide Web–enabling information on sales, inventory, and shipments is a little more complicated to acquire. The Gap brought in CORBA along with Java, the cross-platform language designed to speed across the Internet. The Gap uses the CORBA ORB from Visigenic Software (Visibroker) to serve as the middleware plumbing that connects users' browsers to information in various databases.

Because the ORB is cross-platform, it can usher information to and from any database, where it is sitting on a UNIX machine, a mainframe, or an NT server. Running Java on the front end allows the IT division to easily send that information over the Internet.

The Gap, Inc.
Harrison Street
San Francisco, CA 94105
(*Source:* S. Gaudin, *Computerworld,* June 9, 1997, pp. 6, 45.)

U.K. Home Office's Suspect Index System for Immigration Control/ICL

The U.K. Home Office Suspect Index System (SIS) scans machine-readable passports at major ports of entry to the United Kingdom 7 days a week, 24 hours a day, 365 days a year. Its primary function is to check scans against a central database of information and images of individuals who might be refused entry to the United Kingdom. The SIS contains Dais, ICL's object request broker, making it the world's first and largest mission-critical CORBA-based application.

Operational as of January 1995, SIS is successfully implemented at major U.K. points of entry including Heathrow, Gatwick, the Channel Tunnel, and Dover. It has handled some 6 million passengers and identified approximately 10,000 suspects. Each day an average of up to 700 images are downloaded across a conventional wide area network (WAN).

An annual influx of approximately 10 million foreign nationals from outside the European Economic Area seek entry to the United Kingdom. According to Immigration Services project director Ken Richardson, the Home Office determined that high-technology support was called for to support the work of its frontline immigration staff. A year later, SIS was considered responsible for increasing immigration officers' ability to identify intending illegal immigrants and other individuals to be refused entry into the country, as well as for speeding up the clearance of bona fide visitors.

ICL supplied a secure system that provides U.K. immigration staff with instant access to consistent and comprehensive information. Nearly 400,000 entries are stored on two resilient top-end UNIX systems, each with 30 gigabytes of data storage. Imaging techniques enable the use of photographs to increase user time efficiency.

More than 300 PCs with integrated passport readers are used on control desks in immigration halls at airports and seaports. Immigration officers simply swipe a machine-readable passport through the automatic reader or key in names to quickly receive files enabling them to make individual determinations. The computer search takes less than a second compared to the time it would take to manually search a 300-page record book.

In addition, 280 personal computers with high-resolution graphics screens and image printers are available in nonpublic areas including ports and Channel Tunnel passenger trains. These enable closer review of records held on the database including photographs, handwritten reports, and documents compiled by immigration staff and consular officials around the world. The system is now being planned for extension to cover all U.K. points of entry.

Anne Prine
11490 Commerce Park Drive
Reston, VA 22091
703-648-3300
Fax: 703-648-3350
E-mail: aprine@iclretail.com

Nokia Telecommunications/IONA Technologies

Nokia Telecommunications is using IONA's Orbix as the primary ORB for the organization. Nokia is using Orbix to develop and produce telecommunication products, enabling service providers to rapidly create, deploy, and manage value-added services based on a common intelligent network (IN) architecture.

"We are now seeing the delivery of second and third generation CORBA projects as the technology continues to mature and be deployed in mainstream applications," said Colin Newman, vice president of marketing at IONA. "Nokia's decision to use Orbix in the IN Solution application development process, highlights the continuing adoption of CORBA and is recognition of the fast, effective, scaleable and open approach to the development of powerful, intelligent, mission critical network services that CORBA offers."

Nokia Telecommunications develops and manufactures infrastructure equipment and systems for cellular and fixed networks. Nokia is the second largest in the world for supplying GSM/DCS networks and is a market leader in mobile data infrastructure. In addition, Nokia is a significant supplier of advanced transmission and switching solutions to the fast-growing segment of access networks. Nokia also provides its customers with comprehensive support in building, operating, and developing both cellular and fixed networks.

West Coast Financial Institution/Digital Equipment Corporation

Two years ago the bank decided to streamline customer service and other banking operations by converting from the traditional stovepipe application structure to one that is more customer-centric in structure. In keeping with this goal, the bank began by looking at its customer service department and how the service reps could have better access to customer information and at the same time attain a high level of customer satisfaction. The bank also needed a way to handle a widely distributed customer base, which was the result of a number of bank mergers and acquisitions that had happened or which were about to happen. Of course, the ongoing business need was to continue to grow the bank's business.

Description of application

Several new applications have been implemented, most notably:

- *Internet banking* Written in C++ on an Alpha UNIX platform in conjunction with a Netscape Commerce server. Provides direct customer online home banking to over 55,000 customers and is growing by 300 customers per day.
- *Agent desktop* Written in Visual C++ on Win 3.x PCs primarily. Has also been installed on Win 95 and Win NT in the lab and in a pilot but is only in production on the Win 3.x. Supports agents working with customers that have called in to the bank for banking information and account maintenance types of activities. Currently supports 400 desktops and is in the process of being rolled out to approximately 4000 over the next year.

The applications run on Win 3.x, Win 95, and Win NT on the PC platform and Digital UNIX, HP-UX 9.x, and HP-UX 10.x on the server side. IBM mainframes holding bank's legacy online data are integrated on the third tier.

ROI/benefits

Overall benefits for the IS department are increased software efficiency, faster application development time, integration of legacy applications with new client GUIs, reuse of application objects in the future, and investment protection of hardware, software, and databases.

For the agent desktop application, there is faster, more accurate access to customer information. This provides the ability to more easily see the customer's entire business with the bank at once and thus enables the recommendation of additional banking services that may be of interest. This system has generally resulted in higher customer satisfaction levels.

The Internet banking application enables more direct customer access to their own accounts, bank operational cost savings, and an increase of new accounts due to the easy home banking style of access.

Size

The Internet banking application supports a base of 60,000 business invocations per day with a projected monthly growth rate of 30 percent. The customer agent application currently supports 300 desktops and 1300 business invocations per day with 600,000 per day projected in the future.

Paulette Rio
110 Spitbrook Road
Nashua, NH 03062
603-881-1650
Fax: 603-881-2550
E-mail: paulette.rio@zko.mts.dec.com

Zeneca Pharmaceuticals/Digital Equipment Corporation

Not long after Zeneca initiated the supply chain reengineering program, it became clear that global information flows would be critical to its success. It was also clear that this was not to be a technology-led project, a factor strongly supported by the Zeneca sponsor. Business needs would lead the project. These facts, together with a history and culture of local autonomy that had resulted in every major supply chain location having different systems, provided the challenge to be faced. In summary, the key challenges were how to:

- Underpin the new business processes by defining, providing, and sustaining the necessary information exchange
- Align and integrate the IS activities so as not to unnecessarily constrain the reengineering program or impact on its timescales, and achieve this in a cost-effective manner

Description of application

Digital sold its Framework-Based Environment (FBE) and BEA ObjectBroker SI services and products to integrate the manufacturing supply chain. This involved modeling the desired business process within FBE and implementing this model using Digital's CORBA middleware, BEA ObjectBroker. This integration was undertaken in a total IBM environment, with a mix of MRPII applications to be wrapped, including SAP/R3. This has enabled the integration across 9 countries worldwide, with another 10 to be included in the very near future. The BEA ObjectBroker server is a Digital UNIX Alpha, and the clients are Windows 95.

Business benefits/ROI

This implementation has enabled Zeneca to access stock supply information from anywhere in the world, with a consistent view, in seconds or minutes rather than days or weeks.

The use of BEA ObjectBroker has provided an information infrastructure independent of specific detailed business requirements. It has also enabled Zeneca to maximize use of the existing legacy applications, while creating a plug-and-play environment.

Overall supply chain costs since 1996 have decreased by $50 million to $90 million, and overall stock supply should be reduced by $45 million to $85 million.

Size

Middleware integration across 9 countries worldwide, with another 10 to follow, is expected. The solution integrated seven different enterprise systems running five different applications.

Paulette Rio
110 Spitbrook Road
Nashua, NH 03062
603-881-1650
Fax: 603-881-2550
E-mail: paulette.rio@zko.mts.dec.com

Index

ABOUT THE AUTHORS

JAG SODHI is a well-known author, lecturer, and consultant. He has developed and conducted training in software engineering for government and industry organizations, and is the author of six best-selling books, including *Software Engineering: Methods, Management, and CASE Tools; Software Requirements: Analysis and Specifications;* and *Object-Oriented Methods for Software Development,* all published by McGraw-Hill.

PRINCE SODHI is a senior consultant for IBIS Consulting. He is an expert in several programming languages and in distributed computing applications in multiple-tier, client-server environments. He is completing a doctorate in scientific computing, and is co-author of the book *Object-Oriented Methods for Software Development,* from McGraw-Hill.